Less managing. More teaching. Greater learning.

 INSTRUCTORS...

Would you like your **students** to show up for class more **prepared**? *(Let's face it, class is much more fun if everyone is engaged and prepared...)*

Want ready-made application-level **interactive assignments,** student progress reporting, and auto-assignment grading? *(Less time grading means more time teaching...)*

Want an **instant view of student or class performance** relative to learning objectives? *(No more wondering if students understand...)*

Need to **collect data and generate reports** required for administration or accreditation? *(Say goodbye to manually tracking student learning outcomes...)*

Want to **record and post your lectures** for students to view online?

 With **McGraw-Hill's *Connect*® Plus MIS,**

INSTRUCTORS GET:

- Interactive Applications – **book-specific interactive assignments** that require students to APPLY what they've learned.

- Simple **assignment management,** allowing you to spend more time teaching.

- **Auto-graded** assignments, quizzes, and tests.

- **Detailed Visual Reporting** where student and section results can be viewed and analyzed.

- Sophisticated **online testing** capability.

- A **filtering and reporting** function that allows you to easily assign and report on materials that are correlated to accreditation standards, learning outcomes, and Bloom's taxonomy.

- An easy-to-use **lecture capture** tool.

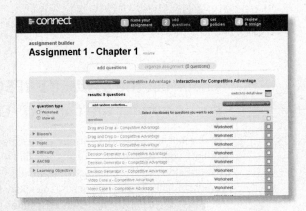

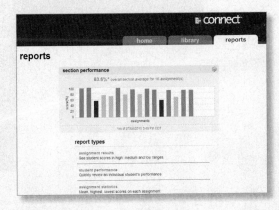

Want an online, **searchable version** of your textbook?

Wish your textbook could be **available online** while you're doing your assignments?

 ### *Connect® Plus MIS* eBook

If you choose to use *Connect™ Plus MIS*, you have an affordable and searchable online version of your book integrated with your other online tools.

Connect® Plus MIS eBook offers features like:

- Topic search
- Direct links from assignments
- Adjustable text size
- Jump to page number
- Print by section

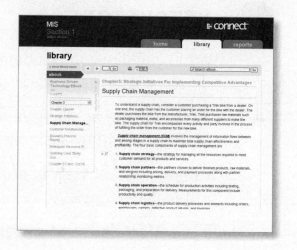

 Want to get more **value** from your textbook purchase?

Think learning MIS should be a bit more **interesting**?

 ### Check out the **STUDENT RESOURCES** section under the *Connect®* Library tab.

Here you'll find a wealth of resources designed to help you achieve your goals in the course. You'll find things like **quizzes, PowerPoints, and Internet activities** to help you study. Every student has different needs, so explore the STUDENT RESOURCES to find the materials best suited to you.

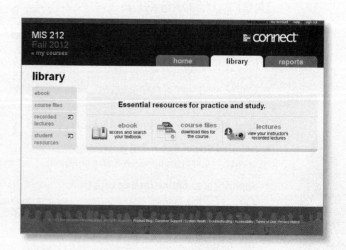

information
systems 2e

Paige Baltzan
Daniels College of Business
University of Denver

McGraw-Hill
Irwin

information
systems 2e

VICE PRESIDENT AND EDITOR-IN-CHIEF	**Brent Gordon**
EDITORIAL DIRECTOR	**Paul Ducham**
EXECUTIVE DIRECTOR OF DEVELOPMENT	**Ann Torbert**
SENIOR DEVELOPMENT EDITOR	**Trina Hauger**
VICE PRESIDENT AND DIRECTOR OF MARKETING	**Robin J. Zwettler**
MARKETING DIRECTOR	**Amee Mosley**
VICE PRESIDENT OF EDITING, DESIGN, AND PRODUCTION	**Sesha Bolisetty**
SENIOR MANAGER, PUBLISHING TOOLS	**Mary Conzachi**
SENIOR BUYER	**Michael R. McCormick**
SENIOR DESIGNER	**Mary Kazak Sander**
SENIOR PHOTO RESEARCH COORDINATOR	**Keri Johnson**
LEAD MEDIA PROJECT MANAGER	**Daryl Horrocks**
COVER AND INTERIOR DESIGN	**Mary Kazak Sander**
COVER IMAGES	**Scott Dunlap**
TYPEFACE	**10/12 Minion Pro Regular**
COMPOSITOR	**Laserwords Private Limited**
PRINTER	**Quad/Graphics**

M: INFORMATION SYSTEMS, 2e

Published by McGraw-Hill/Irwin, a business unit of The McGraw-Hill Companies, Inc., 1221 Avenue of the Americas, New York, NY, 10020. Copyright © 2013, 2011 by The McGraw-Hill Companies, Inc. All rights reserved. Printed in the United States of America. No part of this publication may be reproduced or distributed in any form or by any means, or stored in a database or retrieval system, without the prior written consent of The McGraw-Hill Companies, Inc., including, but not limited to, in any network or other electronic storage or transmission, or broadcast for distance learning.

Some ancillaries, including electronic and print components, may not be available to customers outside the United States.

This book is printed on acid-free paper.

2 3 4 5 6 7 8 9 0 QBD/QDB 1 0 9 8 7 6 5 4 3 2

ISBN 978-0-07-337686-8
MHID 0-07-337686-8

Library of Congress Control Number: 2011940366

brief contents

module one

BUSINESS DRIVEN MIS 3

Chapter 1   Management Information Systems: Business Driven MIS 5

Chapter 2   Decisions + Processes: Value Driven Business 27

Chapter 3   Ebusiness: Electronic Business Value 59

Chapter 4   Ethics + Information Security: MIS Business Concerns 85

module two

TECHNICAL FOUNDATIONS OF MIS 105

Chapter 5   Infrastructures: Sustainable Technologies 107

Chapter 6   Data: Business Intelligence 129

Chapter 7   Networks: Mobile Business 151

module three

ENTERPRISE MIS 177

Chapter 8   Enterprise Applications: Business Communications 179

Chapter 9   Systems Development + Project Management: Corporate Responsibility 205

ONLINE APPENDICES 224

GLOSSARY 225

NOTES 237

CREDITS 243

INDEX 245

contents

module one   BUSINESS DRIVEN MIS 3

CHAPTER 1   MANAGEMENT INFORMATION SYSTEMS: BUSINESS DRIVEN MIS 5

SECTION 1-1 >> Business Driven MIS 6

COMPETING IN THE INFORMATION AGE 6
- **FYI** People in China and India are Starving for Your Jobs 7
- Data 7
- Information 8
- Business Intelligence 9
- **DUE DILIGENCE** Wikiblunders 9
- Knowledge 10
- **DUE DILIGENCE** What's Wrong with This Bathroom? 10

THE CHALLENGE: DEPARTMENTAL COMPANIES 10

THE SOLUTION: MANAGEMENT INFORMATION SYSTEMS 12
- MIS Department Roles and Responsibilities 13

SECTION 1-2 >> Business Strategy 14

IDENTIFYING COMPETITIVE ADVANTAGES 14
- **MY NOT TO-DO LIST** What Happens on YouTube Stays on YouTube—FOREVER 15

THE FIVE FORCES MODEL—EVALUATING INDUSTRY ATTRACTIVENESS 16
- Buyer Power 16
- Supplier Power 17
- Threat of Substitute Products or Services 17
- Threat of New Entrants 18
- Rivalry among Existing Competitors 18
- Analyzing the Airline Industry 18
- **SHOW ME THE MONEY** Death of a Product 19

THE THREE GENERIC STRATEGIES—CHOOSING A BUSINESS FOCUS 19

VALUE CHAIN ANALYSIS—EXECUTING BUSINESS STRATEGIES 20
- **LIVING THE DREAM** One Laptop per Child 21
- **BUSTED** Listen to Spider-Man; He Knows What He's Talking About! 23

CHAPTER 2   DECISIONS + PROCESSES: VALUE DRIVEN BUSINESS 27

SECTION 2-1 >> Decision Support Systems 28

MAKING BUSINESS DECISIONS 28
- The Decision-Making Process 29
- Decision-Making Essentials 29

METRICS: MEASURING SUCCESS 32
- **DUE DILIGENCE** Driving While Breast Feeding—For Real? 32
- Efficiency and Effectiveness Metrics 33
- The Interrelationship Between Efficiency and Effectiveness MIS Metrics 33

SUPPORT: ENHANCING DECISION MAKING WITH MIS 35
- Operational Support Systems 35
- **LIVING THE DREAM** Virtual Nonprofits Helping Sustainability—What Are You Talking About? 36
- Managerial Support Systems 36
- Strategic Support Systems 37
- **BUSTED** The Criminal in the Cube Next Door 40
- **FYI** Got Junk? Get a Hunk! 41

THE FUTURE: ARTIFICIAL INTELLIGENCE 41
- Expert Systems 41
- Neural Networks 42
- Genetic Algorithms 43
- Intelligent Agents 43
- Virtual Reality 44
- **SHOW ME THE MONEY** If It Ain't Broke, Don't Fix It 44

SECTION 2-2 >> Business Processes 44

EVALUATING BUSINESS PROCESSES 45

MODELS: MEASURING PERFORMANCE 46

SUPPORT: CHANGING BUSINESS PROCESSES WITH MIS 50
Improving Operational Business Processes—Automation 51
Improving Managerial Business Processes—Streamlining 52
MY NOT TO-DO LIST You Accidentally Sent Your Confidential Email to Your Significant Other to Your Grandmother—Ouch! 53
Improving Strategic Business Processes—Reengineering 53
DUE DILIGENCE Sue Your College for $70,000 56

THE FUTURE: BUSINESS PROCESS MANAGEMENT 56

CHAPTER 3 EBUSINESS: ELECTRONIC BUSINESS VALUE 59

SECTION 3-1 >> Web 1.0: Ebusiness 60

DISRUPTIVE TECHNOLOGIES AND WEB 1.0 60
Disruptive Versus Sustaining Technology 60
The Internet and World Wide Web—The Ultimate Business Disruptors 61
Web 1.0: The Catalyst for Ebusiness 62
DUE DILIGENCE Excuse Me, but You Are Sitting on My Domain Name 63

ADVANTAGES OF EBUSINESS 63
Expanding Global Reach 63
Opening New Markets 64
Reducing Costs 64
Improving Operations 65
Improving Effectiveness 65

EBUSINESS MODELS 66
Business-to-Business (B2B) 66
Business-to-Consumer (B2C) 67
Consumer-to-Business (C2B) 67
Consumer-to-Consumer (C2C) 68
Ebusiness Forms and Revenue-Generating Strategies 68

EBUSINESS TOOLS FOR CONNECTING AND COMMUNICATING 69
LIVING THE DREAM Crazy over Access 70
Email 70
Instant Messaging 70
Podcasting 70
Videoconferencing 70
Web Conferencing 70
Content Management Systems 70

THE CHALLENGES OF EBUSINESS 71
Identifying Limited Market Segments 71
Managing Consumer Trust 71
Ensuring Consumer Protection 71
Adhering to Taxation Rules 72

SECTION 3-2 >> Web 2.0: Business 2.0 72
SHOW ME THE MONEY Analyzing Websites 72
WEB 2.0: ADVANTAGES OF BUSINESS 2.0 72
Content Sharing Through Open Sourcing 73
User-Contributed Content 73

Collaboration Inside the Organization 73
Collaboration Outside the Organization 74
MY NOT TO-DO LIST Social Not Working 75
NETWORKING COMMUNITIES WITH BUSINESS 2.0 75
Social Tagging 76
BUSINESS 2.0 TOOLS FOR COLLABORATING 77
Blogs 77
DUE DILIGENCE Welcome to the Anti-Social Networking Revolution 78
Wikis 78
Mashups 79
FYI Don't You Just Love Mötley Crüe? 79
THE CHALLENGES OF BUSINESS 2.0 80
Technology Dependence 80
Information Vandalism 80
Violations of Copyright and Plagiarism 80
WEB 3.0: DEFINING THE NEXT GENERATION OF ONLINE BUSINESS OPPORTUNITIES 80
Egovernment: The Government Moves Online 82
Mbusiness: Supporting Anywhere Business 82

CHAPTER 4 ETHICS + INFORMATION SECURITY: MIS BUSINESS CONCERNS 85

SECTION 4-1 >> Ethics 86

INFORMATION ETHICS 86
LIVING THE DREAM The Circle of Life—Kiva 87
MY NOT TO-DO LIST Do You Really Want to Risk It? 87
Information Does Not Have Ethics; People Do 88

DEVELOPING INFORMATION MANAGEMENT POLICIES 88
Ethical Computer Use Policy 88
Information Privacy Policy 90
Acceptable Use Policy 90
DUE DILIGENCE Can You Get a Ticket for Drunk Emailing? 91
Email Privacy Policy 91
Social Media Policy 92
FYI Spam: It's Not Just for Dinner 93

Usability 116
SHOW ME THE MONEY Ranking the -ilities 116

SECTION 5-2 >> Building Sustainable
MIS Infrastructures 116

MIS AND THE ENVIRONMENT 117
LIVING THE DREAM Recycle Your Phone 117
Increased Electronic Waste 118
Increased Energy Consumption 118
Increased Carbon Emissions 118

SUPPORTING THE ENVIRONMENT: SUSTAINABLE
MIS INFRASTRUCTURE 118
LIVING THE DREAM Smart Cities 119
Grid Computing 119
Cloud Computing 120
Virtualized Computing 124
FYI Virtualization for Your Cell Phone 124
BUSTED Hack Attack 125

Workplace Monitoring Policy 93

SECTION 4-2 >> Information Security 94

PROTECTING INTELLECTUAL ASSETS 94
BUSTED I'm Being Fired for Smoking, but
I Was at Home and It Was Saturday 95
Security Threats Caused by Hackers and Viruses 96

THE FIRST LINE OF DEFENSE—PEOPLE 98

THE SECOND LINE OF DEFENSE—TECHNOLOGY 98
People: Authentication and Authorization 98
Data: Prevention and Resistance 100
DUE DILIGENCE Doodling Passwords 100
SHOW ME THE MONEY Hackers Love Phish,
and I Don't Mean the Band 101
Attack: Detection and Response 102

module two TECHNICAL
FOUNDATIONS OF MIS 105

CHAPTER 5 INFRASTRUCTURES: SUSTAINABLE
TECHNOLOGIES 107

SECTION 5-1 >> MIS Infrastructures 108

THE BUSINESS BENEFITS OF A SOLID MIS
INFRASTRUCTURE 108

SUPPORTING OPERATIONS: INFORMATION
MIS INFRASTRUCTURE 109
Backup and Recovery Plan 110
Disaster Recovery Plan 110
DUE DILIGENCE I Don't Have a Temperature,
but I'm Positive I Have a Virus 111
Business Continuity Plan 112

SUPPORTING CHANGE: AGILE MIS INFRASTRUCTURE 113
Accessibility 113
Availability 114
DUE DILIGENCE Zombies Attack the
University of Florida 114
Maintainability 115
Portability 115
Reliability 115
Scalability 115

CHAPTER 6 DATA: BUSINESS INTELLIGENCE 129

SECTION 6-1 >> Data, Information, and Databases 130

THE BUSINESS BENEFITS OF HIGH-QUALITY
INFORMATION 130
Information Type: Transactional and Analytical 130
Information Timelines 131
Information Quality 132
SHOW ME THE MONEY Determining
Information Quality Issues 133
Information Governance 134

STORING INFORMATION IN A RELATIONAL DATABASE
MANAGEMENT SYSTEM 134
DUE DILIGENCE That's Not My Mother
in the Casket! 135
Storing Data Elements in Entities and Attributes 135
Creating Relationships Through Keys 136
MY NOT TO-DO LIST Yes, I Started the Internet 137

USING A RELATIONAL DATABASE FOR BUSINESS
ADVANTAGES 137
Increased Flexibility 137
Increased Scalability and Performance 137
Reduced Data Redundancy 138
Increased Information Integrity
(Quality) 138
Increased Information
Security 138

DRIVING WEBSITES
WITH DATA 139
DUE DILIGENCE
Sorry, I Didn't
Mean to Post Your
Social Security
Number on the
Internet 139

SECTION 6-2 >>
Business Intelligence 141

THE BUSINESS BENEFITS OF DATA WAREHOUSING 141

PERFORMING BUSINESS ANALYSIS WITH DATA MARTS 142
Multidimensional Analysis 142
Information Cleansing or Scrubbing 143

UNCOVERING TRENDS AND PATTERNS WITH DATA MINING 144
BUSTED   Follow the Data 145
Cluster Analysis 146
Association Detection 146
FYI   Want Free Books? Just Ask Google 146
Statistical Analysis 147

SUPPORTING DECISIONS WITH BUSINESS INTELLIGENCE 147
The Problem: Data Rich, Information Poor 147
LIVING THE DREAM   Ice Cream Social Takes on a Whole New Meaning 148
The Solution: Business Intelligence 148

CHAPTER 7   NETWORKS: MOBILE BUSINESS 151

SECTION 7-1 >> Connectivity: The Business Value of a Networked World 152

OVERVIEW OF A CONNECTED WORLD 152
Network Categories 152
Network Providers 153
Network Access Technologies 154
Network Protocols 155
BUSTED   Never Run with Your iPod 156
Network Convergence 157

BENEFITS OF A CONNECTED WORLD 159
Sharing Resources 159
FYI   Music in the Clouds 160
Providing Opportunities 161
MY NOT TO-DO LIST   Ding-a-Ling Took My $400 161
Reducing Travel 162

CHALLENGES OF A CONNECTED WORLD 162
Security 162
Social, Ethical, and Political Issues 162

SECTION 7-2 >> Mobility: The Business Value of a Wireless World 163

WIRELESS NETWORK CATEGORIES 163
Personal Area Networks 163
Wireless LANs 164
Wireless MANs 165
SHOW ME THE MONEY   Wireless Networks and Streetlamps 165
Wireless WAN—Cellular Communication System 165
Wireless WAN—Satellite Communication System 167
DUE DILIGENCE   Call 911, McNugget Outage 167

BUSINESS APPLICATIONS OF WIRELESS NETWORKS 168
Radio-Frequency Identification (RFID) 168
Global Positioning System (GPS) 169
Geographic Information System (GIS) 169
Location-Based Services (LBS) 170

BENEFITS OF BUSINESS MOBILITY 170
Enhances Mobility 171
Provides Immediate Data Access 171
Increases Location and Monitoring Capability 171
Improves Work Flow 172
Provides Mobile Business Opportunities 172
DUE DILIGENCE   WeatherBots 172
Provides Alternative to Wiring 173

CHALLENGES OF BUSINESS MOBILITY 173
Protecting Against Theft 173
Protecting Wireless Connections 173
Preventing Viruses on a Mobile Device 174
Addressing Privacy Concerns with RFID and LBS 174
LIVING THE DREAM   Geoblogging for Chimpanzees 174

module three
ENTERPRISE MIS 177

CHAPTER 8   ENTERPRISE APPLICATIONS: BUSINESS COMMUNICATIONS 179

SECTION 8-1 >> Supply Chain Management 180

BUILDING A CONNECTED CORPORATION THROUGH INTEGRATIONS 180
Integration Tools 181

SUPPLY CHAIN MANAGEMENT 181

THE BENEFITS OF SCM 183
Improved Visibility 184
Increased Profitability 185
DUE DILIGENCE   Robots Took My Job 185

THE CHALLENGES OF SCM 186

THE FUTURE OF SCM 186
MY NOT TO-DO LIST   Fixing the Post Office 186

SECTION 8-2 >> Customer Relationship Management and Enterprise Resource Planning 187

CUSTOMER RELATIONSHIP MANAGEMENT 187

THE BENEFITS OF CRM 188
Evolution of CRM 189
Operational and Analytical CRM 189
BUSTED   I'm Stuck in London and I've Been Robbed—Help Me! 190
Marketing and Operational CRM 190
Sales and Operational CRM 191
Customer Service and Operational CRM 192
DUE DILIGENCE   Customer Power to the Rescue 193
Analytical CRM 193
Measuring CRM Success 193

THE CHALLENGES OF CRM 194

THE FUTURE OF CRM 194

   LIVING THE DREAM Change.org 194

ENTERPRISE RESOURCE PLANNING 196

THE BENEFITS OF ERP 197

   Core ERP Components 198

   SHOW ME THE MONEY Classic Cars 198

   Extended ERP Components 199

   FYI Bean Integration 200

   Measuring ERP Success 201

THE CHALLENGES OF ERP 202

THE FUTURE OF ENTERPRISE SYSTEMS:
INTEGRATING SCM, CRM, AND ERP 202

OUTSOURCING PROJECTS 219

   Outsourcing Benefits 220

   Outsourcing Challenges 220

   DUE DILIGENCE DUI in a Golf Cart 221

   SHOW ME THE MONEY Keeping Time 222

ONLINE APPENDICES 224

GLOSSARY 225

NOTES 237

CREDITS 243

INDEX 245

CHAPTER 9 SYSTEMS DEVELOPMENT + PROJECT MANAGEMENT: CORPORATE RESPONSIBILITY 205

SECTION 9-1 >> Developing Enterprise Applications 206

DEVELOPING SOFTWARE 206

THE SYSTEMS DEVELOPMENT LIFE CYCLE (SDLC) 206

TRADITIONAL SOFTWARE DEVELOPMENT METHODOLOGY: THE WATERFALL 207

   FYI Have You Met Ted? If Not, You Need To! 207

   FYI Reducing Ambiguity in Business Requirements 208

AGILE SOFTWARE DEVELOPMENT METHODOLOGIES 209

   Rapid Application Development (RAD) Methodology 210

   Extreme Programming Methodology 210

   Rational Unified Process (RUP) Methodology 210

   Scrum Methodology 211

DEVELOPING SUCCESSFUL SOFTWARE 211

   Unclear or Missing Business Requirements 211

   BUSTED Faking Your Own Death 211

   Skipping Phases 212

   Changing Technology 212

   The Cost of Finding Errors in the SDLC 212

SECTION 9-2 >> Project Management 212

MANAGING SOFTWARE DEVELOPMENT PROJECTS 212

   The Triple Constraint 213

   Project Participants 213

CHOOSING STRATEGIC PROJECTS 214

   LIVING THE DREAM CharityFocus.org 215

UNDERSTANDING PROJECT PLANNING 215

MANAGING PROJECTS 217

   Managing People 217

   Managing Communications 218

   MY NOT TO-DO LIST Honestly, It Cost $7,500 for a Steak Dinner 218

   Managing Change 219

information
systems 2e

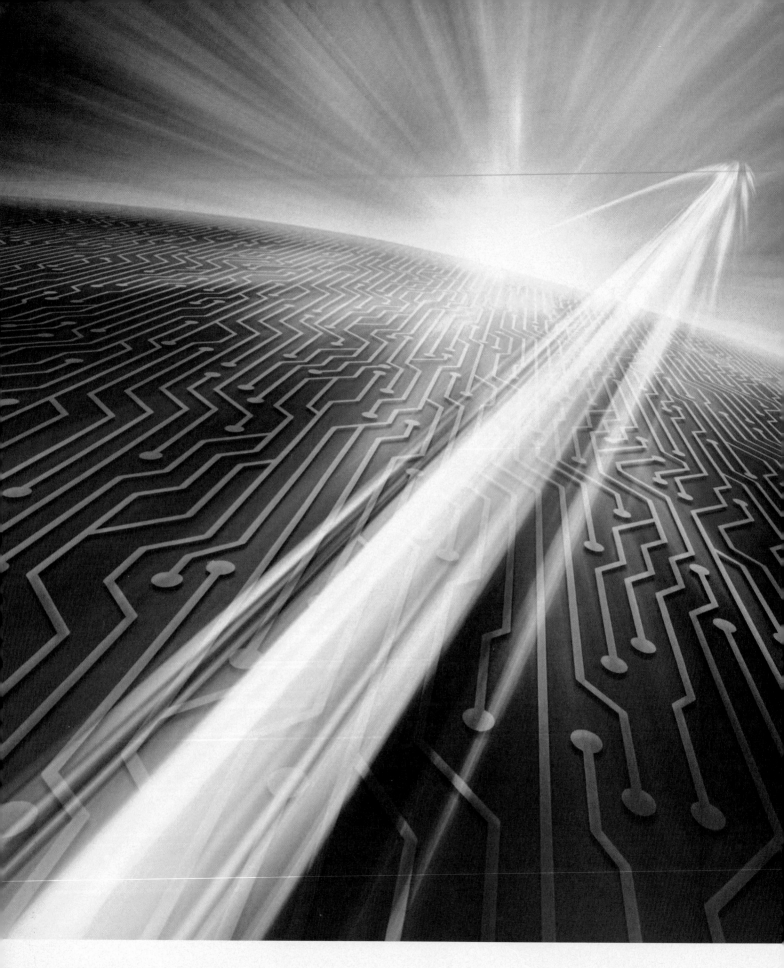

coming up

Most companies today rely heavily on the use of management information systems (MIS) to run various aspects of their businesses. Whether they need to order and ship goods, interact with customers, or conduct other business functions, management information systems are often the underlying infrastructure performing the activities. Management information systems allow companies to remain competitive in today's fast-paced world and especially when conducting business on the Internet. Organizations must adapt to technological advances and innovations to keep pace with today's rapidly changing environment. Their competitors certainly will!

No matter how exciting technology is, successful companies do not use it simply for its own sake. Companies should have a solid business reason for implementing technology. Using a technological solution just because it is available is not a good business strategy.

The purpose of Module 1 is to raise your awareness of the vast opportunities made possible by the tight correlation between business and technology. Business strategies and processes should always drive your technology choices. Although awareness of an emerging technology can sometimes lead us in new strategic directions, the role of information systems, for the most part, is to support existing business strategies and processes. ■

BUSINESS DRIVEN MIS

module one

BUSINESS DRIVEN MIS

CHAPTER 1: Management Information Systems: Business Driven MIS
CHAPTER 2: Decisions + Processes: Value Driven Business
CHAPTER 3: Ebusiness: Electronic Business Value
CHAPTER 4: Ethics + Information Security: MIS Business Concerns

module two
Technical Foundations of MIS

module three
Enterprise MIS

chapter one

What's in IT for me?

This chapter sets the stage for the textbook. It starts from ground zero by providing a clear description of what information is and how it fits into business operations, strategies, and systems. It provides an overview of how companies operate in competitive environments and why they must continually define and redefine their business strategies to create competitive advantages. Doing so allows them to survive and thrive. Information systems are key business enablers for successful operations in competitive environments.

You, as a business student, must understand the tight correlation between business and technology. You must first recognize information's role in daily business activities, and then understand how information supports and helps implement global business strategies

continued on p. 6

management information systems: **business driven MIS**

CHAPTER OUTLINE

SECTION 1-1 >>
Business Driven MIS

- Competing in the Information Age
- The Challenge: Departmental Companies
- The Solution: Management Information Systems

SECTION 1-2 >>
Business Strategy

- Identifying Competitive Advantages
- The Five Forces Model—Evaluating Industry Attractiveness
- The Three Generic Strategies—Choosing a Business Focus
- Value Chain Analysis—Executing Business Strategies

continued from p. 5

and competitive advantages. After reading this chapter, you should have a solid understanding of business driven information systems and their role in managerial decision making and problem solving. ■

{SECTION 1-1}
Business Driven MIS

LEARNING OUTCOMES

LO1-1 Describe the information age and the differences among data, information, business intelligence, and knowledge.

LO1-2 Identify the different departments in a company and why they must work together to achieve success.

LO1-3 Explain systems thinking and how management information systems enable business communications.

COMPETING IN THE INFORMATION AGE LO1-1

Did you know that . . .

- The movie *Avatar* took more than four years to create and cost $450 million.

- Lady Gaga's real name is Stefani Joanne Angelina Germanotta.

- Customers pay $2.6 million for a 30-second advertising time slot during the Super Bowl.[1]

A *fact* is the confirmation or validation of an event or object. In the past, people primarily learned facts from books. Today, by simply pushing a button people can find out anything, from

anywhere, at any time. We live in the *information age,* when infinite quantities of facts are widely available to anyone who can use a computer. The impact of information technology on the global business environment is equivalent to the printing press's impact on publishing and electricity's impact on productivity. College student startups were mostly unheard of before the information age. Now, it's not at all unusual to read about a business student starting a multimillion-dollar company from his or her dorm room. Think of Mark Zuckerberg, who started Facebook from his dorm, or Michael Dell (Dell Computers) and Bill Gates (Microsoft), who both founded their legendary companies as college students.

You may think only students well versed in advanced technology can compete in the information age. This is simply not true. Many business leaders have created exceptional opportunities by coupling the power of the information age with traditional business methods. Here are just a few examples:

- Amazon is not a technology company; its original business focus was to sell books, and it now sells nearly everything.

- Netflix is not a technology company; its primary business focus is to rent videos.

- Zappos is not a technology company; its primary business focus is to sell shoes, bags, clothing, and accessories.

Amazon's founder, Jeff Bezos, at first saw an opportunity to change the way people purchase books. Using the power of the information age to tailor offerings to each customer and speed the payment process, he in effect opened millions of tiny virtual bookstores, each with a vastly larger selection and far cheaper product than traditional bookstores. The success of his original business model led him to expand Amazon to carry many other types of products. The founders of Netflix and Zappos have done the same thing for videos and shoes. All these entrepreneurs were business professionals, not technology experts. However, they understood enough about the information age to apply it to a particular business, creating innovative companies that now lead entire industries.

Students who understand business along with the power associated with the information age will create their own opportunities and perhaps even new industries, as co-founders Chris DeWolfe and Tom Anderson did with MySpace and Mark Zuckerberg did with Facebook. Our primary goal in this course is to arm you with the knowledge you need to compete in the information age. The core drivers of the information age are:

- Data

- Information

- Business intelligence

- Knowledge

LO1-1 Describe the information age and the differences among data, information, business intelligence, and knowledge.

People in China and India Are Starving for Your Jobs[2]

"When I was growing up in Minneapolis, my parents always said, 'Tom, finish your dinner. There are people starving in China and India.' Today I tell my girls, 'Finish your homework, because people in China and India are starving for your jobs.' And in a flat world, they can have them, because there's no such thing as an American job anymore." Thomas Friedman.

In his book, *The World Is Flat,* Thomas Friedman describes the unplanned cascade of technological and social shifts that effectively leveled the economic world and "accidentally made Beijing, Bangalore, and Bethesda next-door neighbors." The video of Thomas Friedman's lecture at MIT discussing the flat world is available at http://mitworld.mit.edu/video/266. If you want to be prepared to compete in a flat world, you must watch this video and answer the following questions:

• Do you agree or disagree with Friedman's assessment that the world is flat?
• What are the potential impacts of a flat world for a student performing a job search?
• What can students do to prepare themselves for competing in a flat world?

Data

Data are raw facts that describe the characteristics of an event or object. Before the information age, managers manually collected and analyzed data, a time-consuming and complicated task without which they would have little insight into how to run their business. Lacking data, managers often found themselves making business decisions about how many products to make, how much material to order, or how many employees to hire based on intuition or gut feelings. In the information age, successful managers compile, analyze, and comprehend massive amounts of data daily, which helps them make more successful business decisions.

Figure 1.1 shows sales data for Tony's Wholesale Company, a fictitious business that supplies snacks to stores. The data highlight characteristics such as order date, customer, sales representative, product, quantity, and profit. The second line in Figure 1.1, for instance, shows that Roberta Cross sold 90 boxes of Ruffles to Walmart for $1,350, resulting in a profit of $450 (note that Profit = Sales − Costs). These data are useful for understanding individual sales; however, they do not provide us much insight

> " In the information age, successful managers compile, analyze, and comprehend massive amounts of data daily. "

into how Tony's business is performing as a whole. Tony needs to answer questions that will help him manage his day-to-day operations such as:

• Who are my best customers?
• Who are my least-profitable customers?
• What is my best-selling product?
• What is my slowest-selling product?
• Who is my strongest sales representative?
• Who is my weakest sales representative?

What Tony needs, in other words, is not data but *information*.

▼**FIGURE 1.1** Tony's Snack Company Data

Order Date	Customer	Sales Representative	Product	Qty	Unit Price	Total Sales	Unit Cost	Total Cost	Profit
4-Jan	Walmart	PJ Helgoth	Doritos	41	$24	$ 984	$18	$738	$246
4-Jan	Walmart	Roberta Cross	Ruffles	90	$15	$1,350	$10	$900	$450
5-Jan	Safeway	Craig Schultz	Ruffles	27	$15	$ 405	$10	$270	$135
6-Jan	Walmart	Roberta Cross	Ruffles	67	$15	$1,005	$10	$670	$335
7-Jan	7-Eleven	Craig Schultz	Pringles	79	$12	$ 948	$ 6	$474	$474
7-Jan	Walmart	Roberta Cross	Ruffles	52	$15	$ 780	$10	$520	$260
8-Jan	Kroger	Craig Schultz	Ruffles	39	$15	$ 585	$10	$390	$195
9-Jan	Walmart	Craig Schultz	Ruffles	66	$15	$ 990	$10	$660	$330
10-Jan	Target	Craig Schultz	Ruffles	40	$15	$ 600	$10	$400	$200
11-Jan	Walmart	Craig Schultz	Ruffles	71	$15	$1,065	$10	$710	$355

BUSTED

Listen to Spider-Man; He Knows What He's Talking About![20]

Spider-Man's infamous advice—"With great power comes great responsibility"—should be applied to every type of technology you encounter in business. Technology provides countless opportunities for businesses, but it can also lead to countless pitfalls and traps. A great example is how many companies profited from online trading and how many people lost their life savings in online trading scams. For example, Bernard Madoff, the owner of a high-profile New York investment company, was able to forge investment statements and allegedly spent almost $50 billion of his client's money.

Texting is a great asset for any company that requires instant communication, but it also digitizes conversations that can be tracked and retrieved. David Colby, the CFO of Wellpoint, was busted

carrying on multiple affairs, even once texting "ABORT!!" to one of his many girlfriends after discovering she was pregnant. Colby carried on relationships with more than 30 women and proposed to at least 12 of them.

AOL brings the power of the Internet to millions of people, and Craigslist allows anyone to become a provider of goods and services. Unfortunately, Craigslist does not describe exactly what types of goods and services are allowed. Adam Vitale was sentenced to two years in prison after he found a way to bypass AOL's spam filters and spammed 1.2 million AOL users. Vitale also had 22 prior convictions, including running an online prostitution ring through Craigslist.

When competing in business, you must analyze the good and the bad associated with every technology you encounter. Choose a company that primarily operates online—such as eBay, Netflix, or Amazon—and analyze all of the business opportunities along with the potential pitfalls you might encounter if you were the owner of the company.

---

sales. One example of a support value activity facilitated by MIS is the development of a human resources system that could more efficiently reward employees based on performance. The system could also identify employees who are at risk of quitting, allowing manager's time to find additional challenges or opportunities that would help retain these employees and thus reduce turnover costs.

Value chain analysis is a highly useful tool that provides hard and fast numbers for evaluating the activities that add value to products and services. Managers can find additional value by analyzing and constructing the value chain in terms of Porter's Five Forces Model (see Figure 1.14). For example, if the goal is to decrease buyer power, a company can construct its value chain activity of "service after the sale" by offering high levels of customer service. This will increase customers' switching costs

and reduce their power. Analyzing and constructing support value activities can help decrease the threat of new entrants. Analyzing and constructing primary value activities can help decrease the threat of substitute products or services.[21]

Revising Porter's three business strategies is critical. Firms must continually adapt to their competitive environments, which can cause business strategy to shift. In the remainder of this text we discuss how managers can formulate business strategies using MIS to create competitive advantages. Figure 1.15 gives an overview of the remaining chapters, along with the relevant business strategy and associated MIS topics.

L01-7 Demonstrate how a company can add value by using Porter's value chain analysis.

FIGURE 1.15
Overview of *Information Systems*

MODULE 1:
BUSINESS DRIVEN MIS

	Business Strategy	MIS Topics
Chapter 1: Management Information Systems	Understanding Business Driven MIS	Data Information Business Intelligence Knowledge Systems Thinking Porter's Business Strategies
Chapter 2: Decisions and Processes	Creating Value Driven Businesses	Transaction Processing Systems Decision Support Systems Executive Information Systems Artificial Intelligence Business Process Reengineering
Chapter 3: Ebusiness	Finding Electronic Business Value	eBusiness eBusiness Models Social Networking Knowledge Management Collaboration
Chapter 4: Ethics and Information Security	Identifying MIS Business Concerns	Information Security Policies Authentication and Authorization Prevention and Resistance Detection and Response

MODULE 2:
TECHNICAL FOUNDATIONS OF MIS

	Business Strategy	MIS Topics
Chapter 5: Infrastructures	Deploying Organizational MIS	Grid Computing Cloud Computing Virtualization Sustainable MIS Infrastructures
Chapter 6: Data	Uncovering Business Intelligence	Database Data Management Systems Data Warehousing Data Mining
Chapter 7: Networks	Supporting Mobile Business	Business Networks Web 1.0, Web 2.0, Web 3.0 Mobile MIS Wireless MIS GPS, GIS, and LBS

MODULE 3:
ENTERPRISE MIS

	Business Strategy	MIS Topics
Chapter 8: Enterprise Applications	Enhancing Business Communications	Customer Relationship Management Supply Chain Management Enterprise Resource Planning
Chapter 9: Systems Development and Project Management	Leading MIS Projects	MIS Development Methodologies Project Management Outsourcing

decisions + processes:
value driven business

What's in IT for me?

Working faster and smarter has become a necessity for companies. A firm's value chain is directly affected by how well it designs and coordinates its business processes. Business processes offer competitive advantages if they enable a firm to lower operating costs, differentiate, or compete in a niche market. They can also be huge burdens if they are outdated, which impedes operations, efficiency, and effectiveness. Thus, the ability of management

information systems to improve business processes is a key advantage.

The goal of Chapter 2 is to provide an overview of specific MIS tools managers can use to support the strategies discussed in Chapter 1. After reading this chapter, you, the business student, should have detailed knowledge of the types of information systems that exist to support decision making and business process reengineering, which in turn can improve organization efficiency and effectiveness and help an organization create and maintain competitive advantages. ■

CHAPTER OUTLINE

SECTION 2-1 >>
Decision Support Systems
- Making Business Decisions
- Metrics: Measuring Success
- Support: Enhancing Decision Making with MIS
- The Future: Artificial Intelligence

SECTION 2-2 >>
Business Processes
- Evaluating Business Processes
- Models: Measuring Performance
- Support: Changing Business Processes with MIS
- The Future: Business Process Management

LEARNING OUTCOMES

LO2-1 Explain the importance of decision making for managers at each of the three primary organization levels along with the associated decision characteristics.

LO2-2 Define critical success factors (CSFs) and key performance indicators (KPIs), and explain how managers use them to measure the success of MIS projects.

LO2-3 Classify the different operational support systems, managerial support systems, and strategic support systems, and explain how managers can use these systems to make decisions and gain competitive advantages.

LO2-4 Describe artificial intelligence, and identify its five main types.

MAKING BUSINESS DECISIONS LO2-1

Porter's strategies outlined in Chapter 1 suggest entering markets with a competitive advantage in either overall cost leadership, differentiation, or focus. To achieve these results,

managers must be able to make decisions and forecast future business needs and requirements. The most important and most challenging question confronting managers today is how to lay the foundation for tomorrow's success while competing to win in today's business environment. A company will not have a future if it is not cultivating strategies for tomorrow. The goal of this section is to expand on Porter's Five Forces Model, three generic strategies, and value chain analysis to demonstrate how managers can learn the concepts and practices of business decision making to add value. It will also highlight how companies heading into the 21st century are taking advantage of advanced MIS capable of generating significant competitive advantages across the value chain.

As we discussed in Chapter 1, decision making is one of the most important and challenging aspects of management. Decisions range from routine choices, such as how many items to order or how many people to hire, to unexpected ones such as what to do if a key employee suddenly quits or needed materials do not arrive. Today, with massive volumes of information available, managers are challenged to make highly complex decisions—some involving far more information than the human brain can comprehend—in increasingly shorter time frames. Figure 2.1 displays the three primary challenges managers face when making decisions.

LO2-1 Explain the importance of decision making for managers at each of the three primary organization levels along with the associated decision characteristics.

> " The most important and most challenging question confronting managers today is how to lay the foundation for tomorrow's success while competing to win in today's business environment. "

▼**FIGURE 2.1** Managerial Decision-Making Challenges

MANAGERIAL DECISION-MAKING CHALLENGES

1. Managers need to analyze large amounts of information: Innovations in communication and globalization have resulted in a dramatic increase in the variables and dimensions people need to consider when making a decision, solving a problem, or appraising an opportunity.

2. Managers must make decisions quickly: Time is of the essence and people simply do not have time to sift through all the information manually.

3. Managers must apply sophisticated analysis techniques, such as Porter's strategies or forecasting, to make strategic decisions: Due to the intensely competitive global business environment, companies must offer far more than just a great product to succeed.

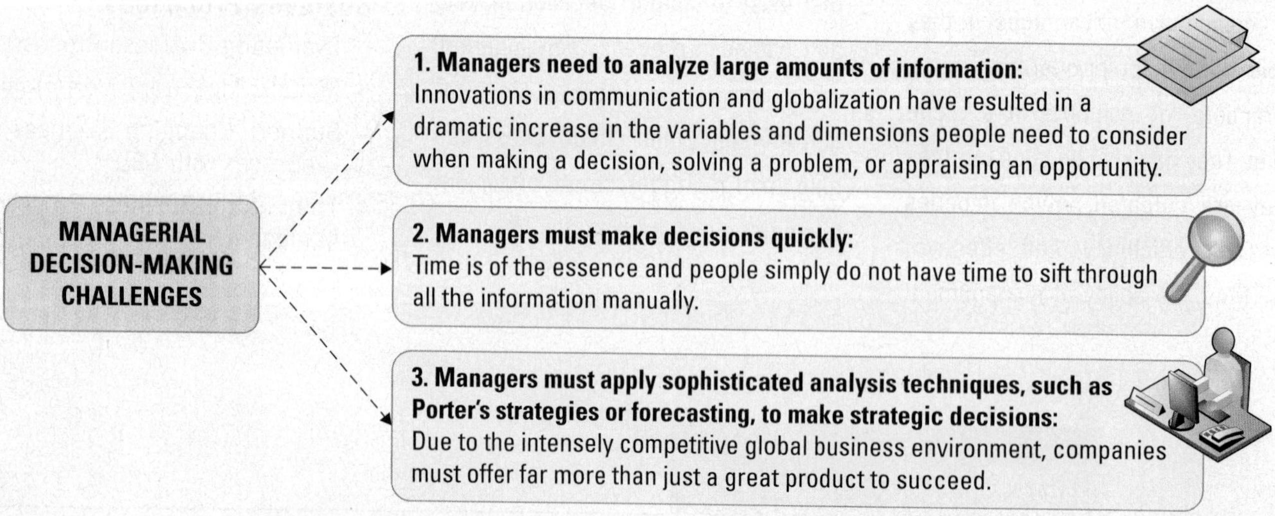

▼**FIGURE 2.2** The Six-Step
Decision-Making Process

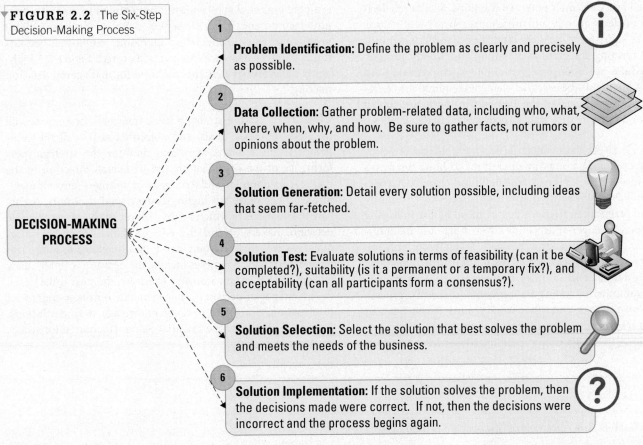

FIGURE 2.2 The Six-Step Decision-Making Process

DECISION-MAKING PROCESS

1. **Problem Identification:** Define the problem as clearly and precisely as possible.

2. **Data Collection:** Gather problem-related data, including who, what, where, when, why, and how. Be sure to gather facts, not rumors or opinions about the problem.

3. **Solution Generation:** Detail every solution possible, including ideas that seem far-fetched.

4. **Solution Test:** Evaluate solutions in terms of feasibility (can it be completed?), suitability (is it a permanent or a temporary fix?), and acceptability (can all participants form a consensus?).

5. **Solution Selection:** Select the solution that best solves the problem and meets the needs of the business.

6. **Solution Implementation:** If the solution solves the problem, then the decisions made were correct. If not, then the decisions were incorrect and the process begins again.

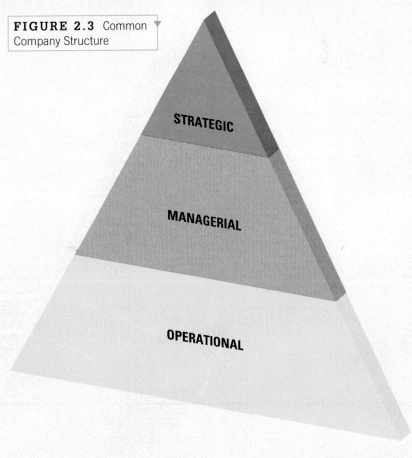

FIGURE 2.3 Common Company Structure

STRATEGIC

MANAGERIAL

OPERATIONAL

The Decision-Making Process

The process of making decisions plays a crucial role in communication and leadership for operational, managerial, and strategic projects. There are numerous academic decision-making models; Figure 2.2 presents just one example.[1]

Decision-Making Essentials

A few key concepts about organizational structure will help our discussion of MIS decision-making tools. The structure of a typical organization is similar to a pyramid, and the different levels require different types of information to assist in decision making, problem solving, and opportunity capturing (see Figure 2.3).

Operational At the operational level, employees develop, control, and maintain core business activities required to run the day-to-day operations. Operational decisions are considered *structured decisions,* which arise in situations where established processes offer potential solutions. Structured decisions are made frequently and are almost repetitive in nature; they affect short-term business strategies. Reordering inventory and creating the employee staffing and weekly production schedules are examples of routine structured decisions. Figure 2.4 highlights the essential elements required for operational decision making. All the elements in the figure should be familiar, except metrics which are discussed in detail below.

Managerial
At the managerial level, employees are continuously evaluating company operations to hone the firm's abilities to identify, adapt to, and leverage change. A company that has a competitive advantage needs to constantly adjust and revise its strategy to remain ahead of fast-following competitors. Managerial decisions cover short- and medium-range plans, schedules, and budgets along with policies, procedures, and business objectives for the firm. They also allocate resources and monitor the performance of organizational subunits, including departments, divisions, process teams, project teams, and other work groups. These types of decisions are considered *semistructured decisions;* they occur in situations in which a few established processes help to

evaluate potential solutions, but not enough to lead to a definite recommended decision. For example, decisions about producing new products or changing employee benefits range from unstructured to semistructured. Figure 2.5 highlights the essential elements required for managerial decision making.

Strategic
At the strategic level, managers develop overall business strategies, goals, and objectives as part of the company's strategic plan. They also monitor the strategic performance of the organization and its overall direction in the political, economic, and competitive business environment. Strategic decisions are highly *unstructured decisions,* occurring in situations in which no procedures or rules exist to guide decision makers toward the correct choice. They are infrequent, extremely important, and typically related to long-term business strategy. Examples include the decision to enter a new market or even a new industry over, say, the next three years. In these types of decisions, managers rely on many sources of information, along with personal knowledge, to find solutions. Figure 2.6 highlights the essential elements required for strategic decision making.

▼**FIGURE 2.4** Overview of Operational Decision Making

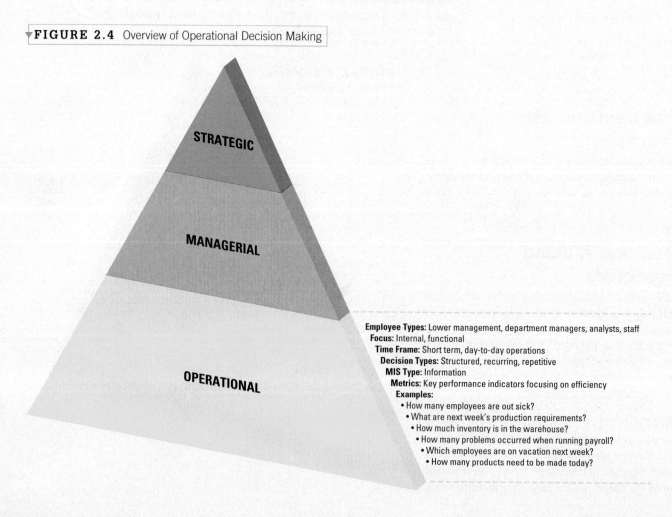

Employee Types: Lower management, department managers, analysts, staff
Focus: Internal, functional
Time Frame: Short term, day-to-day operations
Decision Types: Structured, recurring, repetitive
MIS Type: Information
Metrics: Key performance indicators focusing on efficiency
Examples:
• How many employees are out sick?
• What are next week's production requirements?
• How much inventory is in the warehouse?
• How many problems occurred when running payroll?
• Which employees are on vacation next week?
• How many products need to be made today?

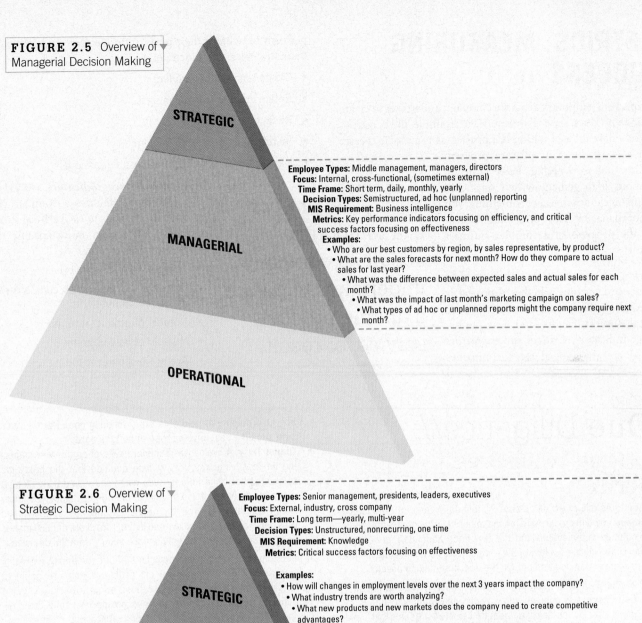

FIGURE 2.5 Overview of Managerial Decision Making

Employee Types: Middle management, managers, directors
Focus: Internal, cross-functional, (sometimes external)
Time Frame: Short term, daily, monthly, yearly
Decision Types: Semistructured, ad hoc (unplanned) reporting
MIS Requirement: Business intelligence
Metrics: Key performance indicators focusing on efficiency, and critical success factors focusing on effectiveness
Examples:
• Who are our best customers by region, by sales representative, by product?
• What are the sales forecasts for next month? How do they compare to actual sales for last year?
• What was the difference between expected sales and actual sales for each month?
• What was the impact of last month's marketing campaign on sales?
• What types of ad hoc or unplanned reports might the company require next month?

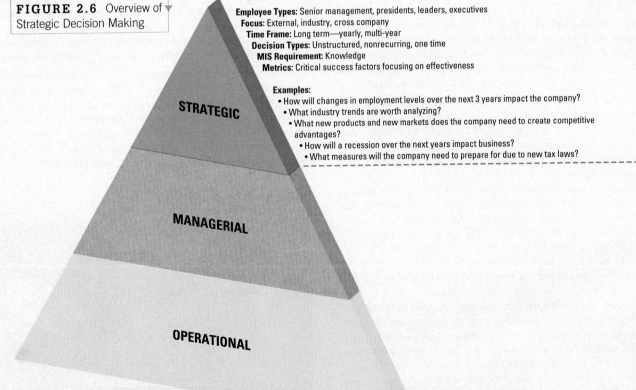

FIGURE 2.6 Overview of Strategic Decision Making

Employee Types: Senior management, presidents, leaders, executives
Focus: External, industry, cross company
Time Frame: Long term—yearly, multi-year
Decision Types: Unstructured, nonrecurring, one time
MIS Requirement: Knowledge
Metrics: Critical success factors focusing on effectiveness

Examples:
• How will changes in employment levels over the next 3 years impact the company?
• What industry trends are worth analyzing?
• What new products and new markets does the company need to create competitive advantages?
• How will a recession over the next years impact business?
• What measures will the company need to prepare for due to new tax laws?

METRICS: MEASURING SUCCESS LO2-2

A *project* is a temporary activity a company undertakes to create a unique product, service, or result. For example, the construction of a new subway station is a project, as is a movie theater chain's adoption of a software program to allow online ticketing. Peter Drucker, a famous management writer, once said that if you cannot measure something, you cannot manage it. How do managers measure the progress of a complex business project?

Metrics are measurements that evaluate results to determine whether a project is meeting its goals. Two core metrics are critical success factors and key performance indicators. **Critical success factors (CSFs)** are the crucial steps companies

> A *project* is a temporary activity a company undertakes to create a unique product, service, or result.

perform to achieve their goals and objectives and implement their strategies. CSFs include:

- Create high-quality products.
- Retain competitive advantages.
- Reduce product costs.
- Increase customer satisfaction.
- Hire and retain the best business professionals.

Key performance indicators (KPIs) are the quantifiable metrics a company uses to evaluate progress toward critical success factors. KPIs are far more specific than CSFs; examples include:

- Turnover rates of employees.
- Percentage of help desk calls answered in the first minute.
- Number of product returns.
- Number of new customers.
- Average customer spending.

Due Diligence//:
Driving While Breast Feeding—For Real?[2]

How do people make decisions? Almost daily you can read about someone who makes a decision the majority of the population finds completely unbelievable and the law finds absolutely unacceptable. Listed here are a few of the recent news headlines that simply defy rational thinking and boggle the decision-making psyche.

- **Mother Caught Driving While Breast-Feeding and Talking on a Cell Phone:** A woman in Ohio was charged with child endangerment after police said she admitted to breastfeeding her child and talking on a cell phone while she was driving her other children to school. We have all heard of multitasking, but this is taking it to the extreme.
- **Souper Drive:** A woman in South Florida was caught driving, talking on a cell phone that she placed on her left shoulder, and eating from a cup of soup placed in her left hand. The woman would take her hands off the wheel and use her right hand to spoon soup, while she continued to talk on the phone. It is common knowledge that it is inappropriate to talk with your mouth full. Perhaps she didn't understand that it was also inappropriate to drive!
- **Driving and Swimming:** A man in California was cited for driving while carrying a swimming pool. Yes, this man decided that it was a good decision to drive with one hand, while he used the other hand to hold onto his new swimming pool that was placed on the roof of his car. Not only was this a bad decision, but he also decided to enlist the help of his three children who were leaning out of the car windows, not wearing seat belts,

and also helping to hold onto the swimming pool. Perhaps this man should invest in some rope or bungee cords?

- **Diaper Duty:** A woman in Baltimore was charged with diapering while driving. Yes, this woman decided that the best time to change her child's diaper was while she was driving 65 mph down the highway. If you have ever changed a diaper, you know that it definitely requires two hands, and the fact that her child was not in a car seat and located in the front of the car just makes you wonder why anyone would make such a dreadful decision.

If people make such terrible decisions about something as highly policed as driving, just imagine the problems that are going to occur when they start making decisions about a business. What can you do to ensure your employees are making solid business decisions? Find an example of a company that found itself in a terrible mess because its employees made bad decisions. What could the company do to protect itself from employee blunders?

It is important to understand the relationship between critical success factors and key performance indicators. CSFs are elements crucial for a business strategy's success. KPIs measure the progress of CSFs with quantifiable measurements, and one CSF can have several KPIs. Of course, both categories will vary by company and industry. Imagine *improve graduation rates* as a CSF for a college. The KPIs to measure this CSF can include:

- Average grades by course and gender.

- Student dropout rates by gender and major.

- Average graduation rate by gender and major.

- Time spent in tutoring by gender and major.

KPIs can focus on external and internal measurements. A common external KPI is **market share,** or the proportion of the market that a firm captures. We calculate it by dividing the firm's sales by the total market sales for the entire industry. Market share measures a firm's external performance relative to that of its competitors. For example, if a firm's total sales (revenues) are $2 million and sales for the entire industry are $10 million, the firm has captured 20 percent of the total market ($2/10 = 20\%$) or a 20 percent market share.

Efficiency and Effectiveness Metrics

Efficiency MIS metrics measure the performance of MIS itself, such as throughput, transaction speed, and system availability. **Effectiveness MIS metrics** measure the impact MIS has on business processes and activities, including customer satisfaction and customer conversion rates. Efficiency focuses on the extent to which a firm is using its resources in an optimal way, while effectiveness focuses on how well a firm is achieving its goals and objectives. Peter Drucker offers a helpful distinction between efficiency and effectiveness: Doing things right addresses efficiency—getting the most from each resource. Doing the right things addresses effectiveness—setting the right goals and objectives and ensuring they are accomplished. Figure 2.7 describes a few of the common types of efficiency and effectiveness MIS metrics. KPIs that measure MIS projects include both efficiency and effectiveness metrics. Of course, these metrics are not as concrete as market share or ROI, but they do offer valuable insight into project performance.[3]

Large increases in productivity typically result from increases in effectiveness, which focus on CSFs. Efficiency MIS metrics are far easier to measure, however, so most managers tend to

Efficiency MIS metrics focus on the technology itself.

A common internal KPI is **return on investment (ROI),** which indicates the earning power of a project. We measure it by dividing the profitability of a project by the costs. This sounds easy, and for many departments where the projects are tangible and self-contained it is; however, for projects that are intangible and cross departmental lines (such as MIS projects), ROI is challenging to measure. Imagine attempting to calculate the ROI of a fire extinguisher. If the fire extinguisher is never used, its ROI is low. If the fire extinguisher puts out a fire that could have destroyed the entire building, its ROI is astronomically high.

Creating KPIs to measure the success of an MIS project offers similar challenges. Think about a firm's email system. How could managers track departmental costs and profits associated with company email? Measuring by volume does not account for profitability, because one sales email could land a million-dollar deal while 300 others might not generate any revenue. Non-revenue-generating departments such as human resources and legal require email but will not be using it to generate profits. For this reason, many managers turn to higher-level metrics, such as efficiency and effectiveness, to measure MIS projects.

focus on them, often incorrectly, to measure the success of MIS projects. Consider measuring the success of automated teller machines (ATMs). Thinking in terms of MIS efficiency metrics, a manager would measure the number of daily transactions, the average amount per transaction, and the average speed per transaction to determine the success of the ATM. Although these offer solid metrics on how well the system is performing, they miss many of the intangible or value-added benefits associated with ATM effectiveness. Effectiveness MIS metrics might measure how many new customers joined the bank due to its ATM locations or the ATMs' ease of use. They can also measure increases in customer satisfaction due to reduced ATM fees or additional ATM services such as the sale of stamps and movie tickets, significant time savers and value-added features for customers. Being a great manager means taking the added viewpoint offered by effectiveness MIS metrics to analyze all benefits associated with an MIS project.

The Interrelationship Between Efficiency and Effectiveness MIS Metrics

Efficiency and effectiveness are definitely related. However, success in one area does not necessarily imply success in the other. Efficiency MIS metrics focus on the technology itself. While these efficiency MIS metrics are important to monitor,

LO2-2 Define critical success factors (CSFs) and key performance indicators (KPIs), and explain how managers use them to measure the success of MIS projects.

FIGURE 2.7 Common Types of Efficiency and Effectiveness Metrics

Efficiency Metrics

Throughput—The amount of information that can travel through a system at any point in time.

Transaction speed—The amount of time a system takes to perform a transaction.

System availability—The number of hours a system is available for users.

Information accuracy—The extent to which a system generates the correct results when executing the same transaction numerous times.

Response time—The time it takes to respond to user interactions such as a mouse click.

Effectiveness Metrics

Usability—The ease with which people perform transactions and/or find information.

Customer satisfaction—Measured by satisfaction surveys, percentage of existing customers retained, and increases in revenue dollars per customer.

Conversion rates—The number of customers an organization "touches" for the first time and persuades to purchase its products or services. This is a popular metric for evaluating the effectiveness of banner, pop-up, and pop-under ads on the Internet.

Financial—Such as return on investment (the earning power of an organization's assets), cost-benefit analysis (the comparison of projected revenues and costs including development, maintenance, fixed, and variable), and break-even analysis (the point at which constant revenues equal ongoing costs).

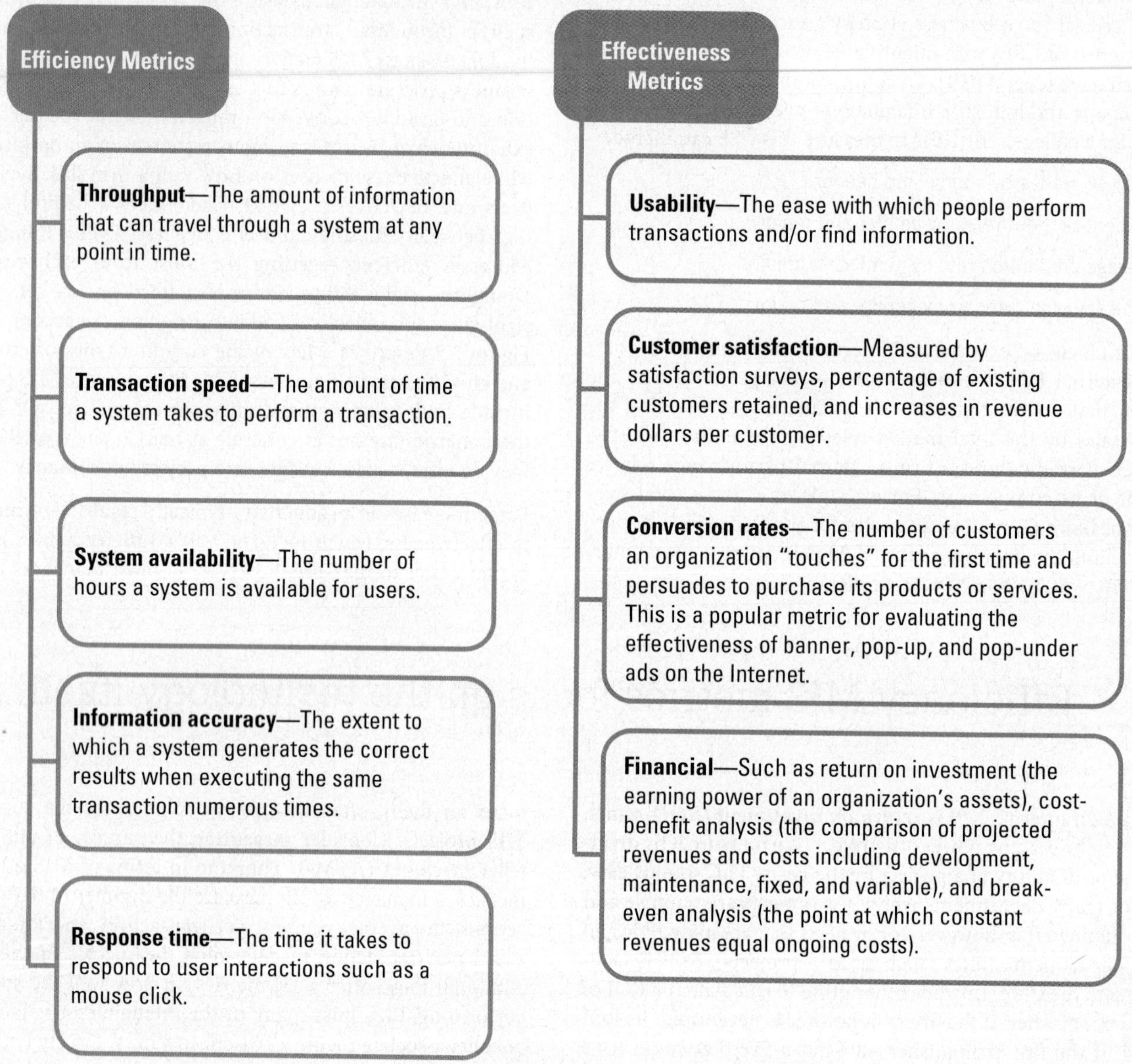

they do not always guarantee effectiveness. Effectiveness MIS metrics are determined according to an organization's goals, strategies, and objectives. Here, it becomes important to consider a company's CSFs, such as a broad cost leadership strategy (Walmart, for example), as well as KPIs such as increasing new customers by 10 percent or reducing new-product development cycle times to six months. In the private sector, eBay continuously benchmarks its MIS projects for efficiency and effectiveness. Maintaining constant website availability and optimal throughput performance are CSFs for eBay.

Figure 2.8 depicts the interrelationships between efficiency and effectiveness. Ideally, a firm wants to operate in the upper right-hand corner of the graph, realizing both significant increases in efficiency and effectiveness. However, operating in the upper

left-hand corner (minimal effectiveness with increased efficiency) or the lower right-hand corner (significant effectiveness with minimal efficiency) may be in line with an organization's particular strategies. In general, operating in the lower left-hand corner (minimal efficiency and minimal effectiveness) is not ideal for the operation of any organization.

Benchmarks Regardless of what process is measured, how it is measured, and whether it is performed for the sake of efficiency or effectiveness, managers must set *benchmarks,* or baseline values the system seeks to attain. *Benchmarking* is a process of continuously measuring system results, comparing those results to optimal system performance (benchmark values), and identifying steps and procedures to improve system performance. Benchmarks help assess how an MIS project

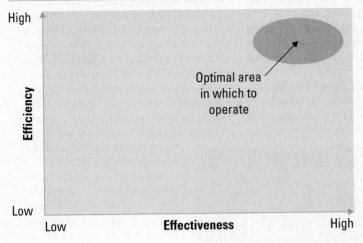

▼FIGURE 2.8
The Interrelationships Between Efficiency and Effectiveness

performs over time. For instance, if a system held a benchmark for response time of 15 seconds, the manager would want to ensure response time continued to decrease until it reached that point. If response time suddenly increased to 1 minute, the manager would know the system was not functioning correctly and could start looking into potential problems. Continuously measuring MIS projects against benchmarks provides feedback so managers can control the system.

SUPPORT: ENHANCING DECISION MAKING WITH MIS LO2-3

Now that we've reviewed the essentials of decision making, we are ready to understand the powerful benefits associated with using MIS to support managers making decisions.

A *model* is a simplified representation or abstraction of reality. Models help managers calculate risks, understand uncertainty, change variables, and manipulate time to make decisions. MIS support systems rely on models for computational and analytical routines that mathematically express relationships among variables. For example, a spreadsheet program, such as Microsoft Office Excel, might contain models that calculate market share or ROI. MIS have the capability and functionality to express far more complex modeling relationships that provide information, business intelligence, and knowledge. Figure 2.9 highlights the three primary types of management information systems available to support decision making across the company levels.

LO2-3 Classify the different operational support systems, managerial support systems, and strategic support systems, and explain how managers can use these systems to make decisions and gain competitive advantages.

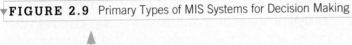

▼FIGURE 2.9 Primary Types of MIS Systems for Decision Making

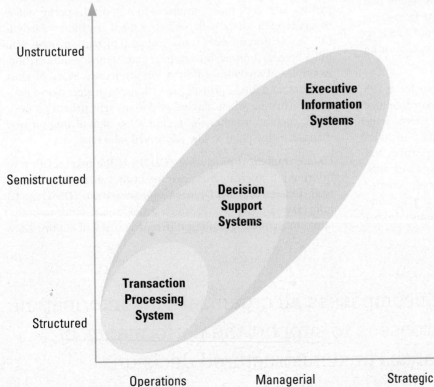

Operational Support Systems

Transactional information encompasses all the information contained within a single business process or unit of work, and its primary purpose is to support the performance of daily operational or structured decisions. Transactional information is created, for example, when customers are purchasing stocks, making an airline reservation, or withdrawing cash from an ATM. Managers use transactional information when making structured decisions at the operational level, such as when analyzing daily sales reports to determine how much inventory to carry.

Online transaction processing (OLTP) is the capture of transaction and event information using technology to (1) process the information according to defined business rules, (2) store the information, and (3) update existing information to

Living the DREAM

Virtual Nonprofits Helping Sustainability—What Are You Talking About?[4]

Second Life is an online 3D virtual world where its millions of residents create the content. Virtual worlds are exciting for any innovative businessperson who wants to find new ways to collaborate, train employees, and market products. A few business possibilities in a virtual world include:

- Holding a virtual meeting with sales managers located in Europe and Asia, which saves money and reduces carbon emissions.
- Presenting new sales initiatives and product ideas

and discussing them with a virtual focus group, which reduces the amount of mail required for promotional materials.

- Selling products and services in Second Life by creating an event to promote the product: a concert, a class, a famous speaker, a party, a contest.

Innovative individuals are pursing ways to use Second Life to help nonprofits such as Global Kids. Global Kids is a nonprofit group working to prepare urban youth to become

global citizens and community leaders. With help from Main Grid content creators and consultants like The Magicians and the Electric Sheep Company, Global Kids created a program in which students in New York City collaborate with Teen Grid Residents from around the world. The teens had to finish the interactive adventure to participate in a real-world essay contest. Winners of the contest received cash prizes (in U.S. dollars) and were part of an awards ceremony co-broadcast into the Teen Grid and on stage in New York City.

The benefits for social entrepreneurship and sustainability in a virtual world are endless. Identify a way you could use Second Life to help tackle an environmental issue, sustainable business idea, or social entrepreneurship endeavor. What types of roadblocks do you expect to encounter as you deploy your Second Life project? What types of security and ethical issues do you anticipate encountering in a virtual world?

---

reflect the new information. During OLTP, the organization must capture every detail of transactions and events. A **transaction processing system (TPS)** is the basic business system that serves the operational level (analysts) and assists in making structured decisions. The most common example of a TPS is an operational accounting system such as a payroll system or an order-entry system.

Using systems thinking, we can see that the inputs for a TPS are **source documents,** the original transaction record. Source documents for a payroll system can include time sheets, wage rates, and employee benefit reports. Transformation includes common procedures such as creating, reading, updating, and deleting (commonly referred to as CRUD) employee records, along with calculating the payroll and summarizing benefits. The output includes cutting the paychecks and generating payroll reports. Figure 2.10 demonstrates the systems thinking view of a TPS.[5]

Managerial Support Systems

Analytical information encompasses all organizational information, and its primary purpose is to support the performance of managerial analysis or semistructured decisions. Analytical information includes transactional information along with other information such as market and industry information. Examples of analytical information are trends, sales, product statistics, and future growth projections. Managers use analytical information when making important semistructured decisions, such as whether the organization should build a new manufacturing plant or hire additional sales reps.

Online analytical processing (OLAP) is the manipulation of information to create business intelligence in support of strategic decision making. **Decision support systems (DSSs)** model information using OLAP, which provides assistance in evaluating and choosing among different courses of action. DSSs

> Analytical information encompasses all organizational information, and its primary purpose is to support the performance of managerial analysis or semistructured decisions.

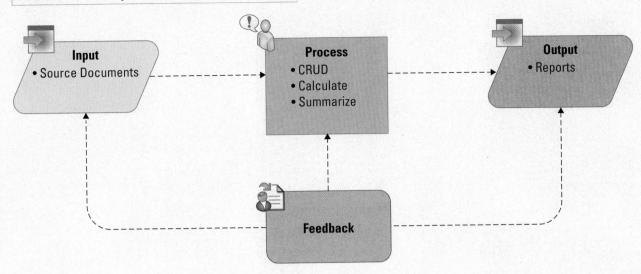

enable high-level managers to examine and manipulate large amounts of detailed data from different internal and external sources. Analyzing complex relationships among thousands or even millions of data items to discover patterns, trends, and exception conditions is one of the key uses associated with a DSS. For example, doctors may enter symptoms into a decision support system so it can help diagnose and treat patients. Insurance companies also use a DSS to gauge the risk of providing insurance to drivers who have imperfect driving records. One company found that married women who are homeowners with one speeding ticket are rarely cited for speeding again. Armed with this business intelligence, the company achieved a cost advantage by lowering insurance rates to this specific group of customers. The following are common DSS analysis techniques.

What-If Analysis
What-if analysis checks the impact of a change in a variable or assumption on the model. For example, "What will happen to the supply chain if a hurricane in South Carolina reduces holding inventory from 30 percent to 10 percent?" A user would be able to observe and evaluate any changes that occurred to the values in the model, especially to a variable such as profits. Users repeat this analysis with different variables until they understand all the effects of various situations.

Sensitivity Analysis
Sensitivity analysis, a special case of what-if analysis, is the study of the impact on other variables when one variable is changed repeatedly. Sensitivity analysis is useful when users are uncertain about the assumptions made in estimating the value of certain key variables. For example, repeatedly changing revenue in small increments to determine its effects on other variables would help a manager understand the impact of various revenue levels on other decision factors.

Goal-Seeking Analysis
Goal-seeking analysis finds the inputs necessary to achieve a goal such as a desired level of output. It is the reverse of what-if and sensitivity analysis. Instead of observing how changes in a variable affect other variables, goal-seeking analysis sets a target value (a goal) for a variable and then repeatedly changes other variables until the target value is achieved. For example, goal-seeking analysis could determine how many customers must purchase a new product to increase gross profits to $5 million.

Optimization Analysis
Optimization analysis, an extension of goal-seeking analysis, finds the optimum value for a target variable by repeatedly changing other variables, subject to specified constraints. By changing revenue and cost variables in an optimization analysis, managers can calculate the highest potential profits. Constraints on revenue and cost variables can be taken into consideration, such as limits on the amount of raw materials the company can afford to purchase and limits on employees available to meet production needs.

Figure 2.11 shows the common systems view of a DSS. Figure 2.12 shows how TPSs supply transactional data to a DSS. The DSS then summarizes and aggregates the information from the different TPSs, which assist managers in making semistructured decisions.

Strategic Support Systems

Decision making at the strategic level requires both business intelligence and knowledge to support the uncertainty and complexity associated with business strategies. An *executive information system (EIS)* is a specialized DSS that supports senior-level executives and unstructured, long-term, nonroutine decisions requiring judgment, evaluation, and insight. These decisions do not have a right or wrong answer, only efficient and effective answers. Moving up through th

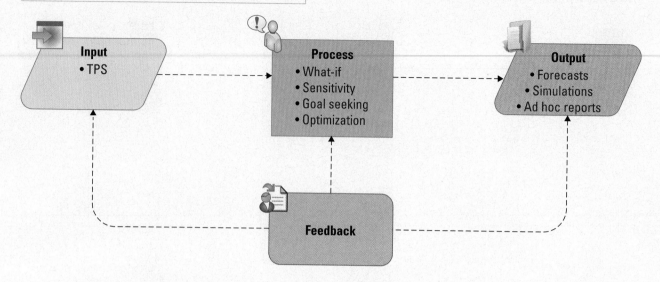

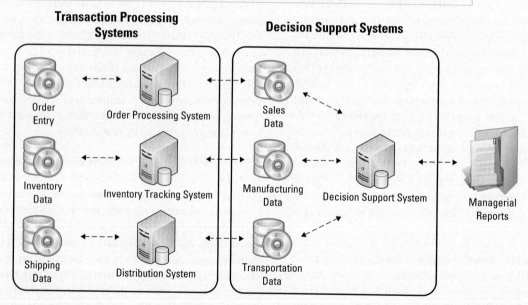

organizational pyramid, managers deal less with the details ("finer" information) and more with meaningful aggregations of information ("coarser" information). *Granularity* refers to the level of detail in the model or the decision-making process. The greater the granularity, the deeper the level of detail or fineness of data (see Figure 2.13).

A DSS differs from an EIS in that an EIS requires data from external sources to support unstructured decisions (see Figure 2.14). This is not to say that DSSs never use data from external sources, but typically DSS semistructured decisions rely on int___ data only.

___*on* produces graphical displays of patterns and ___ationships in large amounts of data. Executive ___stems use visualization to deliver specific key

information to top managers at a glance, with little or no interaction with the system. A common tool that supports visualization is a *digital dashboard,* which tracks KPIs and CSFs by compiling information from multiple sources and tailoring it to meet user needs. Following is a list of potential features included in a dashboard designed for a manufacturing team:

- A hot list of key performance indicators, refreshed every 15 minutes.

- A running line graph of planned versus actual production for the past 24 hours.

- A table showing actual versus forecasted product prices and inventories.

- A list of outstanding alerts and their resolution status.

- A graph of stock market prices.

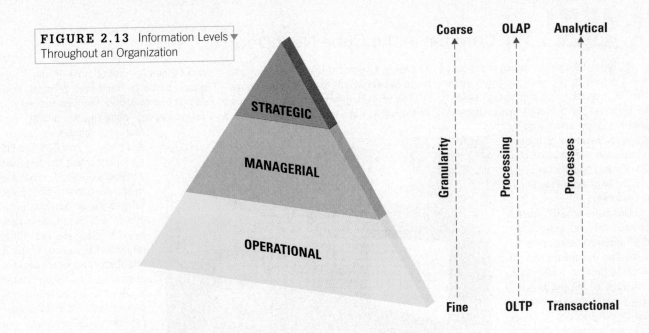

FIGURE 2.13 Information Levels Throughout an Organization

STRATEGIC

MANAGERIAL

OPERATIONAL

Coarse — OLAP — Analytical

Granularity — Processing — Processes

Fine — OLTP — Transactional

FIGURE 2.14 Interaction Between a TPS and EIS

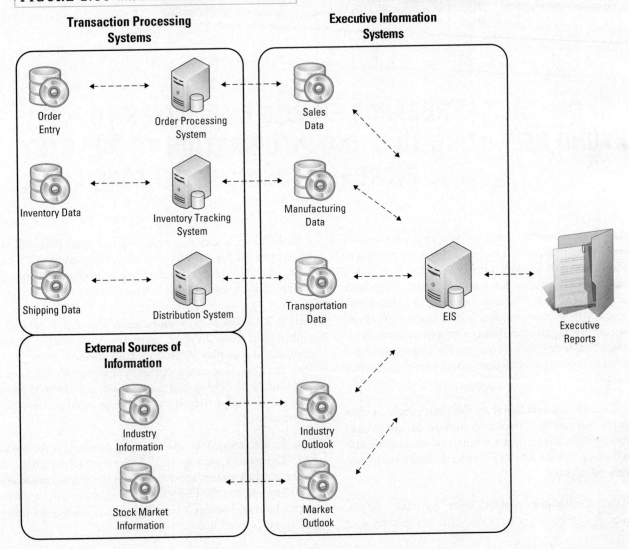

Transaction Processing Systems

Executive Information Systems

Order Entry

Order Processing System

Inventory Data

Inventory Tracking System

Shipping Data

Distribution System

Sales Data

Manufacturing Data

Transportation Data

EIS

Executive Reports

External Sources of Information

Industry Information

Stock Market Information

Industry Outlook

Market Outlook

BUSTED

The Criminal in the Cube Next Door[6]

What if the person sitting in the cube next to you was running a scam that cost your company $7 billion? An employee at a French bank allegedly used his inside knowledge of business processes to bypass the systems and make roughly $73 billion in bogus trades that cost the bank more than $7 billion to unwind.

Findings from the U.S. Secret Service and its examination of 23 incidents conducted by 26 insiders determined that 70 percent of the time, insiders took advantage of failures in business process rules and authorization mechanisms to steal from the company. Seventy-eight percent of the time, insiders were authorized and active computer users, and a surprising 43 percent used their own username and passwords to commit their crime.

This is a daunting reminder that every employee has the potential to become a knowledgeable insider, and if they ever turned bad in a fraudulent, criminal, even destructive way, they could do tremendous damage to your company. You need to protect your company's assets, and many of your DSS and EIS systems contain the business intelligence your company needs to operate effectively. What types of sensitive information is housed in a company's TPS, DSS, and EIS? What issues could you encounter if one of your employees decided to steal the information housed in your DSS? How could you protect your EIS from unethical users? What would you do if you thought the person sharing your cube was a rogue insider?

" DIGITAL DASHBOARDS ENABLE EMPLOYEES TO MOVE BEYOND REPORTING TO USING INFORMATION TO DIRECTLY INCREASE BUSINESS PERFORMANCE. "

Digital dashboards, whether basic or comprehensive, deliver results quickly. As they become easier to use, more employees can perform their own analyses without inundating MIS staff with questions and requests for reports. Digital dashboards enable employees to move beyond reporting to using information to directly increase business performance. With them, employees can react to information as soon as it becomes available and make decisions, solve problems, and change strategies daily instead of monthly. Digital dashboards offer the following capabilities:

Consolidation *Consolidation* is the aggregation of data from simple roll-ups to complex groupings of interrelated information. For example, data for different sales representatives can then be rolled up to an office level, then a state level, then a regional sales level.

Drill-Down *Drill-down* enables users to view details, and details of details, of information. This is the reverse of consolidation; a user can view regional sales data and then drill down all the way to each sales representative's data at each office. Drill-down capability lets managers view monthly, weekly, daily, or even hourly information.

Slice-and-Dice *Slice-and-dice* is the ability to look at information from different perspectives. One slice of information could display all product sales during a given promotion. Another slice could display a single product's sales for all promotions. Slicing and dicing is often performed along a time axis to analyze trends and find time-based patterns in the information.

One thing to remember when making decisions is the old saying, "Garbage in, garbage out." If the transactional data used in the support system are wrong, then the managerial analysis will be wrong and the DSS will simply assist in making a wrong decision faster. Managers should also ask, "What is the DSS *not* telling me before I make my final decision?"

THE FUTURE: ARTIFICIAL INTELLIGENCE LO2-4

Executive information systems are starting to take advantage of artificial intelligence to facilitate unstructured strategic decision making. *Artificial intelligence (AI)* simulates human thinking and behavior, such as the ability to reason and learn. Its ultimate goal is to build a system that can mimic human intelligence.

Intelligent systems are various commercial applications of artificial intelligence. They include sensors, software, and devices that emulate and enhance human capabilities, learn or understand from experience, make sense of ambiguous or contradictory information, and even use reasoning to solve problems and make decisions effectively. Intelligent systems perform such tasks as boosting productivity in factories by monitoring equipment and signaling when preventive maintenance is required. They are beginning to show up everywhere:

- At Manchester Airport in England, the Hefner AI Robot Cleaner alerts passengers to security and nonsmoking rules while it scrubs up to 65,600 square feet of floor per day. Laser scanners and ultrasonic detectors keep it from colliding with passengers.

- Shell Oil's SmartPump keeps drivers in their cars on cold, wet winter days. It can service any automobile built after 1987

that has been fitted with a special gas cap and a windshield-mounted transponder that tells the robot where to insert the pump.

- Matsushita's courier robot navigates hospital hallways, delivering patient files, X-ray films, and medical supplies.

- The FireFighter AI Robot can extinguish flames at chemical plants and nuclear reactors with water, foam, powder, or inert gas. The robot puts distance between human operators and the fire.[8]

AI systems increase the speed and consistency of decision making, solve problems with incomplete information, and resolve complicated issues that cannot be solved by conventional computing. There are many categories of AI systems; five of the most familiar are (1) expert systems, (2) neural networks, (3) genetic algorithms, (4) intelligent agents, and (5) virtual reality (see Figure 2.15).

LO2-4 Describe artificial intelligence, and identify its five main types.

Expert Systems

Expert systems are computerized advisory programs that imitate the reasoning processes of experts in solving difficult problems. Typically, they include a knowledge base containing various accumulated experience and a set of rules for applying

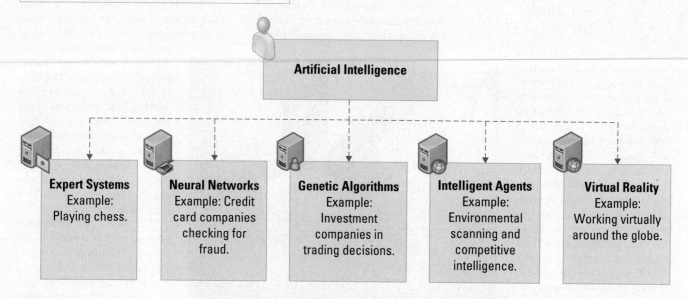

the knowledge base to each particular situation. Expert systems are the most common form of AI in the business arena because they fill the gap when human experts are difficult to find or retain or are too expensive. The best-known systems play chess and assist in medical diagnosis.

Neural Networks

A **neural network,** also called an artificial neural network, is a category of AI that attempts to emulate the way the human brain works. Neural networks analyze large quantities of information to establish patterns and characteristics in situations where the logic or rules are unknown. Neural networks' many features include:

- Learning and adjusting to new circumstances on their own.
- Lending themselves to massive parallel processing.
- Functioning without complete or well-structured information.
- Coping with huge volumes of information with many dependent variables.
- Analyzing nonlinear relationships in information (they have been called fancy regression analysis systems).

The finance industry is a veteran in the use of neural network technology and has been relying on various forms for over two decades. It uses neural networks to review loan applications and create patterns or profiles of applications that fall into two categories—approved or denied. Here are some examples of neural networks in finance:

- Citibank uses neural networks to find opportunities in financial markets. By carefully examining historical stock market data with neural network software, Citibank financial managers learn of interesting coincidences or small anomalies (called market inefficiencies). For example, it could be that whenever IBM stock goes up, so does Unisys stock, or that a U.S. Treasury note is selling for 1 cent less in Japan than in the United States. These snippets of information can make a big difference to Citibank's bottom line in a very competitive financial market.

- Visa, MasterCard, and many other credit card companies use a neural network to spot peculiarities in individual accounts and follow up by checking for fraud. MasterCard estimates neural networks save it $50 million annually.

- Insurance companies along with state compensation funds and other carriers use neural network software to identify fraud. The system searches for patterns in billing charges, laboratory tests, and frequency of office visits. A claim for which the diagnosis was a sprained ankle but treatment included an electrocardiogram would be flagged for the account manager.[9]

> Expert systems are the most common form of AI in the business arena because they fill the gap when human experts are difficult to find or retain or are too expensive.

Fuzzy logic is a mathematical method of handling imprecise or subjective information. The basic approach is to assign values between 0 and 1 to vague or ambiguous information. Zero represents information not included, while 1 represents inclusion or membership. For example, fuzzy logic is used in washing machines that determine by themselves how much water to use or how long to wash (they continue washing until the water is clean). In accounting and finance, fuzzy logic allows people to analyze information with subjective financial values (intangibles such as goodwill) that are very important considerations in economic analysis. Fuzzy logic and neural networks are often combined to express complicated and subjective concepts in a form that makes it possible to simplify the problem and apply rules that are executed with a level of certainty.[10]

Genetic Algorithms

A *genetic algorithm* is an artificial intelligence system that mimics the evolutionary, survival-of-the-fittest process to generate increasingly better solutions to a problem. A genetic algorithm is essentially an optimizing system: It finds the combination of inputs that gives the best outputs.

Genetic algorithms are best suited to decision-making environments in which thousands, or perhaps millions, of solutions are possible. Genetic algorithms can find and evaluate solutions with many more possibilities, faster and more thoroughly than a human. Organizations face decision-making environments for all types of problems that require optimization techniques, such as the following:

- Business executives use genetic algorithms to help them decide which combination of projects a firm should invest in, taking complicated tax considerations into account.

- Investment companies use genetic algorithms to help in trading decisions.

- Telecommunication companies use genetic algorithms to determine the optimal configuration of fiber-optic cable in a network that may include as many as 100,000 connection points. The genetic algorithm evaluates millions of cable configurations and selects the one that uses the least amount of cable.[11]

Intelligent Agents

An *intelligent agent* is a special-purpose knowledge-based information system that accomplishes specific tasks on behalf of its users. Intelligent agents usually have a graphical representation, such as "Sherlock Holmes" for an information search agent.

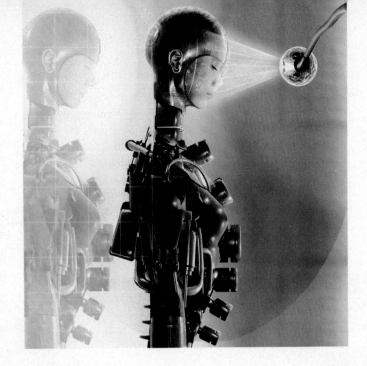

One of the simplest examples of an intelligent agent is a shopping bot. A *shopping bot* is software that will search several retailer websites and provide a comparison of each retailer's offerings including price and availability. Increasingly, intelligent agents handle the majority of a company's Internet buying and selling and complete such processes as finding products, bargaining over prices, and executing transactions. Intelligent agents also have the capability to handle all supply chain buying and selling.

Another application for intelligent agents is in environmental scanning and competitive intelligence. For instance, an intelligent agent can learn the types of competitor information users want to track, continuously scan the web for it, and alert users when a significant event occurs.

Multiagent Systems and Agent-Based Modeling

What do cargo transport systems, book distribution centers, the video game market, and a flu epidemic have in common with an ant colony? They are all complex adaptive systems. By observing parts of Earth's ecosystem, like ant colonies, artificial intelligence scientists can use hardware and software models that incorporate insect characteristics and behavior to (1) learn how people-based systems behave, (2) predict how they will behave under a given set of circumstances, and (3) improve human systems to make them more efficient and effective. This process of learning from ecosystems and

"A genetic algorithm is essentially an optimizing system: It finds the combination of inputs that gives the best outputs."

adapting their characteristics to human and organizational situations is called biomimicry.

In the past few years, AI research has made much progress in modeling complex organizations as a whole with the help of multiagent systems. In a multiagent system, groups of intelligent agents have the ability to work independently and to interact with each other. Agent-based modeling is a way of simulating human organizations using multiple intelligent agents, each of which follows a set of simple rules and can adapt to changing conditions.

Agent-based modeling systems are being used to model stock market fluctuations, predict the escape routes people seek in a burning building, estimate the effects of interest rates on consumers with different types of debt, and anticipate how changes in conditions will affect the supply chain, to name just a few.

Virtual Reality

Virtual reality is a computer-simulated environment that can be a simulation of the real world or an imaginary world. Virtual reality is a fast-growing area of artificial intelligence that had its origins in efforts to build more natural, realistic, multisensory human-computer interfaces. Virtual reality enables telepresence where users can be anywhere in the world and use virtual reality systems to work alone or together at a remote site.

show me *the* MONEY

If It Ain't Broke, Don't Fix It

Do you hate waiting in line at the grocery store? Do you find it frustrating when you go to the video store and cannot find the movie you wanted to rent? Do you get annoyed when the pizza delivery person brings you the wrong order? This is your chance to reengineer the annoying process that drives you crazy. Choose a problem you are currently experiencing, and reengineer the process to make it more efficient and effective. Be sure to provide an As-Is and To-Be business process model.

real estate expenses. Drawbacks include the fear among workers that they will jeopardize their careers by working from home, and some workers need a busy environment to stay productive. Virtual workers also tend to feel alone, secluded, and deprived of vital training and mentoring.[12]

> ## " VIRTUAL REALITY IS A FAST-GROWING AREA OF ARTIFICIAL INTELLIGENCE THAT HAD ITS ORIGINS IN EFFORTS TO BUILD MORE NATURAL, REALISTIC, MULTISENSORY HUMAN-COMPUTER INTERFACES. "

Typically, this involves using a virtual reality system to enhance the sight and touch of a human who is remotely manipulating equipment to accomplish a task. Examples range from virtual surgery, where surgeon and patient may be on opposite sides of the globe, to the remote use of equipment in hazardous environments such as chemical plants and nuclear reactors.

Virtual Workforce At Microsoft's headquarters in Redmond, Washington, traffic congestion occurs daily for the 35,000 commuters. To alleviate the congestion Microsoft is offering its employees the ability to work virtually from home. Over 42 percent of IBMs 330,000 employees work virtually saving over $100 million per year in real estate–related expenses. Working virtually offers several advantages such as fewer cars on the road, increases in worker productivity, and decreasing

{SECTION 2-2}
Business Processes

LEARNING OUTCOMES

LO2-5 Explain the value of business processes for a company, and differentiate between customer-facing and business-facing processes.

LO2-6 Demonstrate the value of business process modeling, and compare As-Is and To-Be models.

LO2-7 Differentiate among business process improvements, streamlining, and reengineering.

LO2-8 Describe business process management and its value to an organization.

EVALUATING BUSINESS PROCESSES LO2-5

Most companies pride themselves on providing breakthrough products and services for customers. But if customers do not receive what they want quickly, accurately, and hassle-free, even fantastic offerings will not prevent a company from annoying customers and ultimately eroding its own financial performance. To avoid this pitfall and protect its competitive advantage, a company must continually evaluate all the business processes in its value chain. Recall from Chapter 1 that a *business process* is a standardized set of activities that accomplish a specific task, such as processing a customer's order. Business processes transform a set of inputs into a set of outputs—goods or services—for another person or process by using people and tools. Understanding business processes helps a manager envision how the entire company operates.

Improving the efficiency and effectiveness of its business processes will improve the firm's value chain. The goal of this section is to expand on Porter's value chain analysis by detailing the powerful value-adding relationships between business strategies and core business processes. Figure 2.16 illustrates several common business processes.

The processes outlined in Figure 2.16 reflect functional thinking. Some processes, such as a programming process, may be contained wholly within a single department. However, most, such as ordering a product, are cross-functional or cross-departmental processes and span the entire organization. The process of "order to delivery" focuses on the entire customer order process across functional departments (see Figure 2.17). Another example is "product realization," which includes not only the way a product is developed, but also the way it is marketed and serviced. Some other cross-functional business processes are taking a product from concept to market, acquiring customers, loan processing, providing post-sales service, claim processing, and reservation handling.

Accounting and Finance
- Creating financial statements
- Paying of Accounts Payable
- Collecting of Accounts Receivable

Marketing and Sales
- Promoting of discounts
- Communicating marketing campaigns
- Attracting customers
- Processing sales

Operations Management
- Ordering inventory
- Creating production schedules
- Manufacturing goods

Human Resources
- Hiring employees
- Enrolling employees in health care
- Tracking vacation and sick time

▼ **FIGURE 2.17** Five Steps in the Order-to-Delivery Business Process

Step One
- Create campaign
- Check inventory

Step Two
- Place order
- Notify production
- Check credit

Step Three
- Manufacture goods

Step Four
- Deliver goods
- Bill customer

Step Five
- Support sale

Marketing

Sales

Operations Management

Accounting and Finance

Customer Service

Customer-Facing Processes	Industry-Specific Customer-Facing Processes	Business-Facing Processes
Order processing Customer service Sales process Customer billing Order shipping	Banking – Loan processing Insurance – Claims processing Government – Grant allocation Hotel – Reservation handling Airline – Baggage handling	Strategic planning Tactical planning Budget forecasting Training Purchasing raw materials

Customer-facing processes, also called front-office processes, result in a product or service received by an organization's external customer. They include fulfilling orders, communicating with customers, and sending out bills and marketing information. *Business-facing processes,* also called back-office processes, are invisible to the external customer but essential to the effective management of the business; they include goal setting, day-to-day planning, giving performance feedback and rewards, and allocating resources. Figure 2.18 displays the different categories of customer-facing and business-facing processes along with an example of each.[13]

A company's strategic vision should provide guidance on which business processes are core, that is, which are directly linked to the firm's critical success factors. Mapping these core business processes to the value chain reveals where the processes touch the customers and affect their perceptions of value. This type of map conceptualizes the business as a value delivery system, allowing managers to ensure all core business processes are operating as efficiently and effectively as possible.

and distribution. As this example demonstrates, changing business processes can generate significant competitive advantages across the value chain.[14]

L02-5 Explain the value of business processes for a company, and differentiate between customer-facing and business-facing processes.

MODELS: MEASURING PERFORMANCE L02-6

Business process modeling, or *mapping,* is the activity of creating a detailed flowchart or process map of a work process that shows its inputs, tasks, and activities in a structured sequence. A *business process model* is a graphic description of a process, showing the sequence of process tasks, which is

" MAPPING THESE CORE BUSINESS PROCESSES TO THE VALUE CHAIN REVEALS WHERE THE PROCESSES TOUCH THE CUSTOMERS AND AFFECT THEIR PERCEPTIONS OF VALUE. "

A firm can even create a value chain map of the entire industry to extend critical success factors and business process views beyond its boundaries. This type of evaluation allowed National Semiconductor to identify the core business processes required to move assembly plants to Southeast Asia. The map identified logistics and distribution as critical to the success of the move. Thus, to ensure reliable delivery of its products, National Semiconductor contracted with Federal Express, combining its outstanding manufacturing process and Federal Express's exceptional distribution processes. The move allowed National Semiconductor to save money by closing nine warehouses while maintaining excellence in logistics

developed for a specific purpose and from a selected viewpoint. A set of one or more process models details the many functions of a system or subject area with graphics and text, and its purpose is to:

- Expose process detail gradually and in a controlled manner.

- Encourage conciseness and accuracy in describing the process model.

- Focus attention on the process model interfaces.

- Provide a powerful process analysis and consistent design vocabulary. (Figures 2.19 through 2.22 provide examples of business process modeling.)[15]

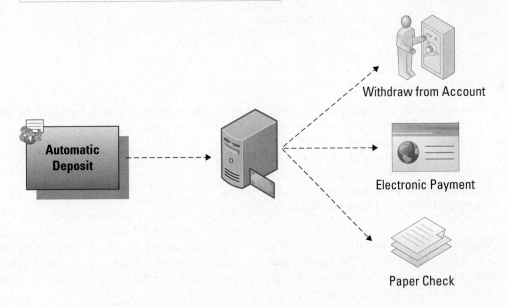

Business process modeling usually begins with a functional process representation of *what* the process problem is, or an As-Is process model. **As-Is process models** represent the current state of the operation that has been mapped, without any specific improvements or changes to existing processes. The next step is to build a To-Be process model that displays *how* the process problem will be solved or implemented. **To-Be** *process models* show the results of applying change improvement opportunities to the current (As-Is) process model. This approach ensures that the process is fully and clearly understood before the details of a process solution are decided upon. The To-Be process model shows *how* the *what* is to be realized. Figure 2.23 displays the As-Is and To-Be process models for ordering a hamburger.

FIGURE 2.21 Order Fulfillment Process Model

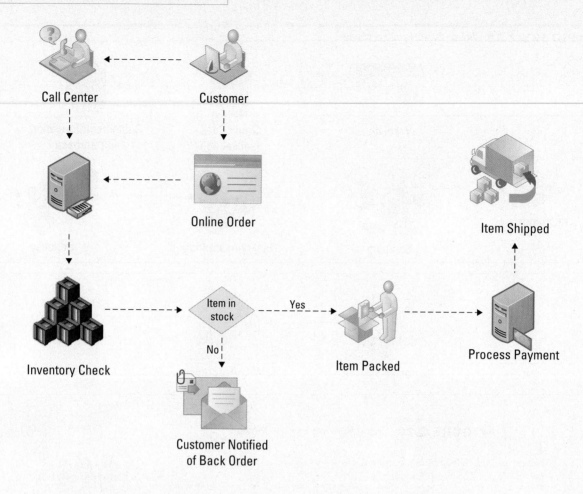

As-Is and To-Be process models are both integral in business process reengineering projects, since these diagrams are very powerful in visualizing the activities, processes, and data flow of an organization. Figure 2.24 illustrates an As-Is process model of the order-to-delivery process using swim lanes to represent the relevant departments. The *swim lane* layout arranges the steps of a business process into a set of rows depicting the various elements.

You need to be careful not to become inundated in excessive detail when creating an As-Is process model. The primary goal is to simplify, eliminate, and improve the To-Be processes. Process improvement efforts focus on defining the most efficient and effective process identifying all of the illogical, missing, or irrelevant processes.

Investigating business processes can help an organization find bottlenecks, remove redundant tasks, and recognize smooth-running processes. For example, a florist might have a key success factor of reducing delivery time. A florist that has an inefficient ordering process or a difficult distribution process will be unable to achieve this goal. Taking down inaccurate orders, incorrect addresses, or shipping delays can cause errors in the delivery process. Improving order entry, production, or scheduling processes can improve the delivery process.

> ❝ INVESTIGATING BUSINESS PROCESSES CAN HELP AN ORGANIZATION FIND BOTTLENECKS, REMOVE REDUNDANT TASKS, AND RECOGNIZE SMOOTH-RUNNING PROCESSES. ❞

FIGURE 2.22
Purchasing an Item on eBay and Selling
an Item on eBay Process Model

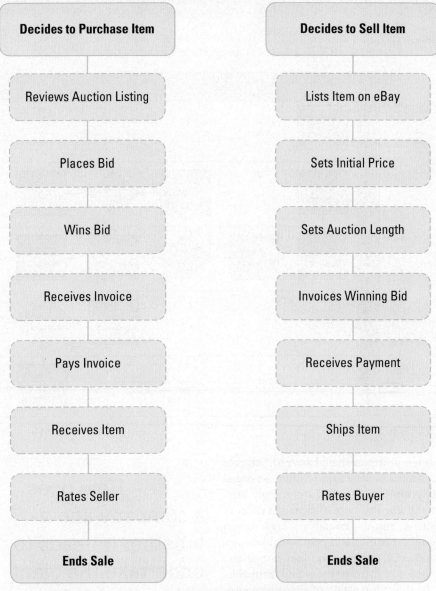

Decides to Purchase Item	Decides to Sell Item
Reviews Auction Listing	Lists Item on eBay
Places Bid	Sets Initial Price
Wins Bid	Sets Auction Length
Receives Invoice	Invoices Winning Bid
Pays Invoice	Receives Payment
Receives Item	Ships Item
Rates Seller	Rates Buyer
Ends Sale	**Ends Sale**

FIGURE 2.23
As-Is and To-Be Process Model for
Ordering a Hamburger

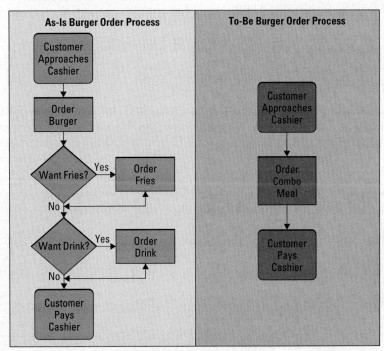

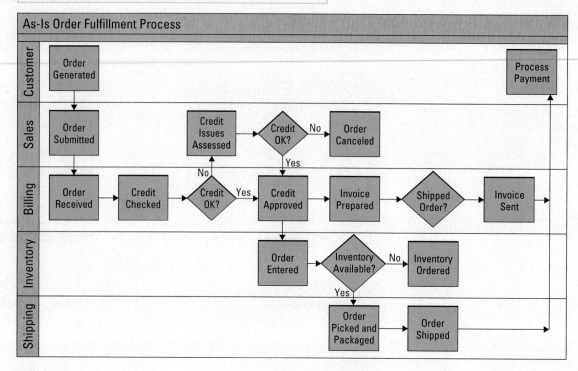

Business processes should drive MIS choices and should be based on business strategies and goals (see Figure 2.25A). Only after determining the most efficient and effective business process should an organization choose the MIS that supports that business process. Of course, this does not always happen, and managers may find themselves in the difficult position of changing a business process because the system cannot support the ideal solution (see Figure 2.25B). Managers who make MIS choices and only then determine how their business processes should perform typically fail.

> **How does a company know whether it needs to undertake the giant step of changing core business processes?**

L02-6 Demonstrate the value of business process modeling, and compare As-Is and To-Be models.

SUPPORT: CHANGING BUSINESS PROCESSES WITH MIS L02-7

Workflow includes the tasks, activities, and responsibilities required to execute each step in a business process. Understanding workflow, customers' expectations, and the competitive environment provides managers with the necessary ingredients to design and evaluate alternative business processes in order to maintain competitive advantages when internal or external circumstances change.

Alternative business processes should be effective (they deliver the intended results) and efficient (they consume the least amount of resources for the intended value). They should also be adaptable or flexible and support change as customers, market forces, and technology shift. Figure 2.26 shows the three primary types of business process change available to firms and the business areas in which they are most often effective. How does a company know whether it needs to undertake the giant step of changing core business processes? Three conditions indicate the time is right to initiate a business process change:

1. There has been a pronounced shift in the market the process was designed to serve.

2. The company is markedly below industry benchmarks on its core processes.

3. To regain competitive advantage, the company must leapfrog competition on key dimensions.[16]

L02-7 Differentiate among business process improvements, streamlining, and reengineering.

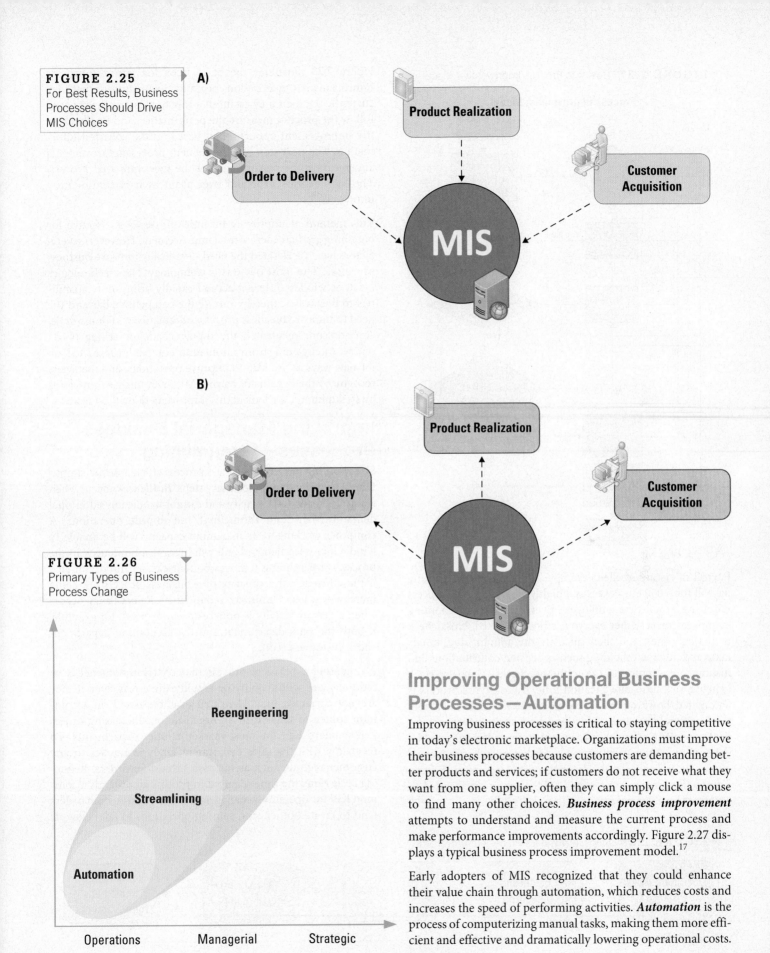

FIGURE 2.25
For Best Results, Business Processes Should Drive MIS Choices

A)

Order to Delivery

Product Realization

Customer Acquisition

MIS

B)

Order to Delivery

Product Realization

Customer Acquisition

MIS

FIGURE 2.26
Primary Types of Business Process Change

Reengineering

Streamlining

Automation

Operations   Managerial   Strategic

Improving Operational Business Processes—Automation

Improving business processes is critical to staying competitive in today's electronic marketplace. Organizations must improve their business processes because customers are demanding better products and services; if customers do not receive what they want from one supplier, often they can simply click a mouse to find many other choices. *Business process improvement* attempts to understand and measure the current process and make performance improvements accordingly. Figure 2.27 displays a typical business process improvement model.[17]

Early adopters of MIS recognized that they could enhance their value chain through automation, which reduces costs and increases the speed of performing activities. *Automation* is the process of computerizing manual tasks, making them more efficient and effective and dramatically lowering operational costs.

FIGURE 2.27 Business Process Improvement Model

Process Improvement Model

```
                                    ┌──────────────┐
                                    │  Identify    │
                                    │  a Process   │
                                    └──────┬───────┘
                                           ↓
        ◇◇◇◇◇◇◇◇◇◇◇         Yes      ┌──────────────┐
       ◇ Is there an ◇──────────────→│ Identify one │
       ◇  additional  ◇              │ of the steps │
       ◇    step?     ◇              │ in the process│
        ◇◇◇◇◇◇◇◇◇◇◇              └──────┬───────┘
                                           ↓
    ┌──────────┐     No       ◇◇◇◇◇◇◇◇◇◇
    │Remove the│←─────────────◇ Is the step ◇
    │   step   │              ◇  necessary? ◇
    └────┬─────┘               ◇◇◇◇◇◇◇◇◇◇
         ↑                          │ Yes
         │                          ↓
    ┌──────────┐     No       ◇◇◇◇◇◇◇◇◇◇
    │ Keep the │←─────────────◇ Can the step ◇
    │   step   │              ◇ be improved? ◇
    └────┬─────┘               ◇◇◇◇◇◇◇◇◇◇
         ↑                          │ Yes
         │                          ↓
 No      │               ◇◇◇◇◇◇◇◇◇◇◇◇
         │               ◇ Are resources  ◇
         │               ◇   available to  ◇
         │      No       ◇  implement the  ◇
         │               ◇     change?     ◇
         │                ◇◇◇◇◇◇◇◇◇◇◇◇
    ┌──────────┐    Yes           │ Yes
    │ Document │←─────────────────┘
    │ improved │
    │   step   │
    └────┬─────┘
         ↓
    ┌──────────┐
    │  Model   │
    │ improved │
    │ process  │
    └────┬─────┘
         ↓
    ┌──────────────┐
    │Implement New │
    │   Process    │
    └──────────────┘
```

Payroll offers an excellent example. Calculating and tracking payroll for 5,000 employees is a highly labor-intensive process requiring 30 full-time employees. Every two weeks accounting employees must gather everyone's hours worked, cross-check with wage rates, and then calculate the amount due, minus taxes and other withholding such as pension contributions and insurance premiums, to create the paychecks. They also track benefits, sick time, and vacation time. If the payroll process is automated, however, one employee can easily calculate payroll, track withholding and deductions, and create paychecks for 5,000 people in a few hours, since everything is performed by the system. Automation improves efficiency and effectiveness and reduces head count, lowering overall operational costs. Transaction processing systems (TPSs) are primarily used to automate business processes.

Figure 2.28 illustrates the basic steps for business process improvement. Organizations begin by documenting what they currently do; then they establish a way to measure the process, follow the process, measure the performance, and finally identify improvement opportunities based on the collected information. The next step is to implement process improvements and measure the performance of the new improved process. The loop repeats over and over again as it is continuously improved.[18]

This method of improving business processes is effective for obtaining gradual, incremental improvement. However, several factors have accelerated the need to radically improve business processes. The most obvious is technology. New technologies (such as wireless Internet access) rapidly bring new capabilities to businesses, thereby raising the competitive bar and the need to improve business processes dramatically. For example, Amazon.com reinvented the supply chain for selling books online. After gaining from automation, companies began to look for new ways to use MIS to improve operations, and managers recognized the benefits of pairing MIS with business processes by streamlining. We look at this improvement method next.

Improving Managerial Business Processes—Streamlining

Streamlining improves business process efficiencies by simplifying or eliminating unnecessary steps. *Bottlenecks* occur when resources reach full capacity and cannot handle any additional demands; they limit throughput and impede operations. A computer working at its maximum capacity will be unable to handle increased demand and will become a bottleneck in the process. Streamlining removes bottlenecks, an important step if the efficiency and capacity of a business process are being increased. It also eliminates redundancy. *Redundancy* occurs when a task or activity is unnecessarily repeated, for example, if both the sales department and the accounting department check customer credit.

Automating a business process that contains bottlenecks or redundancies will magnify or amplify these problems if they are not corrected first. Here's an example based on a common source of tension in an organization. Increasing orders is a standard KPI for most marketing/sales departments. To meet this KPI, the sales department tends to say yes to any customer request, such as for rush or custom orders. Reducing *cycle time,* the time required to process an order, is a common KPI for operations management. Rush and custom orders tend to create bottlenecks, causing operations to fall below its

FIGURE 2.28 Steps in Business Process Improvement

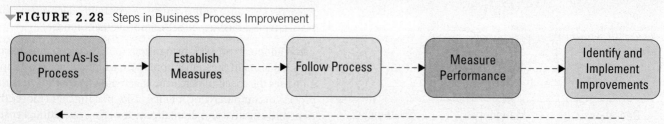

Document As-Is Process - - -→ Establish Measures - - -→ Follow Process - - -→ Measure Performance - - -→ Identify and Implement Improvements

You Accidently Sent Your Confidential Email to Your Significant Other to Your Grandmother—Ouch![19]

If someone at your work currently looked through your email, would they find anything unacceptable? There is a 99 percent chance that at some point you have been guilty of using your work email for personal use. Not only are you wasting company time and resources, but you are also putting yourself at serious risk of violating company policies. There is no doubt some of these mistakes are funny, like the embarrassing story of how a woman sent a racy email to her husband, only to have accidentally sent it to her boss instead. However, you stop laughing when you are fired because it was you who sent the unsuitable email!

You do not own your email; it is that simple. Your employer owns your email, and they have every right to read every single piece of email that you send or is sent to you. Some people argue that it is an invasion of privacy to read someone else's email, but it is not private when you are sitting in the company's office building, at the company's desk, using the company's computer equipment and email software. Technology is so advanced that your employer can flag anything with inappropriate language or keywords such as "résumé," "job search," or "confidential."

How do you prevent email blunders? It is a good idea to create a free Google Gmail account or a Hotmail account for your personal email. Also, before sending any email, ask yourself: If my boss was looking over my shoulder right now, would he or she approve? This is the true litmus test that can be applied to anything an employee does at work.

Now, here comes the hard part: What if you are working from home, using your own computer? Does the company still have a right to monitor your email? If you are using your own personal iPhone to work remotely and you receive the company's emails on your device, is it still company property? What do you think? What additional dilemmas do you see being created as innovative technologies such as BlackBerrys and iPhones continue to change the fundamental business process of how we work?

---

benchmarked cycle time. Removing these bottlenecks, however, can create master streamlined business processes that deliver both standard and custom orders reliably and profitably. The goal of streamlining is not only to automate but also to improve by monitoring, controlling, and changing the business process.

FedEx streamlined every business process to provide a CSF of speedy and reliable delivery of packages. It created one central hub in Memphis, Tennessee, that processed all its orders. It its traditional delivery process to handle increased volume faster and more reliably, it could have missed an entire customer segment.[20]

Improving Strategic Business Processes—Reengineering

The flat world (see Chapter 1) is bringing more companies and more customers into the marketplace, greatly increasing

> **"The goal of streamlining is not only to automate but also to improve by monitoring, controlling, and changing the business process."**

purchased its own planes to be sure it could achieve the desired level of service. FedEx combined MIS and traditional distribution and logistics processes to create a competitive advantage. FedEx soon identified another market segment of customers who cared a little less about speed and were willing to trade off early-morning delivery for delivery any time *within* the next day at a significantly lower price. The firm had to reevaluate its strategy and realign its business processes to capture this market segment. Had Federal Express focused only on improving competition. Wine wholesalers in the United States must now compete globally, for instance, because customers can just as easily order a bottle of wine from a winery in France as from them. Companies need breakthrough performance and business process changes just to stay in the game. As the rate of change increases, companies looking for rapid change and dramatic improvement are turning to **business process reengineering (BPR),** the analysis and redesign of workflow within and between enterprises. Figure 2.29 highlights an analogy

FIGURE 2.29 Different Ways to Travel the Same Route

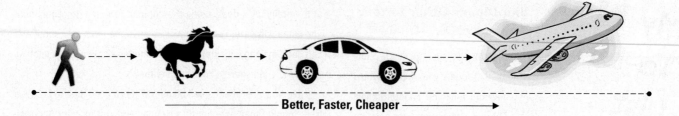

Better, Faster, Cheaper

to process improvement by explaining the different means of traveling along the same route. A company could improve the way it travels by changing from foot to horse and then from horse to car. With a BPR mind-set, however, it would look beyond automating and streamlining to find a completely different approach. It would ignore the road and travel by air to get from point A to point B. Companies often follow the same indirect path for doing business, not realizing there might be a different, faster, and more direct way.

An organization can reengineer its cross-departmental business processes or an individual department's business processes to help meet its CSFs and KPIs. When selecting a business process to reengineer, wise managers focus on those core processes that

- Does it have a high impact on the agency's strategic direction?
- Does it significantly impact customer satisfaction?
- Is it antiquated?
- Does it fall far below best-in-class?
- Is it crucial for productivity improvement?
- Will savings from automation be clearly visible?
- Is the return on investment from implementation high and preferably immediate?

BPR relies on a different school of thought than business process improvement. *In the extreme,* BPR assumes the current process is irrelevant, does not work, or is broken and

> When selecting a business process to reengineer, wise managers focus on those core processes that are critical to performance, rather than marginal processes that have little impact.

are critical to performance, rather than marginal processes that have little impact. The effort to reengineer a business process as a strategic activity requires a different mind-set than that required in continuous business process improvement programs. Because companies have tended to overlook the powerful contribution that processes can make to strategy, they often undertake process improvement efforts using their current processes as the starting point. Managers focusing on reengineering can instead use several criteria to identify opportunities:

- Is the process broken?
- Is it feasible that reengineering of this process will succeed?

must be overhauled from scratch. Starting from such a clean slate enables business process designers to disassociate themselves from today's process and focus on a new process. It is as if they are projecting themselves into the future and asking: What should the process look like? What do customers want it to look like? What do other employees want it to look like? How do best-in-class companies do it? How can new technology facilitate the process?

Figure 2.30 displays the basic steps in a business process reengineering effort. It begins with defining the scope and objectives of the reengineering project and then takes the process

FIGURE 2.30 Business Process Reengineering Model

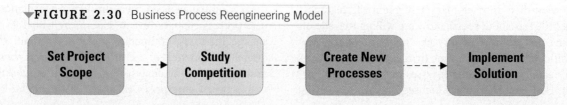

designers through a learning process with customers, employees, competitors, and new technology. Given this knowledge base, the designers can create a plan of action based on the gap between current processes, technologies, and structures and their vision of the processes of the future. It is then top management's job to implement the chosen solution.[21]

System thinking plays a big role in BPR. Automation and streamlining operate departmentally, whereas BPR occurs at the systems level or companywide level and the end-to-end view of a process.

Creating value for the customer is the leading reason for instituting BPR, and MIS often plays an important enabling role. Fundamentally new business processes enabled Progressive Insurance to slash its claims settlement time from 31 days

A true BPR effort does more for a company than simply improve a process by performing it better, faster, and cheaper. Progressive Insurance's BPR effort redefined best practices for an entire industry.[22]

The Business Process Systems View
Leveraging business processes has enormous implications for the business system as a whole. It requires recognition that any meaningful change within the organization affects the entire organization. Without a systems view, the identification of business process flaws and implementation of proposed solutions will often fix only symptoms. Many times what can make one process effective is what makes another process ineffective. Therefore, the redesign of any process within an integrated system requires appreciating the impact of the redesign on other processes.

> "Leveraging business processes has enormous implications for the business system as a whole."

to four hours, for instance. Typically, car insurance companies follow this standard claims resolution process: The customer gets into an accident, has the car towed, and finds a ride home. The customer then calls the insurance company to begin the claims process, which includes an evaluation of the damage, assignment of fault, and an estimate of the cost of repairs, and which usually takes about a month (see Figure 2.31). Progressive Insurance's innovation was to offer a mobile claims process. When a customer has a car accident, he or she calls in the claim on the spot. The Progressive claims adjuster comes to the accident site, surveying the scene and taking digital photographs. The adjuster then offers the customer on-site payment, towing services, and a ride home.

For example, operations management often wants to wait until a truck is full before sending it out for deliveries because the department's KPI measures cost-per-mile-transported. Conversely, the customer satisfaction KPIs measure the ability to make the order-to-delivery cycle time as short as possible, requiring the truck to leave as soon as the product is available, whether it is full or not. Changing business processes to meet operations management KPIs will thus reduce customer satisfaction KPIs. Changing business processes to meet customer satisfaction KPIs will lower operations management KPIs. A systems view, on the other hand, will allow managers to understand the impact business processes have across the entire organization, so both can be improved.

FIGURE 2.31 Auto Insurance Claims Processes

Company A: Claims Resolution Process

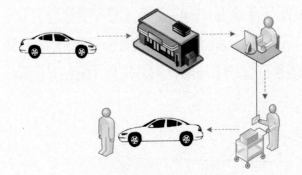

Resolution Cycle Time: 3–8 weeks

Progressive Insurance: Claims Resolution Process

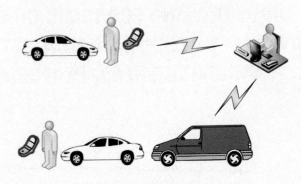

Resolution Cycle Time: 30 minutes–3 hours

THE FUTURE: BUSINESS PROCESS MANAGEMENT L02-8

Creating a company that can quickly adapt to market, industry, and economic changes to create a competitive advantage requires a new set of operating rules based on achieving speed, performance, and improved delivery. Until recently, business process improvement initiatives focused on improving workflow or document-based processes that were completed by hand. Now, however, *business process management (BPM) systems* focus on evaluating and improving processes that include both person-to-person workflow and system-to-system communications. BPM systems include advanced features such as enhanced process modeling, simulation, execution, and monitoring, providing a high level of flexibility while reducing costs. Think of BPM as a way to build, implement, and monitor automated processes that span organizational boundaries—a kind of next-generation workflow. BPM not only allows a business process to be executed more efficiently, but it also provides the tools to measure performance and identify opportunities for improvement, as well as to easily capture opportunities such as:

- Bringing processes, people, and information together.
- Breaking down the barriers between business areas and finding "owners" for the processes.
- Managing front-office and back-office business processes.

BPM uniquely offers two types of systems: (1) Customer-facing or front-office BPM focuses on person-to-person workflow and (2) business-facing or back-office BPM focuses on system-to-system workflow. With BPM the two systems function as one, allowing continual improvements to many business processes simultaneously and in real time. BPM's unified environment encourages people to observe, think, and provide feedback, harnessing the power of ideas and insight and promoting systems thinking throughout the organization. Providing the flexibility for quick BPM change drives efficiency and effectiveness, creating optimal business processes. This ability is the foundation for creating an operation that gives a company competitive advantage.

L02-8 Describe business process management and its value to an organization.

> CREATING A COMPANY THAT CAN QUICKLY ADAPT TO MARKET, INDUSTRY, AND ECONOMIC CHANGES TO CREATE A COMPETITIVE ADVANTAGE REQUIRES A NEW SET OF OPERATING RULES BASED ON ACHIEVING SPEED, PERFORMANCE, AND IMPROVED DELIVERY.

GET ONLINE

mhhe.com/BaltzanM2e

for study materials including
quizzes, iPod downloads,
and video

chapter three

ebusiness: electronic business value

What's in IT for Me?

Internet and communication technologies have revolutionized the way business operates, improving upon traditional methods and even introducing new opportunities and ventures that were simply not possible before. More than just giving organizations another means of conducting transactions, online business provides the ability to develop and maintain customer relationships, supplier relationships, and even employee relationships between and within enterprises.

As future managers and organizational knowledge workers, you need to understand the benefits ebusiness can offer an organization and your career, the challenges that accompany web technologies, and their impact on organizational communication and collaboration. You need to be aware of the strategies organizations can use to deploy ebusiness and the methods of measuring ebusiness success. This chapter will give you this knowledge and help prepare you for success in tomorrow's electronic global marketplace. ■

CHAPTER OUTLINE

SECTION 3-1 >>
WEB 1.0: Ebusiness
- Disruptive Technologies and Web 1.0
- Advantages of Ebusiness
- Ebusiness Models
- Ebusiness Tools for Connecting and Communicating
- The Challenges of Ebusiness

SECTION 3-2 >>
WEB 2.0: Business 2.0
- Web 2.0: Advantages of Business 2.0
- Networking Communities with Business 2.0
- Business 2.0 Tools for Collaborating
- The Challenges of Business 2.0
- Web 3.0: Defining the Next Generation of Online Business Opportunities

FIGURE 3.17 Characteristics of Business 2.0

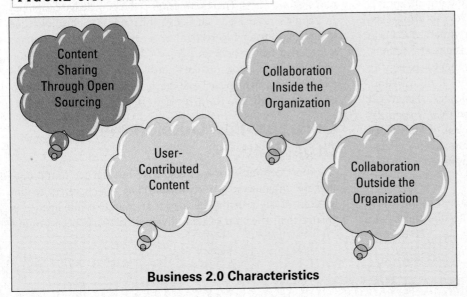

Content Sharing Through Open Sourcing

User-Contributed Content

Collaboration Inside the Organization

Collaboration Outside the Organization

Business 2.0 Characteristics

threat to Microsoft's Internet Explorer. How do open source software companies generate revenues? Many people are still awaiting an answer to this very important question.[21]

User-Contributed Content

Ebusiness was characterized by a few companies or users posting content for the masses. Business 2.0 is characterized by the masses posting content for the masses. *User-contributed content* (or *user-generated content*) is created and updated by many users for many users. Websites such as Flickr, Wikipedia, and YouTube, for example, move control of online media from the hands of leaders to the hands of users. Netflix and Amazon both use user-generated content to drive their recommendation tools, and websites such as Yelp use customer reviews to express opinions on products and services. Companies are embracing user-generated content to help with everything from marketing to product development and quality assurance.

One of the most popular forms of user-generated content is a *reputation system*, where buyers post feedback on sellers. EBay

Content Sharing Through Open Sourcing

An *open system* consists of nonproprietary hardware and software based on publicly known standards that allow third parties to create add-on products to plug into or interoperate with the system. Thousands of hardware devices and

> ## Companies are embracing user-generated content to help with everything from marketing to product development and quality assurance.

software applications created and sold by third-party vendors interoperate with computers, such as iPods, drawing software, and mice.

Source code contains instructions written by a programmer specifying the actions to be performed by computer software. *Open source* refers to any software whose source code is made available free (not on a fee or licensing basis as in ebusiness) for any third party to review and modify. Business 2.0 is capitalizing on open source software. Mozilla, for example, offers its Firefox web browser and Thunderbird email software free. Mozilla believes the Internet is a public resource that must remain open and accessible to all; it continuously develops free products by bringing together thousands of dedicated volunteers from around the world. Mozilla's Firefox now holds over 20 percent of the browser market and is quickly becoming a

buyers voluntarily comment on the quality of service, their satisfaction with the item traded, and promptness of shipping. Sellers comment about prompt payment from buyers or respond to comments left by the buyer. Companies ranging from Amazon to restaurants are using reputation systems to improve quality and enhance customer satisfaction.

Collaboration Inside the Organization

A *collaboration system* is a set of tools that supports the work of teams or groups by facilitating the sharing and flow of information. Business 2.0's collaborative mind-set generates more information faster from a wider audience. *Collective intelligence* is collaborating and tapping into the core knowledge of all employees, partners, and customers. Knowledge can be a real competitive advantage for an organization. The most common form of collective intelligence found inside the organization is **knowledge management (KM)**, which involves capturing, classifying, evaluating, retrieving, and sharing information assets in a way that provides context for effective decisions and actions. The primary objective of knowledge management is to be sure that a company's knowledge of facts, sources of information, and solutions is readily available to all employees whenever it is needed. A **knowledge management system (KMS)** supports the capturing, organization, and dissemination of knowledge (i.e., know-how) throughout an organization. KMS can distribute an organization's knowledge base by interconnecting people and digitally gathering their expertise.

A great example of a knowledge worker is a golf caddie. Golf caddies give advice such as, "The rain makes the third hole

such as patents, trademarks, business plans, marketing research, and customer lists. **Tacit knowledge** is the knowledge contained in people's heads. The challenge inherent in tacit knowledge is figuring out how to recognize, generate, share, and manage knowledge that resides in people's heads. While information technology in the form of email, instant messaging, and related technologies can help facilitate the dissemination of tacit knowledge, identifying it in the first place can be a major obstacle.

Collaboration Outside the Organization

The most common form of collective intelligence found outside the organization is **crowdsourcing,** which refers to the wisdom of the crowd. The idea that collective intelligence is greater than the sum of its individual parts has been around

> " THE MOST COMMON FORM OF COLLECTIVE INTELLIGENCE FOUND INSIDE THE ORGANIZATION IS *KNOWLEDGE MANAGEMENT (KM)*, WHICH INVOLVES CAPTURING, CLASSIFYING, EVALUATING, RETRIEVING, AND SHARING INFORMATION ASSETS IN A WAY THAT PROVIDES CONTEXT FOR EFFECTIVE DECISIONS AND ACTIONS. "

play 10 yards shorter." If a golf caddie is good and gives accurate advice it can lead to big tips. Collaborating with other golf caddies can provide bigger tips for all. How can knowledge management make this happen? Caddies could be rewarded for sharing course knowledge by receiving prizes for sharing knowledge. The course manager could compile all of the tips and publish a course notebook for distribution to all caddies. The goal of a knowledge management system is that everyone wins. Here the caddies make bigger tips and golfers improve their play by benefiting from the collaborative experiences of the caddies, and the course owners win as business increases.

KM has assumed greater urgency in American business over the past few years as millions of baby boomers prepare to retire. When they punch out for the last time, the knowledge they gleaned about their jobs, companies, and industries during their long careers will walk out with them—unless companies take measures to retain their insights.

Explicit and Tacit Knowledge Not all information is valuable. Individuals must determine what information qualifies as intellectual and knowledge-based assets. In general, intellectual and knowledge-based assets fall into one of two categories: explicit or tacit. As a rule, **explicit knowledge** consists of anything that can be documented, archived, and codified, often with the help of IT. Examples of explicit knowledge are assets

for a long time (see Figure 3.18). With Business 2.0 the ability to efficiently tap into its power is emerging. For many years organizations believed that good ideas came from the top.

FIGURE 3.18 Crowdsourcing: The Crowd Is Smarter Than the Individual

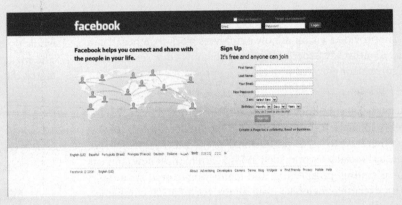
CEOs collaborated only with the heads of sales and marketing, the quality assurance expert, or the road warrior salesman. The organization chart governed who should work with whom and how far up the chain of command a suggestion or idea would travel. With Business 2.0 this belief is being challenged, as firms capitalize on crowdsourcing by opening up a task or problem to a wider group to find better or cheaper results from outside the box.

With Business 2.0, people can be continuously connected, a driving force behind collaboration. Traditional ebusiness communications were limited to face-to-face conversations and one-way technologies that used *asynchronous communications*, or communication such as email in which the message and the response do not occur at the same time. Business 2.0 brought *synchronous communication,* or communications that occur at the same time such as IM or chat. Ask a group of college students when they last spoke to their parents. For most the answer is less than an hour ago, as opposed to the traditional response of a few days ago. In business too, continuous connections are now expected in today's collaborative world.

NETWORKING COMMUNITIES WITH BUSINESS 2.0 LO3-7

Social media refers to websites that rely on user participation and user-contributed content, such as Facebook, YouTube, and Digg. A *social network* is an application that connects people by matching profile information. Providing individuals with the ability to network is by far one of the greatest advantages of Business 2.0. *Social networking* is the practice of expanding your business and/or social contacts by constructing a personal network (see Figure 3.19). Social networking sites provide two basic functions. The first is the ability to create and maintain a profile that serves as an online identity within the environment. The second is the ability to create connections between other people within the network. *Social networking analysis (SNA)* maps group contacts (personal and professional) identifying who knows each other and who works together. In a company

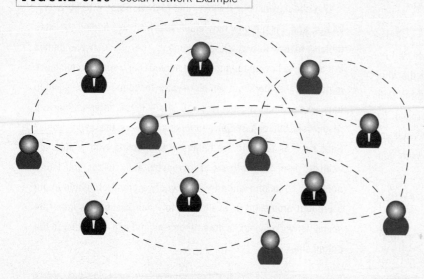

it can provide a vision of how employees work together. It can also identify key experts with specific knowledge such as how to solve a complicated programming problem or launch a new product.

Business 2.0 simplifies access to information and improves the ability to share it. Instead of spending $1,000 and two days at a conference to meet professional peers, businesspeople can now use social networks such as LinkedIn to meet new contacts for recruiting, prospecting, and identifying experts on a topic. With executive members from all the *Fortune* 500 companies, LinkedIn has become one of the more useful recruiting tools on the web.

Social networking sites can be especially useful to employers trying to find job candidates with unique or highly specialized skill sets that may be harder to locate in larger communities. Many employers also search social networking sites to find "dirt" and character references for potential employees. Keep in mind that what you post on the Internet stays on the Internet.[24]

LO3-7 Explain how Business 2.0 is helping communities network and collaborate.

Social Tagging

Tags are specific keywords or phrases incorporated into website content for means of classification or taxonomy. An item can have one or more tags associated with it, to allow for multiple browsable paths through the items, and tags can be changed with minimal effort (see Figure 3.20). *Social tagging* describes the collaborative activity of marking shared online content with keywords or tags as a way to organize it for future navigation, filtering, or search. The entire user community is invited to tag, and thus essentially defines, the content. Flickr allows users

to upload images and tag them with appropriate keywords. After enough people have done so, the resulting tag collection will identify images correctly and without bias.

Folksonomy is similar to taxonomy except that crowdsourcing determines the tags or keyword-based classification system. Using the collective power of a community to identify and classify content significantly lowers content categorization costs, because there is no complicated nomenclature to learn. Users simply create and apply tags as they wish. For example, while cell phone manufacturers often refer to their products as mobile devices, the folksonomy could include mobile phone, wireless phone, smart phone, iPhone, BlackBerry, and so on. All these keywords, if searched, should take a user to the same site. Folksonomies reveal what people truly call things (see Figure 3.21). They have been a point of discussion on the web because the whole point of having a website is for your customers to find it. The majority of websites are found through search terms that match the content.[25]

▼**FIGURE 3.20** Social Tagging Occurs When Many Individuals Categorize Content

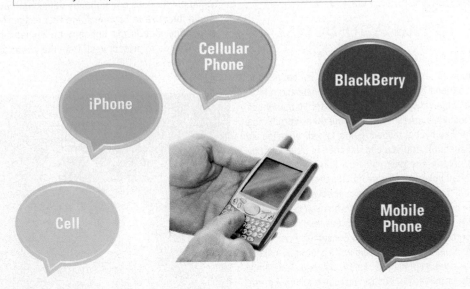

FIGURE 3.21
Folksonomy Example: The User-Generated Names for Cellular Phones

A **website bookmark** is a locally stored URL or the address of a file or Internet page saved as a shortcut. **Social bookmarking** allows users to share, organize, search, and manage bookmarks. Del.icio.us, a website dedicated to social bookmarking, provides users with a place to store, categorize, annotate, and share favorites. StumbleUpon is another popular social bookmarking website that allows users to locate interesting websites based on

Blogs

A **blog,** or **web log,** is an online journal that allows users to post their own comments, graphics, and video. Unlike traditional HTML web pages, blog websites let writers communicate—and reader's respond—on a regular basis through a simple yet customizable interface that does not require any programming.

> "Social networking and collaborating are leading businesses in new directions."

their favorite subjects. The more you use the service, the more the system "learns" about your interests and the better it can show you websites that interest you. StumbleUpon represents a new social networking model in which content finds the users instead of the other way around. StumbleUpon is all about the users and the content they enjoy.[26]

From a business perspective, blogs are no different from marketing channels such as video, print, audio, or presentations. They all deliver results of varying kinds. Consider Sun Microsystem's Jonathan Schwartz and GM's Bob Lutz, who use their blogs for marketing, sharing ideas, gathering feedback, press

BUSINESS 2.0 TOOLS FOR COLLABORATING L03-8

Social networking and collaborating are leading businesses in new directions, and Figure 3.22 provides an overview of the tools that harness the "power of the people," allowing users to share ideas, discuss business problems, and collaborate on solutions.

L03-8 Describe the three Business 2.0 tools for collaborating.

FIGURE 3.22
Business 2.0 Communication and Collaboration Tools

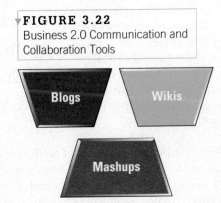

Due Diligence //:

Welcome to the Anti-Social Networking Revolution[27]

Have you ever received a friend application on Facebook and thought you are not a friend but an enemyface? Well one smart individual has created an application that allows you to tell your enemies as well as your friends what you really think about them: introducing the Enemybook. The Enemybook allows users to add enemies as well as friends on Facebook, and you can describe in detail exactly how you know the person and why you truly hate them. Another great feature, instead of poking them, you can flip them the bird.

Have you noticed that individuals have a great deal of power when it comes to the Internet? That wimpy kid who used to be picked on in high school can now Enemybook those bullies all over Facebook. The same power has been given to the consumer. Prior to the Internet, if a customer was angry, they could write a letter or make a phone call, but their individual power was relatively weak. Now, they can create a website or upload a video to YouTube bashing a product or service, and their efforts can be viewed by millions and millions of people. The power has shifted to the hands of the consumer.

What issues can your company anticipate from consumers? What power does one unhappy consumer have and what methods could they use to communicate their issues? What role does viral marketing play in the unhappy consumer scenario? What can a company do to protect itself from the wrath of an unhappy blogger or tweeter?

response, and image shaping. Starbucks has developed a blog called My Starbucks Idea, allowing customers to share ideas, tell Starbucks what they think of other people's ideas, and join discussions. Blogs are an ideal mechanism for many businesses since they can focus on topic areas more easily than traditional media, with no limits on page size, word count, or publication deadline.[28]

Microblogs *Microblogging* is the practice of sending brief posts (140 to 200 characters) to a personal blog, either publicly or to a private group of subscribers who can read the posts as IMs or as text messages. The main advantage of microblogging is that posts can be submitted by a variety of means, such as instant messaging, email, or the web. By far the most popular microblogging tool is Twitter, which allows users to send microblog entries called tweets to anyone who has registered to "follow" them. Senders can restrict delivery to people they want to follow them or, by default, allow open access. Microblogging is covered in detail in Chapter 7.[29]

Real Simple Syndication (RSS) *Real Simple Syndication (RSS)* is a web format used to publish frequently updated works, such as blogs, news headlines, audio, and video, in a standardized format. An RSS document or feed includes full or summarized text, plus other information such as publication date and authorship. News websites, blogs, and podcasts use RSS, constantly feeding news to consumers instead of having them search for it. In addition to facilitating syndication, RSS allows a website's frequent readers to track updates on the site.

> **While blogs have largely drawn on the creative and personal goals of individual authors, wikis are based on open collaboration with any- and everybody.**

Wikis

A *wiki* (the word is Hawaiian for quick) is a type of collaborative web page that allows users to add, remove, and change content, which can be easily organized and reorganized as required. While blogs have largely drawn on the creative and personal goals of individual authors, wikis are based on open collaboration with any- and everybody. Wikipedia, the open encyclopedia that launched in 2001, has become one of the 10 most popular web destinations, reaching an estimated 217 million unique visitors a month.[30]

A wiki user can generally alter the original content of any article, while the blog user can only add information in the form of comments. Large wikis, such as Wikipedia, protect the quality and accuracy of their information by assigning users roles such as reader, editor, administrator, patroller, policy maker, subject matter expert, content maintainer, software developer, and system operator. Access to some important or sensitive Wikipedia material is limited to users in these authorized roles.[31]

The **network effect** describes how products in a network increase in value to users as the number of users increases. The more users and content managers on a wiki, the greater the network effect because more users attract more contributors, whose work attracts more users, and so on. For example, Wikipedia becomes more valuable to users as the number of its contributors increases.

Wikis internal to firms can be vital tools for collecting and disseminating knowledge throughout an organization, across geographic distances, and between functional business areas. For example, what U.S. employees call a "sale" may be called "an order booked" in the United Kingdom, an "order scheduled" in Germany, and an "order produced" in France. The corporate wiki can answer any questions about a business process or definition. Companies are also using wikis for documentation, reporting, project management, online dictionaries, and discussion groups. Of course, the more employees who use the corporate wiki, the greater the network effect and valued added for the company.

Mashups

A **mashup** is a website or web application that uses content from more than one source to create a completely new product or service. The term is typically used in the context of music; putting Jay-Z lyrics over a Radiohead song makes something old new. The web version of a mashup allows users to mix map data, photos, video, news feeds, blog entries, and so on to create content with a new purpose. Content used in mashups is typically sourced from an **application programming interface (API)**, which is a set of routines, protocols, and tools for building software applications. A programmer then puts these building blocks together.

Most operating environments, such as Microsoft Windows, provide an API so that programmers can write applications consistent with them. Many people experimenting with mashups are using Microsoft, Google, eBay, Amazon, Flickr, and Yahoo APIs, leading to the creation of mashup editors. **Mashup editors** are WYSIWYG, or What You See Is What You Get, tools. They provide a visual interface to build a mashup, often allowing the user to drag and drop data points into a web application.

Whoever thought technology could help sell bananas? Dole Organic now places three-digit farm codes on each banana and creates a mashup using Google Earth and its banana database. Socially and environmentally conscious buyers can plug the numbers into Dole's website and look at a bio of the farm where the bananas were raised. The site tells the story of the farm and its surrounding community, lists its organic certifications, posts some photos, and offers a link to satellite images of the farm in Google Earth. Customers can personally monitor the production and treatment of their fruit from the tree to the grocer. The process assures customers that their bananas have been raised to proper organic standards on an environmentally friendly, holistically minded plantation.[32]

THE CHALLENGES OF BUSINESS 2.0 LO3-9

As much as Business 2.0 has positively changed the global landscape of business, a few challenges remain in open source software, user-contributed content systems, and collaboration systems, all highlighted in Figure 3.23. We'll briefly describe each one.

LO3-9 Explain the three challenges associated with Business 2.0.

Technology Dependence

Many people today expect to be continuously connected, and their dependence on technology glues them to their web connections for everything from web conferencing for a university class or work project to making plans with friends for dinner. If a connection is down, how will they function? How long can people go without checking email, text messaging, or listening to free music on Pandora or watching on-demand television? As society becomes more technology-dependent, outages hold the potential to cause ever-greater havoc for people, businesses, and educational institutions.

to Attorney General Robert F. Kennedy in the early 1960s and was thought to have been directly involved in the assassinations of both Kennedy and his brother, President John F. Kennedy. Seigenthaler did work as an assistant to Robert Kennedy, but he was never involved in the assassinations. Wiki vandalism is a hot issue and for this reason wiki software can now store all versions of a web page, tracking updates and changes and ensuring the site can be restored to its original form if the site is vandalized. It can also color-code the background ensuring the user understands which areas have been validated and which areas have not. The real trick to wiki software is to determine which statements are true and which are false, a huge issue when considering how easily and frequently wiki software is updated and changed.[34]

Violations of Copyright and Plagiarism

Online collaboration makes plagiarism as easy as clicking a mouse. Unfortunately a great deal of copyrighted material tends to find its way to blogs and wikis where many times blame cannot be traced to a single person. Clearly stated copyright and plagiarism policies are a must for all corporate blogs and wikis. These topics are discussed in detail in Chapter 4.

> **Many people today expect to be continuously connected.**

Information Vandalism

Open source and sharing are both major advantages of Business 2.0, and ironically they are major challenges as well. Allowing anyone to edit anything opens the door for individuals to purposely damage, destroy, or vandalize website content. One of the most famous examples of wiki vandalism occurred when a false biography entry read that John Seigenthaler Sr. was assistant

WEB 3.0: DEFINING THE NEXT GENERATION OF ONLINE BUSINESS OPPORTUNITIES LO3-10

While Web 1.0 refers to static text-based information websites and Web 2.0 is about user-contributed content, Web 3.0 is based on "intelligent" web applications using natural language processing, machine-based learning and reasoning, and intelligent applications. Web 3.0 is the next step in the evolution of the Internet and web applications. Business leaders who explore its opportunities will be the first to market with competitive advantages.

Web 3.0 offers a way for people to describe information such that computers can start to understand the relationships among concepts and topics. To demonstrate the power of Web 3.0, let's look at a few sample relationships, such as Adam Sandler

▼**FIGURE 3.23** Challenges of Business 2.0

- Technology Dependence
- Information Vandalism
- Violations of Copyright and Plagiarism

is a comedian, Lady Gaga is a singer, and Hannah is friends with Sophie. These are all examples of descriptions that can be added to web pages allowing computers to learn about relationships while displaying the information to humans. With this kind of information in place, there will be a far richer interaction between people and machines with Web 3.0.

Applying this type of advanced relationship knowledge to a company can create new opportunities. After all, businesses run on information. Where Web 2.0 brings people closer together with information using machines, Web 3.0 brings *machines* closer together using *information*. These new relationships unite people, machines, and information so a business can be smarter, quicker, more agile, and more successful.

One goal of Web 3.0 is to tailor online searches and requests specifically to users' preferences and needs. For example, instead of making multiple searches, the user might type a complex sentence or two in a Web 3.0 browser, such as "I want to see a funny movie and then eat at a good Mexican restaurant. What are my options?" The Web 3.0 browser will analyze the request, search the web for all possible answers, organize the results, and present them to the user.

Tim Berners-Lee, one of the founders of the Internet, has described the **semantic web** as a component of Web 3.0 that describes things in a way that computers can understand. The semantic web is not about links between web pages; rather it describes the relationships between *things* (such as A is a part of B and Y is a member of Z) and the properties of things (size, weight, age, price). If information about music, cars, concert tickets, and so on is stored in a way that describes the information and associated resource files, semantic web applications can collect information from many different sources, combine it, and present it to users in a meaningful way. Although Web 3.0 is still a bit speculative, some topics and features are certain to be included in it, such as:[35]

- Integration of legacy devices: the ability to use current devices such as iPhones, laptops, and so on, as credit cards, tickets, and reservations tools.

- Intelligent applications: the use of agents, machine learning, and semantic web concepts to complete intelligent tasks for users.

- Open ID: the provision of an online identity that can be easily carried to a variety of devices (cell phones, PCs) allowing for easy authentication across different websites.

- Open technologies: the design of websites and other software so they can be easily integrated and work together.

- A worldwide database: the ability for databases to be distributed and accessed from anywhere.

LO3-10 Describe Web 3.0 and the next generation of online business.

> **Web 3.0 offers a way for people to describe information such that computers can start to understand the relationships among concepts and topics.**

Egovernment: The Government Moves Online

Recent business models that have arisen to enable organizations to take advantage of the Internet and create value are within egovernment. *Egovernment* involves the use of strategies and technologies to transform government(s) by improving the delivery of services and enhancing the quality of interaction between the citizen-consumer and all branches of government.

One example of an egovernment portal, FirstGov.gov, the official U.S. gateway to all government information, is the catalyst for a growing electronic government. Its powerful search engine and ever-growing collection of topical and customer-focused links connect users to millions of web pages, from the federal government, to local and tribal governments, to foreign nations around the world. Figure 3.24 highlights specific egovernment models.

Mbusiness: Supporting Anywhere Business

Internet-enabled mobile devices are quickly outnumbering personal computers. *Mobile business* (or *mbusiness, mcommerce*) is the ability to purchase goods and services through a wireless Internet-enabled device. The emerging technology behind mbusiness is a mobile device equipped with a web-ready micro-browser that can perform the following services:

- Mobile entertainment—downloads for music, videos, games, voting, ring tones, as well as text-based messaging services.

- Mobile sales/marketing—advertising, campaigns, discounts, promotions, and coupons.

FIGURE 3.24 Extended Ebusiness Models

	Business	Consumer	Government
Business	B2B conisint.com	B2C dell.com	B2G lockheedmartin.com
Consumer	C2B priceline.com	C2C ebay.com	C2G egov.com
Government	G2B export.gov	G2C medicare.gov	G2G disasterhelp.gov

- Mobile banking—manage accounts, pay bills, receive alerts, and transfer funds.

- Mobile ticketing—purchase tickets for entertainment, transportation, and parking including the ability to automatically feed parking meters.

- Mobile payments—pay for goods and services including in-store purchases, home delivery, vending machines, taxis, gas, and so on.

Organizations face changes more extensive and far reaching in their implications than anything since the modern industrial revolution occurred in the early 1900s. Technology is a primary force driving these changes. Organizations that want to survive must recognize the immense power of technology, carry out required organizational changes in the face of it, and learn to operate in an entirely different way.

EGOVERNMENT INVOLVES THE USE OF STRATEGIES AND TECHNOLOGIES TO TRANSFORM GOVERNMENT(S) BY IMPROVING THE DELIVERY OF SERVICES AND ENHANCING THE QUALITY OF INTERACTION BETWEEN THE CITIZEN-CONSUMER AND ALL BRANCHES OF GOVERNMENT.

GET ONLINE

mhhe.com/BaltzanM2e

for study materials including
quizzes, iPod downloads,
and video

ethics +
information security:
MIS business
concerns

What's in IT for me?

This chapter concerns itself with protecting information from potential misuse. Organizations must ensure they collect, capture, store, and use information in an ethical manner. This means any type of information they collect and utilize, including about customers, partners, and employees. Companies must ensure that personal information collected about someone remains private. This is not just a nice thing to do. The law requires it. Perhaps more important, information must be kept physically secure to prevent access and possible dissemination and use by unauthorized sources.

You, the business student, must understand ethics and security because they are the top concerns voiced by customers today. The way they are handled directly influences a customer's likelihood of embracing electronic technologies and conducting business over the web—and thus the company's bottom line. You can find evidence in recent news reports about how the stock price of organizations falls dramatically when information privacy and security breaches are made known. Further, organizations face potential litigation if they fail to meet their ethical, privacy, and security obligations in the handling of information. ■

CHAPTER OUTLINE

SECTION 4-1 >>
Ethics
■ Information Ethics
■ Developing Information Management Policies

SECTION 4-2 >>
Information Security
■ Protecting Intellectual Assets
■ The First Line of Defense—People
■ The Second Line of Defense—Technology

LEARNING OUTCOMES

LO4-1 Explain the ethical issues in the use of information technology.

LO4-2 Identify the six epolicies organizations should implement to protect themselves.

INFORMATION ETHICS LO4-1

Ethics and security are two fundamental building blocks for all organizations. In recent years, enormous business scandals along with 9/11 have shed new light on the meaning of ethics and security. When the behavior of a few individuals can destroy billion-dollar organizations, the value of ethics and security should be evident.

Copyright is the legal protection afforded an expression of an idea, such as a song, book, or video game. *Intellectual property* is intangible creative work that is embodied in physical form and includes copyrights, trademarks, and patents. As it becomes easier for people to copy everything from words and data to music and video, the ethical issues surrounding copyright infringement and the violation of intellectual property rights are consuming the ebusiness world. Technology poses new challenges for our *ethics*—the principles and standards that guide our behavior toward other people.

The protection of customers' privacy is one of the largest, and murkiest, ethical issues facing organizations today. *Privacy* is the right to be left alone when you want to be, to have control over your personal possessions, and not to be observed without your consent. Privacy is related to *confidentiality,* which is the assurance that messages and information remain available only to those authorized to view them. Each time employees make a decision about a privacy issue, the outcome could sink the company.

Trust among companies, customers, partners, and suppliers is the support structure of ebusiness. Privacy is one of its main ingredients. Consumers' concerns that their privacy will be violated because of their interactions on the web continue to be one of the primary barriers to the growth of ebusiness.

> **Ethics and security are two fundamental building blocks for all organizations.**

Information ethics govern the ethical and moral issues arising from the development and use of information technologies, as well as the creation, collection, duplication, distribution, and processing of information itself (with or without the aid of computer technologies). Ethical dilemmas in this area usually arise not as simple, clear-cut situations but as clashes among competing goals, responsibilities, and loyalties. Inevitably, there will be more than one socially acceptable or "correct" decision. The two primary areas concerning software include pirated software and counterfeit software. *Pirated software* is the unauthorized use, duplication, distribution, or sale of copyrighted software. *Counterfeit software* is software that is manufactured to look like the real thing and sold as such. Figure 4.1 contains examples of ethically questionable or unacceptable uses of information technology.[1]

Unfortunately, few hard and fast rules exist for always determining what is ethical. Many people can either justify or condemn the actions in Figure 4.1, for example. Knowing the law is important but that knowledge will not always help, because what is legal might not always be ethical, and what might be ethical is not always legal. For example, Joe Reidenberg received an offer for AT&T cell phone service. AT&T used Equifax, a credit reporting agency, to identify potential customers such as

---

FIGURE 4.1 Ethically Questionable or Unacceptable Information Technology Use

Individuals copy, use, and distribute software.

Employees search organizational databases for sensitive corporate and personal information.

Organizations collect, buy, and use information without checking the validity or accuracy of the information.

Individuals create and spread viruses that cause trouble for those using and maintaining IT systems.

Individuals hack into computer systems to steal proprietary information.

Employees destroy or steal proprietary organization information such as schematics, sketches, customer lists, and reports.

Joe Reidenberg. Overall, this seemed like a good business opportunity between Equifax and AT&T Wireless. Unfortunately, the Fair Credit Reporting Act (FCRA) forbids repurposing credit information except when the information is used for "a firm offer of credit or insurance." In other words, the only product that can be sold based on credit information is credit. A representative for Equifax stated, "As long as AT&T Wireless (or any company for that matter) is offering the cell phone service on a credit basis, such as allowing the use of the service before the consumer has to pay, it is in compliance with the FCRA." However, the question remains—is it ethical?[3]

This is a good example of the ethical dilemmas, many still being defined, that organizations face. Figure 4.2 shows the four

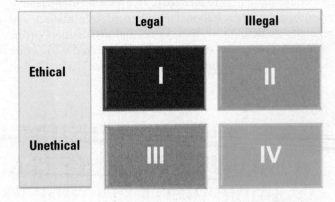

FIGURE 4.2
Acting Ethically and Acting Legally Are Not Always the Same

	Legal	Illegal
Ethical	I	II
Unethical	III	IV

Do You Really Want to Risk It?[4]

My Not To-Do List

Ethics. It's just one tiny word, but it has monumental impact on every area of business. From the magazines, blogs, and newspapers you read to the courses you take, you will encounter ethics because it is a hot topic in today's electronic world. Technology has provided so many incredible opportunities, but it has also provided those same opportunities to unethical people. Discuss the ethical issues surrounding each of the following situations (yes, these are true stories):

- A girl raises her hand in class and states "I can legally copy any DVD I get from Netflix because Netflix purchased the DVD and the copyright only applies to the company who purchased the product."
- A student stands up the first day of class before the professor arrives and announces that his fraternity scans textbooks and that he has the textbook for this course on his thumb drive, which he will gladly sell for $20. Several students pay on the spot and upload the scanned textbook to their PCs. One student takes down the student information and contacts the publisher about the incident.
- A senior manager is asked to monitor his employee's email because there is a rumor that the employee is looking for another job.
- A vice president of sales asks her employee to burn all of the customer data onto an external hard drive because she made a deal to provide customer information to a strategic partner.
- A senior manager is asked to monitor his employee's email to discover if she is sexually harassing another employee.
- An employee is looking at the shared network drive and discovers his boss's entire hard drive, including his email backup, has been copied to the network and is visible to all.
- An employee is accidentally copied on an email that lists the targets for the next round of layoffs.

quadrants of ethical and legal behavior. The goal for organizations is to make decisions within quadrant I that are *both* legal and ethical.

L04-1 Explain the ethical issues in the use of information technology.

Information Does Not Have Ethics; People Do

Information itself has no ethics. It does not care how it is used. It will not stop itself from spamming customers, sharing itself if it is sensitive or personal, or revealing details to third parties. Information cannot delete or preserve itself. Therefore, it falls to those who own the information to develop ethical guidelines about how to manage it. *Information management* examines the organizational resource of information and regulates its definitions, uses, value, and distribution ensuring it has the types of data/information required to function and grow effectively. *Information governance* is a method or

does information governance and information compliance. Figure 4.3 provides an overview of some of the important laws individuals and firms must follow in managing and protecting information.[5]

DEVELOPING INFORMATION MANAGEMENT POLICIES L04-2

Treating sensitive corporate information as a valuable resource is good management. Building a corporate culture based on ethical principles that employees can understand and implement is responsible management. Organizations should develop written policies establishing employee guidelines, employee procedures, and organizational rules for information. These policies set employee expectations about the organization's practices and standards and protect the organization from misuse of computer systems and IT resources. If an organization's employees use computers at work, the organization should, at a minimum, implement epolicies. *Epolicies* are policies and

> ## "TREATING SENSITIVE CORPORATE INFORMATION AS A VALUABLE RESOURCE IS GOOD MANAGEMENT. BUILDING A CORPORATE CULTURE BASED ON ETHICAL PRINCIPLES THAT EMPLOYEES CAN UNDERSTAND AND IMPLEMENT IS RESPONSIBLE MANAGEMENT."

system of government for information management or control. *Information compliance* is the act of conforming, acquiescing, or yielding information. A few years ago the ideas of information management, governance, and compliance were relatively obscure. Today, these concepts are a must for virtually every company, both domestic and global, primarily due to the role digital information plays in corporate legal proceedings or litigation. Frequently, digital information serves as key evidence in legal proceedings and it is far easier to search, organize, and filter than paper documents. Digital information is also extremely difficult to destroy especially if it is on a corporate network or sent via email. In fact, the only reliable way to truly obliterate digital information is to destroy the hard drives where the file was stored. *Ediscovery* (or *electronic discovery*) refers to the ability of a company to identify, search, gather, seize, or export digital information in responding to a litigation, audit, investigation, or information inquiry. As the importance of ediscovery grows, so

procedures that address information management along with the ethical use of computers and the Internet in the business environment. Figure 4.4 displays the epolicies a firm should implement to set employee expectations.

L04-2 Identify the six epolicies organizations should implement to protect themselves.

Ethical Computer Use Policy

In a case that illustrates the perils of online betting, a leading Internet poker site reported that a hacker exploited a security flaw to gain an insurmountable edge in high-stakes, no-limit Texas hold-'em tournaments—the ability to see his opponents' hole cards. The cheater, whose illegitimate winnings were estimated at between $400,000 and $700,000 by one victim, was an employee of AbsolutePoker.com and hacked the system to show

Established Information-Related Laws	
Privacy Act—1974	Restricts what information the federal government can collect; allows people to access and correct information on themselves; requires procedures to protect the security of personal information; and forbids the disclosure of name-linked information without permission.
Family Education Rights and Privacy Act—1974	Regulates access to personal education records by government agencies and other third parties and ensures the right of students to see their own records.
Cable Communications Act—1984	Requires written or electronic consent from viewers before cable TV providers can release viewing choices or other personally identifiable information.
Electronic Communications Privacy Act—1986	Allows the reading of communications by a firm and says that employees have no right to privacy when using their companies' computers.
Computer Fraud and Abuse Act—1986	Prohibits unauthorized access to computers used for financial institutions, the U.S. government, or interstate and international trade.
The Bork Bill (officially known as the Video Privacy Protection Act, 1988)	Prohibits the use of video rental information on customers for any purpose other than that of marketing goods and services directly to the customer.
Communications Assistance for Law Enforcement Act—1994	Requires that telecommunications equipment be designed so that authorized government agents are able to intercept all wired and wireless communications being sent or received by any subscriber. The act also requires that subscriber call-identifying information be transmitted to a government when and if required.
Freedom of Information Act—1967, 1975, 1994, and 1998	Allows any person to examine government records unless it would cause an invasion of privacy. It was amended in 1974 to apply to the FBI, and again in 1994 to allow citizens to monitor government activities and information gathering, and once again in 1998 to access government information on the Internet.
Health Insurance Portability and Accountability Act (HIPAA)—1996	Requires that the health care industry formulate and implement regulations to keep patient information confidential.
Identity Theft and Assumption Deterrence Act—1998	Strengthened the criminal laws governing identity theft making it a federal crime to use or transfer identification belonging to another. It also established a central federal service for victims.
USA Patriot Act—2001 and 2003	Allows law enforcement to get access to almost any information, including library records, video rentals, bookstore purchases, and business records when investigating any act of terrorist or clandestine intelligence activities. In 2003, Patriot II broadened the original law.
Homeland Security Act—2002	Provided new authority to government agencies to mine data on individuals and groups including emails and website visits; put limits on the information available under the Freedom of Information Act; and gave new powers to government agencies to declare national health emergencies.
Sarbanes-Oxley Act—2002	Sought to protect investors by improving the accuracy and reliability of corporate disclosures and requires companies (1) to implement extensive and detailed policies to prevent illegal activity within the company, and (2) to respond in a timely manner to investigate illegal activity.
Fair and Accurate Credit Transactions Act—2003	Included provisions for the prevention of identity theft including consumers' right to get a credit report free each year, requiring merchants to leave all but the last five digits of a credit card number off a receipt, and requiring lenders and credit agencies to take action even before a victim knows a crime has occurred when they notice any circumstances that might indicate identity theft.
CAN-Spam Act—2003	Sought to regulate interstate commerce by imposing limitations and penalties on businesses sending unsolicited email to consumers. The law forbids deceptive subject lines, headers, return addresses, etc., as well as the harvesting of email addresses from websites. It requires businesses that send spam to maintain a do-not-spam list and to include a postal mailing address in the message.

FIGURE 4.4 Overview of Epolicies

warnings, the company may terminate an employee who spends significant amounts of time playing computer games at work.

Organizations can legitimately vary in how they expect employees to use computers, but in any approach to controlling such use, the overriding principle should be informed consent. The users should be *informed* of the rules and, by agreeing to use the system on that basis, *consent* to abide by them.

Managers should make a conscientious effort to ensure all users are aware of the policy through formal training and other means. If an organization were to have only one epolicy, it should be an ethical computer use policy because that is the starting point and the umbrella for any other policies the organization might establish.

Information Privacy Policy

An organization that wants to protect its information should develop an *information privacy policy,* which contains general principles regarding information privacy. Visa created Inovant to handle all its information systems including its coveted customer information, which details how people are spending their money, in which stores, on which days, and even at what time of day. Just imagine what a sales and marketing department could do if it gained access to this information. For this reason, Inovant bans the use of Visa's customer information for anything outside its intended purpose—billing. Inovant's privacy specialists developed a strict credit card information privacy policy, which it follows.

Now Inovant is being asked if it can guarantee that unethical use of credit card information will never occur. In a large majority of cases, the unethical use of information happens not through the malicious scheming of a rogue marketer, but rather unintentionally. For instance, information is collected and stored for some purpose, such as record keeping or billing. Then, a sales or marketing professional figures out another way to use it internally, share it with partners, or sell it to a trusted third party. The information is "unintentionally" used for new purposes. The classic example of this type of unintentional information reuse is the Social Security number, which started simply as a way to identify government retirement benefits and then was used as a sort of universal personal ID, found on everything from drivers' licenses to savings accounts.

that it could be done. Regardless of what business a company operates—even one that many view as unethical—the company must protect itself from unethical employee behavior.[6]

One essential step in creating an ethical corporate culture is establishing an ethical computer use policy. An *ethical computer use policy* contains general principles to guide computer user behavior. For example, it might explicitly state that users should refrain from playing computer games during working hours. This policy ensures the users know how to behave at work and the organization has a published standard to deal with infractions. For example, after appropriate

Acceptable Use Policy

An *acceptable use policy (AUP)* requires a user to agree to follow it to be provided access to corporate email, information systems, and the Internet. *Nonrepudiation* is a contractual stipulation to ensure that ebusiness participants do not deny (repudiate) their online actions. A nonrepudiation clause is typically contained in an acceptable use policy. Many businesses and educational facilities require employees or students to sign an acceptable use policy before gaining network access. When signing up with an email provider, each customer is

Due Diligence //:

Can You Get a Ticket for Drunk Emailing?[7]

Have you ever experienced a time when you were a little bit tipsy and not thinking clearly and you decided to send an email to your ex-boyfriend to tell him you still love him or to the girl that got away? The next morning, you were probably embarrassed and humiliated by the email, and you were wondering why your friends allowed you to send drunk email. Well, no more worries, as Google is coming to the rescue. Mail Goggles

is one of Google's latest features, and it is designed to prevent users from sending embarrassing drunk emails. If you are using Gmail and you enable Mail Goggles, you are required to answer a series of mathematical equations within 60 seconds before you are allowed to send an email. Mail Goggles only activates on weekend evenings between 10 P.M. and 4 A.M., so you don't have to worry about answering the questions every time you send an email.

Information security lines of defense are implemented with people first and technology second. How does that apply to Mail Goggles? Besides drinking, in what other instances would it be helpful for people to use Mail Goggles? Are there any ethical issues surrounding Mail Goggles?

---

typically presented with an AUP, which states the user agrees to adhere to certain stipulations. Users agree to the following in a typical acceptable use policy:

- Not using the service as part of violating any law.
- Not attempting to break the security of any computer network or user.
- Not posting commercial messages to groups without prior permission.
- Not performing any nonrepudiation.

Some organizations go so far as to create a unique information management policy focusing solely on Internet use. An **Internet use policy** contains general principles to guide the proper use of the Internet. Because of the large amounts of computing resources that Internet users can expend, it is essential that such use be legitimate. In addition, the Internet contains numerous materials that some believe are offensive, making regulation in the workplace a requirement. Generally, an Internet use policy:

- Describes the Internet services available to users.
- Defines the organization's position on the purpose of Internet access and what restrictions, if any, are placed on that access.

- Describes user responsibility for citing sources, properly handling offensive material, and protecting the organization's good name.
- States the ramifications if the policy is violated.

Email Privacy Policy

An **email privacy policy** details the extent to which email messages may be read by others. Email is so pervasive in organizations that it requires its own specific policy. Most working professionals use email as their preferred means of corporate communications. While email and instant messaging are common business communication tools, there are risks associated with using them. For instance, a sent email is stored on at least three or four computers (see Figure 4.5). Simply deleting an email from one computer does not delete it from the others. Companies can mitigate many of the risks of using electronic messaging systems by implementing and adhering to an email privacy policy.

One major problem with email is the user's expectations of privacy. To a large extent, this expectation is based on the false assumption that email privacy protection exists somehow analogous to that of U.S. first-class mail. Generally, the

---

[**"Companies can mitigate many of the risks of using electronic messaging systems by implementing and adhering to an email privacy policy."**]

▼FIGURE 4.5 Email Is Stored on Multiple Computers

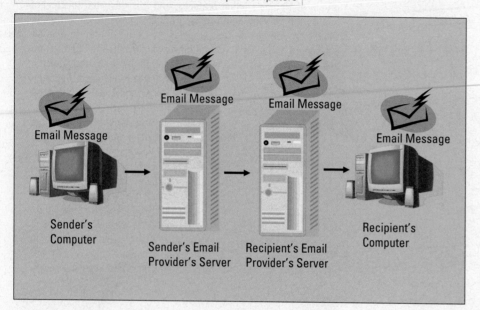

Email Message — Email Message — Email Message — Email Message

Sender's Computer — Sender's Email Provider's Server — Recipient's Email Provider's Server — Recipient's Computer

organization that owns the email system can operate the system as openly or as privately as it wishes. Surveys indicate that the majority of large firms regularly read and analyze employees' email looking for confidential data leaks such as unannounced financial results or the sharing of trade secrets that result in the violation of an email privacy policy and eventual termination of the employee. That means that if the organization wants to read everyone's email, it can do so. Basically, using work email for anything other than work is not a good idea. A typical email privacy policy:

- Defines legitimate email users and explains what happens to accounts after a person leaves the organization.

- Explains backup procedure so users will know that at some point, even if a message is deleted from their computer, it is still stored by the company.

- Describes the legitimate grounds for reading email and the process required before such action is performed.

- Discourages sending junk email or spam to anyone who does not want to receive it.

- Prohibits attempting to mail bomb a site. A *mail bomb* sends a massive amount of email to a specific person or system that can cause that user's server to stop functioning.

- Informs users that the organization has no control over email once it has been transmitted outside the organization.

Spam is unsolicited email. It plagues employees at all levels within an organization, from receptionist to CEO, and clogs email systems and siphons MIS resources away from legitimate business projects. An *anti-spam policy* simply states that email users will not send unsolicited emails (or spam). It is difficult to write anti-spam policies, laws, or software because there is no such thing as a universal litmus test for spam. One person's spam is another person's newsletter.

End users have to decide what spam is, because it can vary widely not just from one company to the next, but from one person to the next.

Social Media Policy

Did you see the YouTube video showing two Domino's Pizza employees violating health codes while preparing food by passing gas on sandwiches? Millions of people did and the company took notice when disgusted customers began posting negative comments all over Twitter. Not having a Twitter account, corporate executives at Domino's did not know about the damaging tweets until it was too late. The use of social media can contribute many benefits to an organization, and implemented correctly it can become a huge opportunity for employees to build brands. But there are also tremendous risks as a few employees representing an entire company can cause tremendous brand damage. Defining a set of guidelines implemented in a social media policy can help mitigate that risk. Companies can protect themselves by implementing a *social media policy* outlining the corporate guidelines or principles governing employee online communications. Having a single social media policy might not be enough to ensure the company's online reputation is protected. Additional, more specific, social media policies a company might choose to implement include:[8]

- Employee online communication policy detailing brand communication.

- Employee blog and personal blog policies.

- Employee social network and personal social network policies.

- Employee Twitter, corporate Twitter, and personal Twitter policies.

- Employee LinkedIn policy.

- Employee Facebook usage and brand usage policy.

- Corporate YouTube policy.

Organizations must protect their online reputations and continuously monitor blogs, message boards, social networking sites, and media sharing sites. However, monitoring the hundreds of different social media sites can quickly become overwhelming. To combat these issues, a number of companies specialize in online social media monitoring; for example, Trackur.com creates digital dashboards allowing executives to view at a glance the date published, source, title, and summary of every item tracked. The dashboard highlights not only what's being said, but also the influence of the particular person, blog, or social media site.

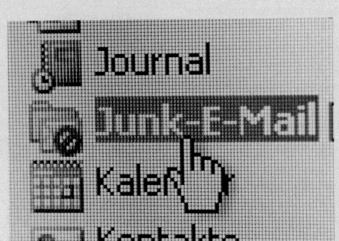
Workplace Monitoring Policy

Increasingly, employee monitoring is not a choice; it is a risk-management obligation. Michael Soden, CEO of the Bank of Ireland, issued a mandate stating that company employees could not surf illicit websites with company equipment. Next, he hired Hewlett-Packard to run the MIS department and illicit websites were discovered on Soden's own computer, forcing Soden to resign. Monitoring employees is one of the biggest challenges CIOs face when developing information management policies.[10]

New technologies make it possible for employers to monitor many aspects of their employees' jobs, especially on telephones, computer terminals, through electronic and voice mail, and when employees are using the Internet. Such monitoring is virtually unregulated. Therefore, unless company policy specifically states otherwise (and even this is not assured), your employer may listen, watch, and read most of your workplace communications. ***Information technology monitoring*** tracks people's activities by such measures as number of keystrokes, error rate, and number of transactions processed (see Figure 4.6 for an overview). The best path for

▼ **FIGURE 4.6** Internet Monitoring Technologies

Common Internet Monitoring Technologies	
Key logger, or key trapper, software	A program that records every keystroke and mouse click.
Hardware key logger	A hardware device that captures keystrokes on their journey from the keyboard to the motherboard.
Cookie	A small file deposited on a hard drive by a website containing information about customers and their web activities. Cookies allow websites to record the comings and goings of customers, usually without their knowledge or consent.
Adware	Software that generates ads that install themselves on a computer when a person downloads some other program from the Internet.
Spyware (sneakware or stealthware)	Software that comes hidden in free downloadable software and tracks online movements, mines the information stored on a computer, or uses a computer's CPU and storage for some task the user knows nothing about.
Web log	Consists of one line of information for every visitor to a website and is usually stored on a web server.
Clickstream	Records information about a customer during a web surfing session such as what websites were visited, how long the visit was, what ads were viewed, and what was purchased.

an organization planning to engage in employee monitoring is open communication including an *employee monitoring policy* stating explicitly how, when, and where the company monitors its employees. Several common stipulations an organization can follow when creating an employee monitoring policy include:

- Be as specific as possible stating when and what (email, IM, Internet, network activity, etc.) will be monitored.

- Expressly communicate that the company reserves the right to monitor all employees.

- State the consequences of violating the policy.

- Always enforce the policy the same for everyone.

Many employees use their company's high-speed Internet access to shop, browse, and surf the web. Most managers do not want their employees conducting personal business during working hours, and they implement a Big Brother approach to employee monitoring. Many management gurus advocate that organizations whose corporate cultures are based on trust are more successful than those whose corporate cultures are based on mistrust. Before an organization implements monitoring technology, it should ask itself, "What does this say about how we feel about our employees?" If the organization really does not trust its employees, then perhaps it should find new ones. If an organization does trust its employees, then it might want to treat them accordingly. An organization that follows its employees' every keystroke might be unwittingly undermining the relationships with its employees, and it might find the effects of employee monitoring are often worse than lost productivity from employee web surfing.

{SECTION 4-2}
Information Security

LEARNING OUTCOMES

LO4-3 Describe the relationships and differences between hackers and viruses.

LO4-4 Describe the relationship between information security policies and an information security plan.

LO4-5 Provide an example of each of the three primary information security areas: (1) authentication and authorization, (2) prevention and resistance, and (3) detection and response.

PROTECTING INTELLECTUAL ASSETS LO4-3

To accurately reflect the crucial interdependence between MIS and business processes, we should update the old business axiom "Time is money" to say "Uptime is money." *Downtime* refers to a period of time when a system is unavailable. Unplanned downtime can strike at any time for any number of reasons, from tornadoes to sink overflows to network failures to power outages (see Figure 4.7). Although natural disasters may appear to be the most devastating causes of MIS outages, they are hardly the most frequent or most expensive. Figure 4.8 demonstrates that the costs of downtime are associated not only with lost revenues, but also with financial

▼**FIGURE 4.7** Sources of Unplanned Downtime

Sources of Unplanned Downtime		
Bomb threat	Frozen pipe	Snowstorm
Burst pipe	Hacker	Sprinkler malfunction
Chemical spill	Hail	Static electricity
Construction	Hurricane	Strike
Corrupted data	Ice storm	Terrorism
Earthquake	Insects	Theft
Electrical short	Lightning	Tornado
Epidemic	Network failure	Train derailment
Equipment failure	Plane crash	Smoke damage
Evacuation	Power outage	Vandalism
Explosion	Power surge	Vehicle crash
Fire	Rodents	Virus
Flood	Sabotage	Water damage (various)
Fraud	Shredded data	Wind

FIGURE 4.8
The Cost of Downtime

Financial Performance

Revenue recognition

Cash flow

Payment guarantees

Credit rating

Stock price

Revenue

Direct loss

Compensatory payments

Lost future revenue

Billing losses

Investment losses

Lost productivity

$

Know your cost of downtime per hour, per day, per week.

Damaged Reputation

Customers

Suppliers

Financial markets

Banks

Business partners

Other Expenses

Temporary employees

Equipment rentals

Overtime costs

Extra shipping charges

Travel expenses

Legal obligations

BUSTED

I'm Being Fired for Smoking, but I Was at Home and It Was Saturday[11]

If on the weekend you like to smoke and eat fast food, you need to be careful, not because it is bad for you but because it just might get you fired. Corporations are starting to implement policies against smoking and obesity and are testing their employees for tobacco use and high-blood pressure. If the tests are positive, the employee can face fines or even dismissal. At Weyco Inc., four employees were fired for refusing to take a test to determine whether they smoke cigarettes. Weyco Inc. adopted a policy that mandates that employees who smoke will be fired, even if the smoking happens after business hours or at home. Howard Weyers, Weyco founder, believes the anti-smoking policies were designed to protect the firm from high health care costs. "I don't want to pay for the results of smoking," states Weyers.

Minority and pregnant women are protected by law from discrimination in the workplace. Unfortunately, if you have a few bad habits, you are on your own. How would you feel if you were fired because you were smoking on the weekend? Do you agree that unhealthy habits warrant disciplinary actions? If companies are allowed to implement policies against smoking and obesity, what unhealthy habit might be next? To date, there have not been any policies on the consumption of alcohol outside of work. Do you agree that overeating and smoking are worse than a drinking habit?

Common Types of Hackers
■ **Black-hat hackers** break into other people's computer systems and may just look around or may steal and destroy information.
■ **Crackers** have criminal intent when hacking.
■ **Cyberterrorists** seek to cause harm to people or to destroy critical systems or information and use the Internet as a weapon of mass destruction.
■ **Hactivists** have philosophical and political reasons for breaking into systems and will often deface the website as a protest.
■ **Script kiddies** or **script bunnies** find hacking code on the Internet and click-and-point their way into systems to cause damage or spread viruses.
■ **White-hat hackers** work at the request of the system owners to find system vulnerabilities and plug the holes.

performance, damage to reputations, and even travel or legal expenses. A few questions managers should ask when determining the cost of downtime are:[12]

• How many transactions can the company afford to lose without significantly harming business?

• Does the company depend upon one or more mission-critical applications to conduct business?

• How much revenue will the company lose for every hour a critical application is unavailable?

• What is the productivity cost associated with each hour of downtime?

• How will collaborative business processes with partners, suppliers, and customers be affected by an unexpected IT outage?

• What is the total cost of lost productivity and lost revenue during unplanned downtime?

The reliability and resilience of IT systems have never been more essential for success as businesses cope with the forces of globalization, 24/7 operations, government and trade regulations, global recession, and overextended IT budgets and resources. Any unexpected downtime in today's business environment has the potential to cause both short- and long-term costs with far-reaching consequences.

Information security is a broad term encompassing the protection of information from accidental or intentional misuse by persons inside or outside an organization. Information security is the primary tool an organization can use to combat the threats associated with downtime. Understanding how to secure information systems is critical to keeping downtime to a minimum and uptime to a maximum. Hackers and viruses are two of the hottest issues currently facing information security.

LO4-3 Describe the relationships and differences between hackers and viruses.

> " **Understanding how to secure information systems is critical to keeping downtime to a minimum and uptime to a maximum.** "

Security Threats Caused by Hackers and Viruses

Hackers are experts in technology who use their knowledge to break into computers and computer networks, either for profit or just motivated by the challenge. Smoking is not just bad for a person's health; it seems it is also bad for company security as hackers regularly use smoking entrances to gain building access. Once inside they pose as employees from the MIS department and either ask for permission to use an employee's computer to access the corporate network, or find a conference room where they simply plug-in their own laptop. Figure 4.9 lists the various types of hackers organizations need to be aware of, and Figure 4.10 shows how a virus is spread.

▼ **FIGURE 4.10** How Computer Viruses Spread

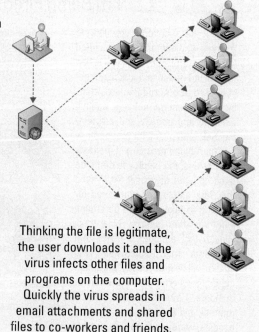

A hacker creates a virus and attaches it to a program, document, or website.

Thinking the file is legitimate, the user downloads it and the virus infects other files and programs on the computer. Quickly the virus spreads in email attachments and shared files to co-workers and friends.

One of the most common forms of computer vulnerabilities is a virus. A *virus* is software written with malicious intent to cause annoyance or damage. Some hackers create and leave viruses causing massive computer damage. Figure 4.11 provides an overview of the most common types of viruses. Two additional computer vulnerabilities include adware and spyware. *Adware* is software that, while purporting to serve some useful function and often fulfilling that function, also allows Internet advertisers to display advertisements without the consent of the computer user. *Spyware* is a special class of adware that collects data about the user and transmits it over the Internet without the user's knowledge or permission. Spyware programs collect specific data about the user, ranging from general demographics such as name, address, and browsing habits to credit card numbers, Social Security numbers, and user names and passwords. Not all adware programs are spyware and used correctly it can generate revenue for a company allowing users to receive free products. Spyware is a clear threat to privacy. Figure 4.12 displays a few

Backdoor programs open a way into the network for future attacks.

Denial-of-service attack (DoS) floods a website with so many requests for service that it slows down or crashes the site.

Distributed denial-of-service attack (DDoS) attacks from multiple computers that flood a website with so many requests for service that it slows down or crashes. A common type is the Ping of Death, in which thousands of computers try to access a website at the same time, overloading it and shutting it down.

Polymorphic viruses and worms change their form as they propagate.

Trojan-horse virus hides inside other software, usually as an attachment or a downloadable file.

Worm spreads itself, not only from file to file, but also from computer to computer. The primary difference between a virus and a worm is that a virus must attach to something, such as an executable file, to spread. Worms do not need to attach to anything to spread and can tunnel themselves into computers.

> " Just as organizations protect their tangible assets, they must also protect their intellectual capital. "

additional weapons hackers use for launching attacks.[13]

Organizational information is intellectual capital. Just as organizations protect their tangible assets—keeping their money in an insured bank or providing a safe working environment for employees—they must also protect their intellectual capital, everything from patents to transactional and analytical information. With security breaches and viruses on the rise and computer hackers everywhere, an organization must put in place strong security measures to survive.

▼ **FIGURE 4.12** Hacker Weapons

Elevation of privilege is a process by which a user misleads a system into granting unauthorized rights, usually for the purpose of compromising or destroying the system. For example, an attacker might log onto a network by using a guest account and then exploit a weakness in the software that lets the attacker change the guest privileges to administrative privileges.

Hoaxes attack computer systems by transmitting a virus hoax, with a real virus attached. By masking the attack in a seemingly legitimate message, unsuspecting users more readily distribute the message and send the attack on to their co-workers and friends, infecting many users along the way.

Malicious code includes a variety of threats such as viruses, worms, and Trojan horses.

Packet tampering consists of altering the contents of packets as they travel over the Internet or altering data on computer disks after penetrating a network. For example, an attacker might place a tap on a network line to intercept packets as they leave the computer. The attacker could eavesdrop or alter the information as it leaves the network.

A sniffer is a program or device that can monitor data traveling over a network. Sniffers can show all the data being transmitted over a network, including passwords and sensitive information. Sniffers tend to be a favorite weapon in the hacker's arsenal.

Spoofing is the forging of the return address on an email so that the message appears to come from someone other than the actual sender. This is not a virus but rather a way by which virus authors conceal their identities as they send out viruses.

Splogs (spam blogs) are fake blogs created solely to raise the search engine rank of affiliated websites. Even blogs that are legitimate are plagued by spam, with spammers taking advantage of the Comment feature of most blogs to comment with links to spam sites.

Spyware is software that comes hidden in free downloadable software and tracks online movements, mines the information stored on a computer, or uses a computer's CPU and storage for some task the user knows nothing about.

THE FIRST LINE OF DEFENSE—PEOPLE LO4-4

Organizations today are able to mine valuable information such as the identity of the top 20 percent of their customers, who usually produce 80 percent of revenues. Most organizations view this type of information as intellectual capital and implement security measures to prevent it from walking out the door or falling into the wrong hands. At the same time, they must enable employees, customers, and partners to access needed information electronically. Organizations address security risks through two lines of defense; the first is people, the second technology.

Surprisingly, the biggest problem is people as the majority of information security breaches result from people misusing organizational information. *Insiders* are legitimate users who purposely or accidentally misuse their access to the environment and cause some kind of business-affecting incident. For example, many individuals freely give up their passwords or write them on sticky notes next to their computers, leaving the door wide open for hackers. Through *social engineering,* hackers use their social skills to trick people into revealing access credentials or other valuable information. *Dumpster diving,* or looking through people's trash, is another way hackers obtain information.

Information security policies identify the rules required to maintain information security, such as requiring users to log off before leaving for lunch or meetings, never sharing passwords with anyone, and changing passwords every 30 days. An *information security plan* details how an organization will

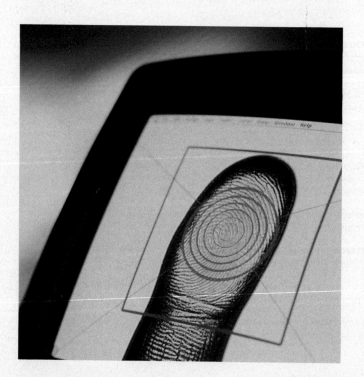

implement the information security policies. The best way a company can safeguard itself from people is by implementing and communicating its information security plan. This becomes even more important with Web 2.0 and as the use of mobile devices, remote workforces, and contractors is growing. A few details managers should consider surrounding people and information security policies include defining the best practices for:[14]

- Applications allowed to be placed on the corporate network, especially various file sharing applications (Kazaz), IM software, and entertainment or freeware created by unknown sources (iPhone applications).

- Corporate computer equipment used for personal reason on personal networks.

- Password creation and maintenance including minimum password length, characters to be included while choosing passwords, and frequency for password changes.

- Personal computer equipment allowed to connect to the corporate network.

- Virus protection including how often the system should be scanned and how frequently the software should be updated. This could also include if downloading attachments is allowed and practices for safe downloading from trusted and untrustworthy sources.

LO4-4 Describe the relationship between information security policies and an information security plan.

THE SECOND LINE OF DEFENSE—TECHNOLOGY LO4-5

Once an organization has protected its intellectual capital by arming its people with a detailed information security plan, it can begin to focus on deploying technology to help combat attackers. Figure 4.13 displays the three areas where technology can aid in the defense against attacks.

LO4-5 Provide an example of each of the three primary information security areas: (1) authentication and authorization, (2) prevention and resistance, and (3) detection and response.

People: Authentication and Authorization

Identity theft is the forging of someone's identity for the purpose of fraud. The fraud is often financial, because thieves apply for and use credit cards or loans in the victim's name. Two means of stealing an identity are phishing and pharming. *Phishing* is a technique to gain personal information for the purpose of identity theft, usually by means of fraudulent emails that look as though they came from legitimate businesses. The messages appear to be genuine, with official-looking formats and logos, and typically ask for verification of important information such as passwords and account numbers, ostensibly for accounting or auditing purposes. Since the emails look authentic, up to one in five recipients responds with the information and subsequently becomes a victim of identity theft and other fraud. Figure 4.14 displays a phishing scam attempting to gain information for Bank of America; you should never click on emails asking you to verify your identity as companies will never contact you directly asking for your user name or password.[15]

Pharming reroutes requests for legitimate websites to false websites. For example, if you were to type in the URL to your bank, pharming could redirect to a fake site that collects your information. Authentication and authorization technologies can prevent identity theft, phishing, and pharming scams. *Authentication* is a method for confirming users' identities. Once a system determines the authentication of a user, it can then determine the access privileges (or authorization) for that user. *Authorization* is the process of providing a user with permission including access levels and abilities such as file access, hours of access, and amount of allocated storage space. Authentication and authorization techniques fall into three categories; the most secure procedures combine all three:

1. Something the user knows, such as a user ID and password.

2. Something the user has, such as a smart card or token.

3. Something that is part of the user, such as a fingerprint or voice signature.

Something the User Knows Such as a User ID and Password

The first type of authentication, using something the user knows, is the most common way to identify individual users and typically consists

FIGURE 4.13 Three Areas of Information Security

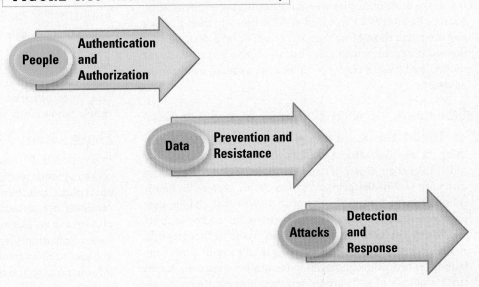

FIGURE 4.13 Three Areas of Information Security

FIGURE 4.14 Bank of America Phishing Scam

From: Bank of America Online [ealert@replies.em.bankofamerica.com]
Sent: Friday, May 21, 2010 5:40 PM
Subject: Customer Alert: Your Account was been Attended

Bank of America ⬆ **Higher Standards**

The sooner you sign in to Online Banking, the simpler your life will get.

Important Notification

Dear **Valued Customer**,

As part of Bank of America Online commitment to provide you with exceptional service, Bank of America Online is taking additional steps to ensure that your account data is secure.

Therefore, we are sending you this e-mail as a security precaution to confirm to you the Inability to accurately verify your account information due to an internal error within server

You are required to confirm your account information to forestall a re-occurence of any future attention with your online banking.

However, failure to update your account information might result in your account being suspended.. Click below to get started.

Get Started

Thank you,
Bank of America Online Banking.

----

* Please do not respond to this email as your reply will not be received.

Bank of America Email, 8th Floor, 101 South Tryon St., Charlotte, NC 28255-0001

of a unique user ID and password. However, this is actually one of the most *ineffective* ways for determining authentication because passwords are not secure. All it typically takes to crack one is enough time. More than 50 percent of help-desk calls are password related, which can cost an organization significant money, and a social engineer can coax a password from almost anybody.

Something the User Has Such as a Smart Card or Token

The second type of authentication, using something the user has, offers a much more effective way to identify individuals than a user ID and password. Tokens and smart cards are two of the primary forms of this type of authentication. **Tokens** are small electronic devices that change user passwords automatically. The user enters his or her user ID and token-displayed password to gain access to the network. A **smart card** is a device about the size of a credit card, containing embedded technologies that can store information and small amounts of software to perform some limited processing. Smart cards can act as identification instruments, a form of digital cash, or a data storage device with the ability to store an entire medical record.

Something That Is Part of the User Such as a Fingerprint or Voice Signature

The third kind of authentication, something that is part of the user, is by far the best and most effective way to manage authentication. **Biometrics** (narrowly defined) is the identification of a user based on a physical characteristic, such as a fingerprint, iris, face, voice, or handwriting. Unfortunately, biometric authentication can be costly and intrusive.

Data: Prevention and Resistance

Prevention and resistance technologies stop intruders from accessing and reading data by means of content filtering, encryption, and firewalls. **Content filtering** occurs when organizations use software that filters content, such as emails, to prevent the accidental or malicious transmission of unauthorized information. Organizations can use content filtering technologies to filter email and prevent emails containing sensitive information from transmitting, whether the transmission was malicious or accidental. It can also filter emails and prevent any suspicious files from transmitting such as potential virus-infected files. Email content filtering can also filter for spam, a form of unsolicited email.

Due Diligence //:
Doodling Passwords[16]

As our online world continues to explode, people are finding the number of usernames and passwords they need to remember growing exponentially. For this reason, many users will assign the same password for every logon, choose easy-to-remember names and dates, or simply write down their passwords on sticky notes and attach them to their computers. Great for the person who needs to remember 72 different passwords, but not so great for system security.

Of course, the obvious answer is to deploy biometrics across the board, but once you start reviewing the costs associated with biometrics, you quickly realize that this is not feasible. What is coming to the rescue to help with the password nightmare we have created? The doodle. Background Draw-a-Secret (BDAS) is a new program created by scientists at Newcastle University in England. BDAS begins by recording the number of strokes it takes a user to draw a

doodle. When the user wants to gain access to the system, he simply redraws the doodle on a touchpad and it is matched against the stored prototype. If the doodle matches, the user is granted access. Doodles are even described as being far more anonymous, therefore offering greater security, than biometrics.

You are probably thinking that you'll end up right back in the same position having to remember all 72 of your password doodles. The good news is that, with doodle passwords, you don't have to remember a thing. The doodle password can be displayed to the user, and they simply have to redraw it since the system analyzes how the user draws or the user's unique hand strokes, not the actual doodle (similar to handwriting recognition technologies).

If you were going to deploy doodle passwords in your organization, what issues and concerns do you think might occur? Do you agree that doodles are easier to remember than text passwords? Do you agree that doodles offer the most effective way to manage authentication, even greater than biometrics? What types of unethical issues do you think you might encounter with doodle passwords?

FIGURE 4.15 Public Key Encryption (PKE)

Originating Business

- Sends the same public key to all customers
- Uses a private key to decrypt the information received

Public Key / Encrypted Information

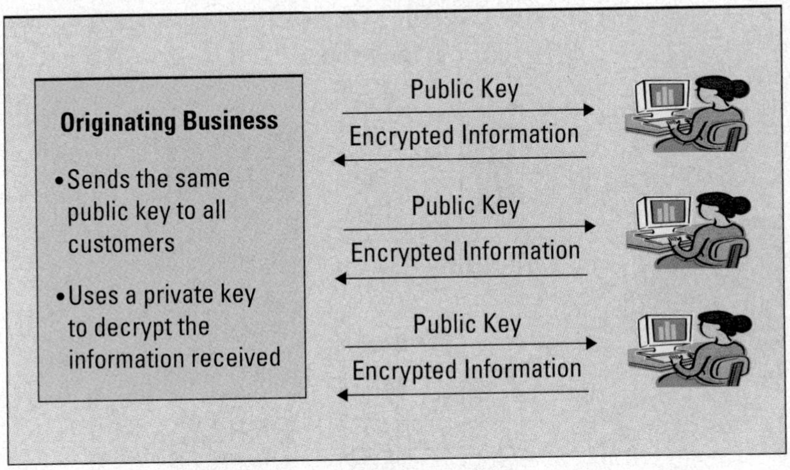

Encryption scrambles information into an alternative form that requires a key or password to decrypt. If there were a security breach and the stolen information were encrypted, the thief would be unable to read it. Encryption can switch the order of characters, replace characters with other characters, insert or remove characters, or use a mathematical formula to convert the information into a code. Companies that transmit sensitive customer information over the Internet, such as credit card numbers, frequently use encryption.

Some encryption technologies use multiple keys. *Public key encryption (PKE)* uses two keys: a public key that everyone can have and a private key for only the recipient (see Figure 4.15). The organization provides the public key to all customers, whether end consumers or other businesses, who use that key to encrypt their information and send it via the Internet. When it arrives at its destination, the organization uses the private key to unscramble it.

Public keys are becoming popular to use for authentication techniques consisting of digital objects in which a trusted third party confirms correlation between the user and the public key. A *certificate authority* is a trusted third party, such as VeriSign, that validates user identities by means of digital certificates. A *digital certificate* is a data file that identifies individuals or organizations online and is comparable to a digital signature.

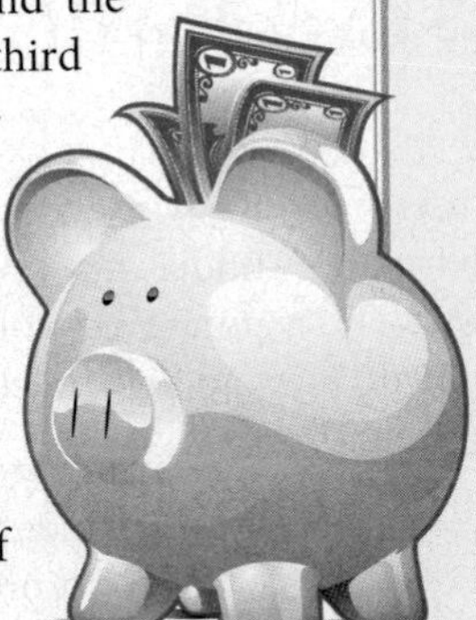

A *firewall* is hardware and/or software that guard a private network by analyzing incoming and outgoing information for the correct markings. If they are missing, the firewall prevents the information from entering the network. Firewalls can even detect computers communicating with the Internet without approval. As Figure 4.16 illustrates, organizations

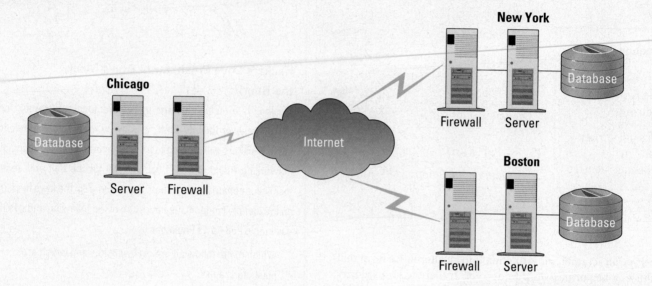

typically place a firewall between a server and the Internet. Think of a firewall as a gatekeeper that protects computer networks from intrusion by providing a filter and safe transfer points for access to and from the Internet and other networks. It screens all network traffic for proper passwords or other security codes and allows only authorized transmissions in and out of the network.

intruders. IDS protects against suspicious network traffic and attempts to access files and data. If a suspicious event or unauthorized traffic is identified, the IDS will generate an alarm and can even be customized to shut down a particularly sensitive part of a network. After identifying an attack, an MIS department can implement response tactics to mitigate the damage.

> RESPONSE TACTICS OUTLINE PROCEDURES SUCH AS HOW LONG A SYSTEM UNDER ATTACK WILL REMAIN PLUGGED IN AND CONNECTED TO THE CORPORATE NETWORK, WHEN TO SHUT DOWN A COMPROMISED SYSTEM, AND HOW QUICKLY A BACKUP SYSTEM WILL BE UP AND RUNNING.

Firewalls do not guarantee complete protection, and users should enlist additional security technologies such as antivirus software and antispyware software. *Antivirus software* scans and searches hard drives to prevent, detect, and remove known viruses, adware, and spyware. Antivirus software must be frequently updated to protect against newly created viruses.

Attack: Detection and Response

The presence of an intruder can be detected by watching for suspicious network events such as bad passwords, the removal of highly classified data files, or unauthorized user attempts. *Intrusion detection software (IDS)* features full-time monitoring tools that search for patterns in network traffic to identify

Response tactics outline procedures such as how long a system under attack will remain plugged in and connected to the corporate network, when to shut down a compromised system, and how quickly a backup system will be up and running.

Guaranteeing the safety of organization information is achieved by implementing the two lines of defense: people and technology. To protect information through people, firms should develop information security policies and plans that provide employees with specific precautions they should take in creating, working with, and transmitting the organization's information assets. Technology-based lines of defense fall into three categories: authentication and authorization; prevention and resistance; and detection and response.

coming up

Module 2 concentrates on the technical foundations of MIS. The power of MIS comes from its ability to carry, house, and support information. And information is power to an organization. This module highlights this point and raises awareness of the significance of information to organizational success. Understanding how the MIS infrastructure supports business operations, how business professionals access and analyze information to make business decisions, and how wireless and mobile technologies can make information continuously and instantaneously available are important for strategically managing any company, large or small. Thus, these are the primary learning outcomes of Module 2.

The module begins by reviewing the role of MIS in supporting business growth, operations, and performance. We quickly turn to the need for MIS to be sustainable given today's focus on being "green," and then dive into databases, data warehousing, networking, and wireless technologies—all fundamental components of MIS infrastructures. A theme throughout the module is the need to leverage and yet safeguard the use of information as key to the survival of any company. Information must be protected from misuse and harm, especially with the continued use, development, and exploitation of the Internet and the web. ■

TECHNICAL FOUNDATIONS OF MIS

module one
BUSINESS DRIVEN MIS

module two
TECHNICAL FOUNDATIONS OF MIS
ch. 5 Infrastructures: Sustainable Technologies
ch. 6 Data: Business Intelligence
ch. 7 Networks: Mobile Business

module three
ENTERPRISE MIS

infrastructures:
sustainable technologies

What's in IT for me?

Why do you, as a business student, need to understand the underlying technology of any company? Most people think "that technical stuff" is something they will never personally encounter and for that reason they do not need to know anything about MIS infrastructures. Well, those people will be challenged in the business world. When your database fails and you lose all of your sales history, you will personally feel the impact when you are unable to receive your bonus. When your computer crashes and you lose all of your confidential information, not to mention your emails, calendars, and messages,

then you will understand why everyone needs to learn about MIS infrastructures. You never want to leave the critical task of backing up your data to your MIS department. You want to personally ensure that your information is not only backed up, but also safeguarded and recoverable. For these reasons, business professionals in the 21st century need to acquire a base-level appreciation of what MIS can and cannot do for their company. Understanding how MIS supports growth, operations, profitability, and most recently sustainability is crucial whether one is new to the workforce or a seasoned *Fortune* 500 employee. One of the primary goals of this chapter is to create a more level playing field between you as a business

continued on p. 108

CHAPTER OUTLINE

SECTION 5-1 >>
MIS Infrastructures

- The Business Benefits of a Solid MIS Infrastructure
- Supporting Operations: Information MIS Infrastructure
- Supporting Change: Agile MIS Infrastructure

SECTION 5-2 >>
Building Sustainable MIS Infrastructures

- MIS and the Environment
- Supporting the Environment: Sustainable MIS Infrastructure

continued from p. 107

professional and the MIS specialists with whom you will work. After reading it you should have many of the skills you need to assist in analyzing current and even some future MIS infrastructures; in recommending needed changes in processes; and in evaluating alternatives that support a company's growth, operations, and profits. ■

{SECTION 5-1}
MIS Infrastructures

LEARNING OUTCOMES

LO5-1 Explain MIS infrastructure and its three primary types.

LO5-2 Identify the three primary areas associated with an information MIS infrastructure.

LO5-3 Describe the characteristics of an agile MIS infrastructure.

is run via a network. A **network** is a communications system created by linking two or more devices and establishing a standard methodology in which they can communicate. As more companies need to share more information, the network takes on greater importance in the infrastructure. Most companies use a specific form of network infrastructure called a client and server network. A **client** is a computer designed to request information from a server. A **server** is a computer dedicated to providing information in response to requests. A good way to understand this is when someone uses a web browser (this would be the client) to access a website (this would be a server that would respond with the web page being requested by the client). Anyone not familiar with the basics of hardware, software, or networks should review Appendix A, "Hardware and Software," and Appendix B, "Networks and Telecommunications," for more information.

In the physical world, a detailed blueprint would show how public utilities, such as water, electricity, and gas, support the foundation of a building. MIS infrastructure is similar as it shows in detail how the hardware, software, and network connectivity support the firm's processes. Every company, regardless of size, relies on some form of MIS infrastructure, whether it is a few personal computers networked together sharing an

["A solid MIS infrastructure can reduce costs, improve productivity, optimize business operations, generate growth, and increase profitability."]

THE BUSINESS BENEFITS OF A SOLID MIS INFRASTRUCTURE LO5-1

Management information systems have played a significant role in business strategies, affected business decisions and processes, and even changed the way companies operate. What is the foundation supporting all of these systems that enable business growth, operations, and profits? What supports the volume and complexity of today's user and application requirements? What protects systems from failures and crashes? It is the **MIS infrastructure,** which includes the plans for how a firm will build, deploy, use, and share its data, processes, and MIS assets. A solid MIS infrastructure can reduce costs, improve productivity, optimize business operations, generate growth, and increase profitability.

Briefly defined, **hardware** consists of the physical devices associated with a computer system, and **software** is the set of instructions the hardware executes to carry out specific tasks. In today's business environment, most hardware and software

Excel file or a large multinational company with thousands of employees interconnected around the world.

An MIS infrastructure is dynamic; it continually changes as the business needs change. Each time a new form of Internet-enabled device, such as an iPhone or BlackBerry, is created and made available to the public, a firm's MIS infrastructure must be revised to support the device. This moves beyond just innovations in hardware to include new types of software and network connectivity. An **enterprise architect** is a person grounded in technology, fluent in business, and able to provide the important bridge between MIS and the business. Firms employ enterprise architects to help manage change and dynamically update MIS infrastructure. Figure 5.1 displays the three primary areas where enterprise architects focus when maintaining a firm's MIS infrastructure.

- **Supporting operations:** *Information MIS infrastructure* identifies where and how important information, such as customer records, is maintained and secured.

- **Supporting change:** *Agile MIS infrastructure* includes the hardware, software, and telecommunications equipment that, when combined, provide the underlying foundation to support the organization's goals.

▼FIGURE 5.1 MIS Infrastructures

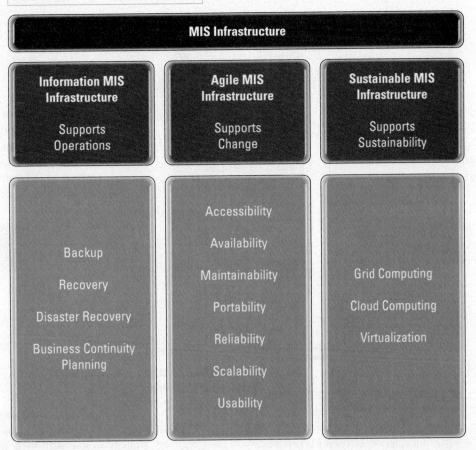

- **Supporting the environment:** *Sustainable MIS infrastructure* identifies ways that a company can grow in terms of computing resources while simultaneously becoming less dependent on hardware and energy consumption.

L05-1 Explain MIS infrastructure and its three primary types.

SUPPORTING OPERATIONS: INFORMATION MIS INFRASTRUCTURE L05-2

Imagine taking a quick trip to the printer on the other side of the room, and when you turn around you find that your laptop has been stolen. How painful would you find this experience? What types of information would you lose? How much time would it take you to recover all of that information? A few things you might lose include music, movies, emails, assignments, saved passwords, not to mention that all-important 40-page paper that took you more than a month to complete. If this sounds painful then you want to pay particular attention to this section and learn how to eliminate this pain.

An information MIS infrastructure identifies where and how important information is maintained and secured. An information infrastructure supports day-to-day business operations and plans for emergencies such as power outages, floods, earthquakes, malicious attacks via the Internet, theft, and security breaches to name just a few. Managers must take every precaution to make sure their systems are operational and protected around the clock every day of the year. Losing a laptop or experiencing bad weather in one part of the country simply cannot take down systems required to operate core business processes. In the past, someone stealing company information would have to carry out boxes upon boxes of paper. Today, as data storage technologies grow in capabilities while shrinking in size, a person can simply walk out the front door of the building with the company's data files stored on a thumb drive or external hard drive. Today's managers must act responsibly to protect one of their most valued assets, information. To support continuous business operations, an information infrastructure provides three primary elements:

- Backup and recovery plan.
- Disaster recovery plan.
- Business continuity plan (see Figure 5.2).

energy to run four separate machines, not to mention created additional amounts of ewaste. Today, you can buy a virtualized computer printer that functions as a fax machine, answering machine, and copy machine all on one physical machine, thereby reducing costs, power requirements, and ewaste. Virtualization is essentially a form of consolidation that can benefit sustainable MIS infrastructures in a variety of ways, for example:

- By increasing availability of applications that can give a higher level of performance depending on the hardware used.

- By increasing energy efficiency by requiring less hardware to run multiple systems or applications.

- By increasing hardware usability by running multiple operating systems on a single computer.

Originally, computers were designed to run a single application on a single operating system. This left most computers vastly underutilized (as mentioned earlier, 75 percent of most computing power is available for other tasks). Virtualization allows multiple virtual computers to exist on a single machine, which allows it to share its resources, such as memory and hard disk space, to run different applications and even different operating systems. Mac computers have the ability to run both the

Apple operating system and the Windows PC operating system, with the use of virtualization software (see Figure 5.12). Unfortunately, virtualization, at least at the moment, is not available for a PC to run Mac software.

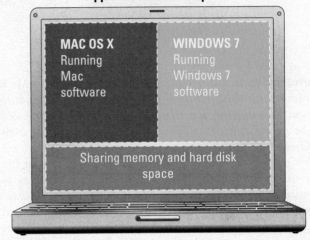

FIGURE 5.12 Virtualization Allows an Apple Macintosh Computer to Run OS X and Windows 7

Apple Macintosh Computer

MAC OS X
Running
Mac
software

WINDOWS 7
Running
Windows 7
software

Sharing memory and hard disk space

BUSTED Hack Attack[15]

A few years ago, it would have been difficult to pull off a hacker attack like the one that took down Twitter. A sophisticated hacker would have needed either the technical savvy to hijack thousands of computers simultaneously or tens of thousands of dollars to pay someone else to do it. Not today. The tools for taking down websites like Twitter, Amazon, or Facebook are getting so cheap and easy to use that the average Joe could easily wreak havoc on any website.

In the Twitter attack, hackers were trying to silence a single blogger who criticized the Russian government, Georgy Jakhaia, who is known online as Cyxymu. The hackers launched a denial-of-service attack, in which thousands of computers try to communicate with the target website at the same time so the site's computers are overwhelmed and can't handle

legitimate requests. In what appears to be collateral damage, the hackers took down the entire Twitter service and hobbled the blogging sites LiveJournal and Facebook, where Jakhaia also posted.

How does it work? Criminal groups and hackers have infected tens of millions of computers around the world with viruses that allow them to control the machines to

launch attacks or send spam. These networks of zombie computers, called "botnets," are then rented out on a per-machine and per-day basis through websites that make executing a denial-of-service attack almost as easy as getting a book from Amazon. No password cracking or software coding is necessary. And it is almost as cheap. A few years ago the cost of renting out 10,000 machines would have been between $2,000 and $5,000. Today you can rent 10,000 machines—enough to take down Twitter—for a mere $200.

With all that you have read in this chapter, highlight the steps an organization can take to protect itself from hacker attacks. Explain how a denial-of-service attack works and why it is illegal. Would using a service-oriented architecture protect a company from a denial-of-service attack? If you were using virtualization, how could you protect your computers from a denial-of-service attack?

▼FIGURE 5.13 Ways for Data Centers to Become Sustainable

Carbon Emissions	Floor Space	Geographic Location
Reduce energy consumption	Stores greater amounts of information in less space	Resources are inexpensive, clean, and available

Virtualization is also one of the easiest and quickest ways to achieve a sustainable MIS infrastructure because it reduces power consumption and requires less equipment that needs to be manufactured, maintained, and later disposed of safely. Managers no longer have to assign servers, storage, or network capacity permanently to single applications. Instead, they can assign the hardware resources when and where they are needed, achieving the availability, flexibility, and scalability a company needs to thrive and grow. Also, by virtually separating the operating system and applications from the hardware, if there is a disaster or hardware failure, it is easy to port the virtual machine to a new physical machine allowing a company to recover quickly from disasters. One of the primary uses of virtualization is for performing backup, recovery, and disaster recovery. Using virtual servers or a virtualization service provider, such as Google, Microsoft, or Amazon, to host disaster recovery is more sustainable than a single company incurring the expense of having redundant physical systems. Also, these providers' data centers are built to withstand natural disasters and are typically located far away from big cities.

Virtual Data Centers

A **data center** is a facility used to house management information systems and associated components, such as telecommunications and storage systems. Data centers, sometimes referred to as server farms, consume power and require cooling and floor space while working to support business growth without disrupting normal business operations and the quality of service. The amount of data a data center stores has grown exponentially over the years as our reliance on information increases. Backups, graphics, documents, presentations, photos, audio and video files all contribute to the ever-expanding information footprint that requires storage.

One of the most effective ways to limit the power consumption and cooling requirements of a data center is to consolidate parts of the physical infrastructure, particularly by reducing the number of physical servers through virtualization. For this reason, virtualization is having a profound impact on data centers as the sheer number of servers a company requires to operate decreases, thereby boosting growth and performance while reducing environmental impact, as shown in Figure 5.13. Google, Microsoft, Amazon, and Yahoo! have all created data centers along the Columbia River in the northwestern United States. In this area, each company can benefit from affordable land, high-speed Internet access, plentiful water for cooling, and even more important, inexpensive electricity. These factors are critical to today's large-scale data centers, whose sheer size and power needs far surpass those of the previous generation. Microsoft's data center in Quincy, Washington, is larger than 10 football fields and is powered entirely by hydroelectricity, power generated from flowing water rather than from the burning of coal or other fossil fuel.[16]

If we take a holistic and integrated approach to overall company growth, the benefits of integrating information MIS infrastructures, environmental MIS infrastructures, and sustainable MIS infrastructures become obvious. For example, a company could easily create a backup of its software and important information in one or more geographically dispersed locations using cloud computing. This would be far cheaper than building its own hot and cold sites in different areas of the country. In the case of a security breach, failover can be deployed as a virtual machine in one location of the cloud can be shut down as another virtual machine in a different location on the cloud comes online.

six

data : business intelligence

What's in IT for me?

This chapter introduces the concepts of information and data and their relative importance to business professionals and firms. It distinguishes between data stored in transactional databases and powerful business intelligence gleaned from data warehouses. Students who understand how to access, manipulate, summarize, sort, and analyze data to support decision making find success. Information has power, and understanding that power will help you compete in the global marketplace. This chapter will provide you with an overview of database fundamentals

continued on p. 130

CHAPTER OUTLINE

SECTION 6-1 >>
Data, Information, and Databases

■ The Business Benefits of High-Quality Information

■ Storing Information in a Relational Database Management System

■ Using a Relational Database for Business Advantages

■ Driving Websites with Data

SECTION 6-2 >>
Business Intelligence

■ The Business Benefits of Data Warehousing

■ Performing Business Analysis with Data Marts

■ Uncovering Trends and Patterns with Data Mining

■ Supporting Decisions with Business Intelligence

continued from p. 129

and the characteristics associated with high-quality information. It will also explain how the various bits of data stored across multiple, operational databases can be transformed in a centralized repository of summarized information in a data warehouse, which can be used for discovering business intelligence.

You, as a business student, need to understand the differences between transactional data and summarized information and the different types of questions you could use a transactional database to answer versus a data warehouse. You need to be aware of the complexity of storing data in databases and the level of effort required to transform operational data into meaningful, summarized information. You need to realize the power of information and the competitive advantage a data warehouse brings an organization in terms of facilitating business intelligence. Armed with the power of information, business students will make smart, informed, and data-supported managerial decisions. ■

{SECTION 6-1}
Data, Information, and Databases

LEARNING OUTCOMES

L06-1 Explain the four primary traits that determine the value of information.

L06-2 Describe a database, a database management system, and the relational database model.

L06-3 Identify the business advantages of a relational database.

L06-4 Explain the business benefits of a data-driven website.

THE BUSINESS BENEFITS OF HIGH-QUALITY INFORMATION L06-1

Information is powerful. Information can tell an organization how its current operations are performing and help it estimate and strategize about how future operations might perform. The ability to understand, digest, analyze, and filter information is key to growth and success to any professional in any industry.

Remember that new perspectives and opportunities can open up when you have the right data that you can turn into information and ultimately business intelligence.

Information is everywhere in an organization. Managers in sales, marketing, human resources, and management need information to run their departments and make daily decisions. When addressing a significant business issue, employees must be able to obtain and analyze all the relevant information so they can make the best decision possible. Information comes at different levels, formats, and granularities. *Information granularity* refers to the extent of detail within the information (fine and detailed or coarse and abstract). Employees must be able to correlate the different levels, formats, and granularities of information when making decisions. For example, a company might be collecting information from various suppliers to make needed decisions, only to find that the information is in different levels, formats, and granularities. One supplier might send detailed information in a spreadsheet, while another supplier might send summary information in a Word document, and still another might send a collection of information from emails. Employees will need to compare these different types of information for what they commonly reveal to make strategic decisions. Figure 6.1 displays the various levels, formats, and granularities of organizational information.

Successfully collecting, compiling, sorting, and finally analyzing information from multiple levels, in varied formats, and exhibiting different granularities can provide tremendous insight into how an organization is performing. Exciting and unexpected results can include potential new markets, new ways of reaching customers, and even new methods of doing business. After understanding the different levels, formats, and granularities of information, managers next want to look at the four primary traits that help determine the value of information:

- Information type: transactional and analytical.
- Information timeliness.
- Information quality.
- Information governance.

L06-1 Explain the four primary traits that determine the value of information.

Information Type: Transactional and Analytical

As discussed previously in the text, the two primary types of information are transactional and analytical. Transactional information encompasses all of the information contained within a single business process or unit of work, and its primary purpose is to support daily operational tasks. Organizations need to capture and store transactional information to perform operational tasks and repetitive decisions such as

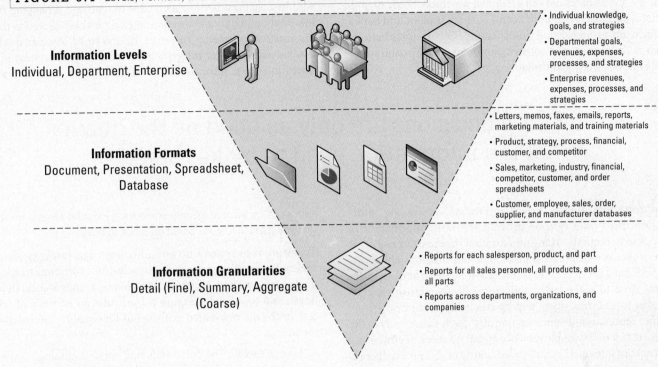

▼FIGURE 6.1 Levels, Formats, and Granularities of Organizational Information

Information Levels
Individual, Department, Enterprise

- Individual knowledge, goals, and strategies
- Departmental goals, revenues, expenses, processes, and strategies
- Enterprise revenues, expenses, processes, and strategies

Information Formats
Document, Presentation, Spreadsheet, Database

- Letters, memos, faxes, emails, reports, marketing materials, and training materials
- Product, strategy, process, financial, customer, and competitor
- Sales, marketing, industry, financial, competitor, customer, and order spreadsheets
- Customer, employee, sales, order, supplier, and manufacturer databases

Information Granularities
Detail (Fine), Summary, Aggregate (Coarse)

- Reports for each salesperson, product, and part
- Reports for all sales personnel, all products, and all parts
- Reports across departments, organizations, and companies

analyzing daily sales reports and production schedules to determine how much inventory to carry. Consider Walmart, which handles more than 1 million customer transactions every hour, and Facebook, which keeps track of 400 million active users (along with their photos, friends, and web links). In addition, every time a cash register rings up a sale, a deposit or withdrawal is made from an ATM, or a receipt is given at the gas pump, capturing and storing of the transactional information are required.[1]

Analytical information encompasses all organizational information, and its primary purpose is to support the performing of managerial analysis tasks. Analytical information is useful when making important decisions such as whether the organization should build a new manufacturing plant or hire additional sales personnel. Analytical information makes it possible to do many things that previously were difficult to accomplish, such as spot business trends, prevent diseases, and fight crime. For example, credit card companies crunch through billions of transactional purchase records to identify fraudulent activity. Indicators such as charges in a foreign country or consecutive purchases of gasoline send a red flag highlighting potential fraudulent activity.

Walmart was able to use its massive amount of analytical information to identify many unusual trends, such as a correlation between storms and Pop-Tarts. Yes, Walmart discovered an increase in the demand for Pop-Tarts during the storm season. Armed with the valuable information the retail chain was able to stock up on Pop-Tarts that were ready for purchase when customers arrived. Figure 6.2 displays different types of transactional and analytical information.[2]

Information Timeliness

Timeliness is an aspect of information that depends on the situation. In some firms or industries, information that is a few

▼FIGURE 6.2 Transactional versus Analytical Information

Transactional Information

Airline Ticket

Sales Receipt

Packing Slip

Database

Analytical Information

Product Statistics

Sales Projections

Future Growth

Trends

days or weeks old can be relevant, while in others information that is a few minutes old can be almost worthless. Some organizations, such as 911 response centers, stock traders, and banks, require up-to-the-second information. Other organizations, such as insurance and construction companies, require only daily or even weekly information.

the amount of work that needs to occur to update a customer who had changed her last name due to marriage. Changing this information in only a few organizational systems will lead to data inconsistencies causing customer 123456 to be associated with two last names. **Data integrity issues** occur when a system produces incorrect, inconsistent, or duplicate data. Data integrity

["Business decisions are only as good as the quality of the information used to make them."]

Real-time information means immediate, up-to-date information. **Real-time systems** provide real-time information in response to requests. Many organizations use real-time systems to uncover key corporate transactional information. The growing demand for real-time information stems from organizations' need to make faster and more effective decisions, keep smaller inventories, operate more efficiently, and track performance more carefully. Information also needs to be timely in the sense that it meets employees' needs, but no more. If employees can absorb information only on an hourly or daily basis, there is no need to gather real-time information in smaller increments.

Most people request real-time information without understanding one of the biggest pitfalls associated with real-time information—continual change. Imagine the following scenario: Three managers meet at the end of the day to discuss a business problem. Each manager has gathered information at different times during the day to create a picture of the situation. Each manager's picture may be different because of the time differences. Their views on the business problem may not match because the information they are basing their analysis on is continually changing. This approach may not speed up decision making, and it may actually slow it down. Business decision makers must evaluate the timeliness for the information for every decision. Organizations do not want to find themselves using real-time information to make a bad decision faster.

Information Quality

Business decisions are only as good as the quality of the information used to make them. **Data inconsistency** occurs when the same data element has different values. Take for example

issues can cause managers to consider the system reports invalid and will make decisions based on other sources.

To ensure your systems do not suffer from data integrity issues, review Figure 6.3 for the five characteristics common to high-quality information: accuracy, completeness, consistency, timeliness, and uniqueness. Figure 6.4 provides an example of several problems associated with using low-quality information including:

1. *Completeness.* The customer's first name is missing.

2. Another issue with *completeness*. The street address contains only a number and not a street name.

3. *Consistency.* There may be a duplication of information since there is a slight difference between the two customers in the spelling of the last name. Similar street addresses and phone numbers make this likely.

▼**FIGURE 6.3** Five Common Characteristics of High-Quality Information

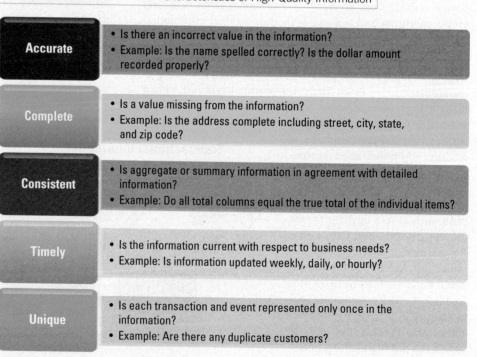

Accurate
- Is there an incorrect value in the information?
- Example: Is the name spelled correctly? Is the dollar amount recorded properly?

Complete
- Is a value missing from the information?
- Example: Is the address complete including street, city, state, and zip code?

Consistent
- Is aggregate or summary information in agreement with detailed information?
- Example: Do all total columns equal the true total of the individual items?

Timely
- Is the information current with respect to business needs?
- Example: Is information updated weekly, daily, or hourly?

Unique
- Is each transaction and event represented only once in the information?
- Example: Are there any duplicate customers?

FIGURE 6.4 Example of Low-Quality Information

1. Missing information (no first name)
2. Incomplete information (no street)
5. Inaccurate information (invalid email)

ID	Last Name	First Name	Street	City	State	Zip	Phone	Fax	Email
113	Smith		123 S. Main	Denver	CO	80210	(303) 777-1258	(303) 777-5544	ssmith@aol.com
114	Jones	Jeff	12A	Denver	CO	80224	(303) 666-6868	(303) 666-6868	(303) 666-6868
115	Roberts	Jenny	1244 Colfax	Denver	CO	85231	759-5654	853-6584	jr@msn.com
116	Robert	Jenny	1244 Colfax	Denver	CO	85231	759-5654	853-6584	jr@msn.com

3. Probable duplicate information (similar names, same address, phone number)
4. Potential wrong information (are the phone and fax numbers the same or is this an error?)
6. Incomplete information (missing area codes)

4. *Accuracy.* This may be inaccurate information because the customer's phone and fax numbers are the same. Some customers might have the same number for phone and fax, but the fact that the customer also has this number in the email address field is suspicious.

5. Another issue with *accuracy.* There is inaccurate information because a phone number is located in the email address field.

6. Another issue with *completeness.* The information is incomplete because there is not a valid area code for the phone and fax numbers.

Nestlé uses 550,000 suppliers to sell more than 100,000 products in 200 countries. However, due to poor information, the company was unable to evaluate its business effectively. After some analysis, it found that it had 9 million records of vendors, customers, and materials, half of which were duplicated, obsolete, inaccurate, or incomplete. The analysis discovered that some records abbreviated vendor names while other records spelled out the vendor names. This created multiple accounts for the same customer, making it impossible to determine the true value of Nestlé's customers. Without being able to identify customer profitability, a company runs the risk of alienating its best customers.[3]

Knowing how low-quality information issues typically occur can help a company correct them. Addressing these errors will significantly improve the quality of company information and the value to be extracted from it. The four primary reasons for low-quality information are:

1. Online customers intentionally enter inaccurate information to protect their privacy.

2. Different systems have different information entry standards and formats.

show me the MONEY

Determining Information Quality Issues

Real People is a magazine geared toward working individuals that provides articles and advice on everything from car maintenance to family planning. *Real People* is currently experiencing problems with its magazine distribution list. More than 30 percent of the magazines mailed are returned because of incorrect address information, and each month it receives numerous calls from angry customers complaining that they have not yet received their magazines. Here is a sample of *Real People*'s customer information. Create a report detailing all of the issues with the information, potential causes of the information issues, and solutions the company can follow to correct the situation.

ID	First Name	Middle Initial	Last Name	Street	City	State	Zip Code
433	M	J	Jones	13 Denver	Denver	CO	87654
434	Margaret	J	Jones	13 First Ave.	Denver	CO	87654
434	Brian	F	Hoover	Lake Ave.	Columbus	OH	87654
435	Nick	H	Schweitzer	65 Apple Lane	San Francisco	OH	65664
436	Richard	A		567 55th St.	New York	CA	98763
437	Alana	B	Smith	121 Tenny Dr.	Buffalo	NY	142234
438	Trevor	D	Darrian	90 Fresrdestil	Dallas	TX	74532

3. Data-entry personnel enter abbreviated information to save time or erroneous information by accident.

4. Third-party and external information contains inconsistencies, inaccuracies, and errors.

Understanding the Costs of Using Low-Quality Information

Using the wrong information can lead managers to make erroneous decisions. Erroneous decisions in turn can cost time, money, reputations, and even jobs. Some of the serious business consequences that occur due to using low-quality information to make decisions are:

- Inability to accurately track customers.
- Difficulty identifying the organization's most valuable customers.

revealed that typical golfers in Phoenix are tourists and conventioneers who usually bring their clubs with them. The analysis further revealed that two of the best places to sell golf clubs in the United States are Rochester, New York, and Detroit, Michigan. Equipped with this valuable information, the company was able to strategically place its stores and launch its marketing campaigns.[4]

High-quality information does not automatically guarantee that every decision made is going to be a good one, because people ultimately make decisions and no one is perfect. However, such information ensures that the basis of the decisions is accurate. The success of the organization depends on appreciating and leveraging the true value of timely and high-quality information.

> "To ensure a firm manages its information correctly, it will need special policies and procedures establishing rules on how the information is organized, updated, maintained, and accessed."

- Inability to identify selling opportunities.
- Lost revenue opportunities from marketing to nonexistent customers.
- The cost of sending nondeliverable mail.
- Difficulty tracking revenue because of inaccurate invoices.
- Inability to build strong relationships with customers.

Understanding the Benefits of Using High-Quality Information

High-quality information can significantly improve the chances of making a good decision and directly increase an organization's bottom line. One company discovered that even with its large number of golf courses, Phoenix, Arizona, is not a good place to sell golf clubs. An analysis

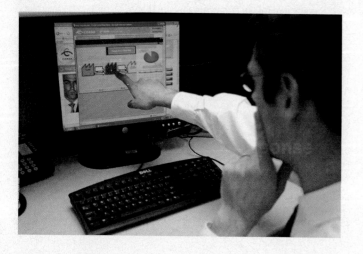

Information Governance

Information is a vital resource and users need to be educated on what they can and cannot do with it. To ensure a firm manages its information correctly, it will need special policies and procedures establishing rules on how the information is organized, updated, maintained, and accessed. Every firm, large and small, should create an information policy concerning data governance. *Data governance* refers to the overall management of the availability, usability, integrity, and security of company data. A company that supports a data governance program has a defined policy that specifies who is accountable for various portions or aspects of the data, including its accuracy, accessibility, consistency, timeliness, and completeness. The policy should clearly define the processes concerning how to store, archive, back up, and secure the data. In addition, the company should create a set of procedures identifying accessibility levels for employees. Then, the firm should deploy controls and procedures that enforce government regulations and compliance with mandates such as Sarbanes-Oxley.

STORING INFORMATION IN A RELATIONAL DATABASE MANAGEMENT SYSTEM LO6-2

The core component of any system, regardless of size, is a database and a database management system. Broadly defined, a *database* maintains information about various types of objects (inventory), events (transactions), people (employees), and places (warehouses). A **database management system (DBMS)** creates, reads, updates, and deletes data in a database while controlling access and security. Managers send requests to the DBMS, and the DBMS performs the actual manipulation of the data in the database. Companies store their information in databases, and managers access these systems to answer operational questions such as how many customers purchased Product A in December or what were the average sales by region. There are two primary tools available for retrieving information from a DBMS. First is a **query-by-example (QBE) tool** that helps users graphically design the answer to a question against a database. Second is a **structured query language (SQL)** that asks users to write lines of code to answer questions against a database. Managers typically interact with QBE tools, and MIS professionals have the skills required to code SQL. Figure 6.5 displays the relationship between a database, a DBMS, and a user. Some of the more popular examples of DBMS include MySQL, Microsoft Access, SQL Server, FileMaker, Oracle, and FoxPro.

A **data element** (or **data field**) is the smallest or basic unit of information. Data elements can include a customer's name, address, email, discount rate, preferred shipping method, product name, quantity ordered, and so on. **Data models** are logical data structures that detail the relationships among data elements using graphics or pictures.

Metadata provides details about data. For example, metadata for an image could include its size, resolution, and date created. Metadata about a text document could contain document length, data created, author's name, and summary. Each data element is given a description, such as Customer Name; metadata is provided for the type of data (text, numeric, alphanumeric, date, image, binary value) and descriptions of potential predefined values such as a certain area code; and finally the relationship is defined. A **data dictionary** compiles all of the metadata about the data elements in the data model. Looking at a data model along with reviewing the data dictionary provides tremendous insight into the database's functions, purpose, and business rules.

DBMS use three primary data models for organizing information—hierarchical, network, and the relational database, the most prevalent. A **relational database model** stores information in the form of logically related two-dimensional tables. A **relational database management system** allows users to create, read, update, and delete data in a relational database. Although the hierarchical and network models are important, this text focuses only on the relational database model.

LO6-2 Describe a database, a database management system, and the relational database model.

Storing Data Elements in Entities and Attributes

For flexibility in supporting business operations, managers need to query or search for the answers to business questions such as which artist sold the most albums during a certain month.

▼**FIGURE 6.5** Relationship of Database, DBMS, and User

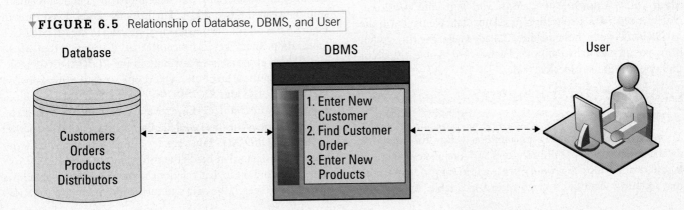

Database

DBMS

User

Customers
Orders
Products
Distributors

1. Enter New Customer
2. Find Customer Order
3. Enter New Products

FIGURE 6.6 Primary Concepts of the Relational Database Model

Entities

Foreign keys

TRACKS

TrackNumber	TrackTitle	TrackLength	RecordingID
1	I Won't	3:45	1
2	Begin Again	4:14	1
3	You Got Me	4:00	1
4	Fallin For you	3:35	1
1	I Gotta Feelin	4:49	2
2	Imma Be	4:17	2
3	Boom Boom Pow	4:11	2
4	Meet Me Halfway	4:44	2

Primary keys

RECORDINGS

RecordingID	RecordingTitle	MuscianID	CategoryID
1	Breakthrough	1	1
2	The E.N.D.	2	1
3	Monkey Business	2	1
4	Elephunk	2	1
5	The Fame Monster	3	1
6	Raymond v. Raymond	4	2

Attributes

MUSICIANS

MusicianID	MusicianName	MusicianPhoto	MusicianNotes
1	Colby Caillat	Colby.jpg	Next concert in Boston 7/1/2011
2	Black Eyed Peas	BYP.bmp	New album due 12/25/2011
3	Lady Gaga	Gaga.tiff	Do not bring young kids to live shows
4	Usher	Usher.bmp	Current album #1 on Billboard

Records

CATEGORIES

CategoryID	CategoryName
1	Pop
2	R&B
3	Rock
4	Country
5	Blues
6	Classical

The relationships in the relational database model help managers extract this information. Figure 6.6 illustrates the primary concepts of the relational database model—entities, attributes, keys, and relationships. An **entity** (also referred to as a table) stores information about a person, place, thing, transaction, or event. The entities, or tables, of interest in Figure 6.6 are TRACKS, RECORDINGS, MUSICIANS, and CATEGORIES. Notice that each entity is stored in a different two-dimensional table (with rows and columns).

Attributes (also called columns or fields) are the data elements associated with an entity. In Figure 6.6 the attributes for the entity TRACKS are TrackNumber, TrackTitle, TrackLength, and RecordingID. Attributes for the entity MUSICIANS are MusicianID, MusicianName, MusicianPhoto, and Musician-Notes. A **record** is a collection of related data elements (in the MUSICIANS table these include "3, Lady Gaga, gag.tiff, Do not bring young kids to live shows"). Each record in an entity occupies one row in its respective table.

Creating Relationships Through Keys

To manage and organize various entities within the relational database model, you use primary keys and foreign keys to create logical relationships. A **primary key** is a field (or group of fields) that uniquely identifies a given record in a table. In the table

RECORDINGS, the primary key is the field RecordingID that uniquely identifies each record in the table. Primary keys are a critical piece of a relational database because they provide a way of distinguishing each record in a table; for instance, imagine you need to find information on a customer named Steve Smith. Simply searching the customer name would not be an ideal way to find the information because there might be 20 customers with the name Steve Smith. This is the reason the relational database model uses primary keys to uniquely identify each record. Using Steve Smith's unique ID allows a manager to search the database to identify all information associated with this customer.

A **foreign key** is a primary key of one table that appears as an attribute in another table and acts to provide a logical relationship between the two tables. For instance, Black Eyed Peas in Figure 6.6 is one of the musicians appearing in the MUSICIANS table. Its primary key, MusicianID, is "2." Notice that MusicianID also appears as an attribute in the RECORDINGS table. By matching these attributes, you create a relationship between the MUSICIANS and RECORDINGS tables that states the Black Eyed Peas (MusicianID 2) have several recordings including The E.N.D., Monkey Business, and Elephunk. In essence, MusicianID in the RECORDINGS table creates a logical relationship (who was the musician that made the recording) to the MUSICIANS table. Creating the logical relationship between the tables allows managers to search the data and turn it into useful information.

USING A RELATIONAL DATABASE FOR BUSINESS ADVANTAGES LO6-3

Many business managers are familiar with Excel and other spreadsheet programs they can use to store business data. Although spreadsheets are excellent for supporting some data analysis, they offer limited functionality in terms of security, accessibility, and flexibility and can rarely scale to support business growth. From a business perspective, relational databases offer many advantages over using a text document or a spreadsheet, including:

- Increased flexibility.
- Increased scalability and performance.
- Reduced information redundancy.
- Increased information integrity (quality).
- Increased information security.

> From a business perspective, relational databases offer many advantages over using a text document or a spreadsheet.

LO6-3 Identify the business advantages of a relational database.

Increased Flexibility

Databases tend to mirror business structures, and a database needs to handle changes quickly and easily, just as any business needs to be able to do. Equally important, databases need to provide flexibility in allowing each user to access the information in whatever way best suits his or her needs. The distinction between logical and physical views is important in understanding flexible database user views. The *physical view* of information deals with the physical storage of information on a storage device.

The *logical view* of information focuses on how individual users logically access information to meet their own particular business needs.

In the database illustration from Figure 6.6, for example, one user could perform a query to determine which recordings had a track length of four minutes or more. At the same time, another user could perform an analysis to determine the distribution of recordings as they relate to the different categories. For example, are there more R&B recordings than rock, or are they evenly distributed? This example demonstrates that while a database has only one physical view, it can easily support multiple logical views that provide for flexibility.

Consider another example—a mail-order business. One user might want a report presented in alphabetical format, in which case last name should appear before first name. Another user, working with a catalog mailing system, would want customer names appearing as first name and then last name. Both are easily achievable but different logical views of the same physical information.

Increased Scalability and Performance

In its first year of operation, the official website of the American Family Immigration History Center, www.ellisisland.org, generated more than 2.5 billion hits. The site offers immigration information about people who entered America through the Port of New York and Ellis Island between 1892 and 1924. The database contains more than 25 million passenger names that are correlated to 3.5 million images of ships' manifests.[7]

The database had to be scalable to handle the massive volumes of information and the large numbers of users expected for the launch of the website. In addition, the database needed to perform quickly under heavy use. Some organizations must be able to support hundreds or thousands of users including employees, partners, customers, and suppliers, who all want to access and share the same information. Databases today scale to exceptional levels, allowing all types of users and programs to perform information-processing and information-searching tasks.

Reduced Data Redundancy

Data redundancy is the duplication of data, or the storage of the same data in multiple places. Redundant data can cause storage issues along with data integrity issues, making it difficult to determine which values are the most current or most accurate. Employees become confused and frustrated when faced with incorrect information causing disruptions to business processes and procedures. One primary

create an order for a nonexistent customer, provide a markup percentage that was negative, or order zero pounds of raw materials from a supplier. *Business-critical integrity constraints* enforce business rules vital to an organization's success and often require more insight and knowledge than relational integrity constraints. Consider a supplier of fresh produce to large grocery chains such as Kroger. The supplier might implement a business-critical integrity constraint stating that no product returns are accepted after 15 days past delivery. That would make sense because of the chance of spoilage of the produce. Business-critical integrity constraints tend to mirror the very rules by which an organization achieves success.

The specification and enforcement of integrity constraints produce higher-quality information that will provide better support for business decisions. Organizations that establish specific procedures for developing integrity constraints typically see an increase in accuracy that then increases the use of organizational information by business professionals.

> # REDUNDANT DATA CAN CAUSE STORAGE ISSUES ALONG WITH DATA INTEGRITY ISSUES, MAKING IT DIFFICULT TO DETERMINE WHICH VALUES ARE THE MOST CURRENT OR MOST ACCURATE.

goal of a database is to eliminate information redundancy by recording each piece of information in only one place in the database. This saves disk space, makes performing information updates easier, and improves information quality.

Increased Information Integrity (Quality)

Information integrity is a measure of the quality of information. *Integrity constraints* are rules that help ensure the quality of information. The database design needs to consider integrity constraints. The database and the DBMS ensures that users can never violate these constraints. There are two types of integrity constraints: (1) relational and (2) business critical.

Relational integrity constraints are rules that enforce basic and fundamental information-based constraints. For example, a relational integrity constraint would not allow someone to

Increased Information Security

Managers must protect information, like any asset, from unauthorized users or misuse. As systems become increasingly complex and highly available over the Internet on many different devices, security becomes an even bigger issue. Databases offer many security features including passwords to provide authentication, access levels to determine who can access the data, and access controls to determine what type of access they have to the information.

For example, customer service representatives might need read-only access to customer order information so they can answer customer order inquiries; they might not have or need the authority to change or delete order information. Managers might require access to employee files, but they should have access only to their own employees' files, not the employee files for the entire company. Various security features of databases can ensure that individuals have only certain types of access to certain types of information.

Security risks are increasing as more and more databases and DBMS systems are moving to data centers run in the cloud. The biggest risks when using cloud computing are ensuring the security and privacy of the information in the database. Implementing data governance policies and procedures that outline the data management requirements can ensure safe and secure cloud computing.

DRIVING WEBSITES WITH DATA L06-4

Websites change for site visitors depending on the type of information they request. Consider, for example, an automobile dealer. The dealer would create a database containing data elements for each car it has available for sale including make, model, color, year, miles per gallon, a photograph, and so on. Website visitors might click on Porsche and then enter their specific requests such as price range or year made. Once the user hits "go" the website automatically provides a custom view of the requested information. The dealer must create, update, and delete automobile information as the inventory changes.

A *data-driven website* is an interactive website kept constantly updated and relevant to the needs of its customers using a database. Data-driven capabilities are especially useful when a firm needs to offer large amounts of information, products, or services. Visitors can become quickly annoyed if they find themselves buried under an avalanche of information when searching a website. A data-driven website can help limit the amount of information displayed to customers based on unique search requirements. Companies even use data-driven websites to make information in their internal databases available to customers and business partners.

There are a number of advantages to using the web to access company databases. First, web browsers are much easier to use than directly accessing the database using a custom-query tool. Second, the web interface requires few or no changes to the database model. Finally, it costs less to add a web interface in front of a DBMS than to redesign and rebuild the system to support changes. Additional data-driven website advantages include:

- **Easy to manage content:** Website owners can make changes without relying on MIS professionals; users can update data-driven websites with little or no training.

- **Easy to store large amounts of data:** Data-driven websites can keep large volumes of information organized. Website owners can use templates to implement changes for layouts, navigation, or website structure. This improves website reliability, scalability, and performance.

- **Easy to eliminate human errors:** Data-driven websites trap data-entry errors, eliminating inconsistencies while ensuring all information is entered correctly.

Zappos credits its success as an online shoe retailer to its vast inventory of nearly 3 million products available through its dynamic data-driven website. The company built its data-driven website catering to a specific niche market: consumers who were tired of finding that their most-desired items were always out of stock at traditional retailers. Zappos' highly flexible, scalable,

Due Diligence //:

Sorry, I Didn't Mean to Post Your Social Security Number on the Internet[8]

Programming 101 teaches all students that security is the crucial part of any system. You must secure your data! It appears that some people working for the state of Oklahoma forgot this important lesson when tens of thousands of Oklahoma residents had their sensitive data—including numbers—posted on the Internet for the general public to access. You have probably heard this type of report before, but have you heard that the error went unnoticed for three years? A programmer reported the problem, explaining how he could easily change the page his browser was pointing to and grab the entire database for the state of Oklahoma. Also, because of the programming, malicious users could easily tamper with the database by changing data or adding fictitious data. If you are still thinking that isn't such a big deal, it gets worse. The website also posted the Sexual and Violent Offender Registry. Yes, the Department of Corrections employee data were also available for the general public to review.

Why is it important to secure data? What can happen if someone accesses your customer database? What could happen if someone changes the information in your customer database and adds fictitious data? Who should be held responsible for the state of Oklahoma data breech? What are the business risks associated with data security?

and secure database helped it rank as the most-available Internet retailer. Figure 6.7 displays Zappos' data-driven website illustrating a user querying the database and receiving information that satisfies the user's request.[9]

Companies can gain valuable business knowledge by viewing the data accessed and analyzed from their website. Figure 6.8 displays how running queries or using analytical tools, such as a PivotTable, on the database that is attached to the website can offer insight into the business, such as items browsed, frequent requests, items bought together, and so on.

LO6-4 Explain the business benefits of a data-driven website.

FIGURE 6.7
Zappos.com—A Data-Driven Website

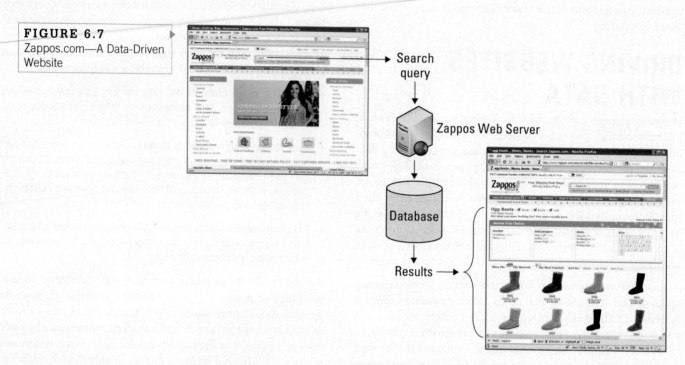

FIGURE 6.8
BI in a Data-Driven website

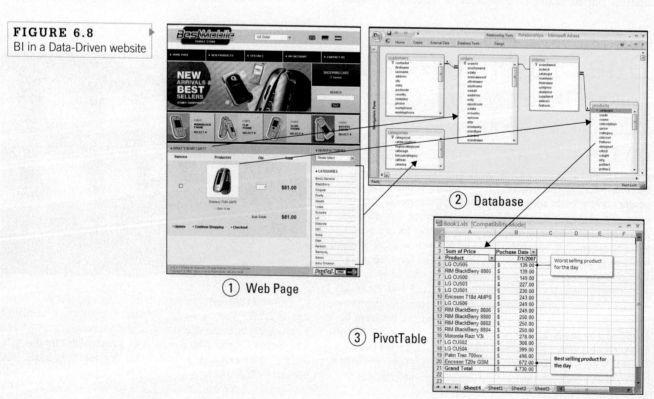

{SECTION 6-2}
Business Intelligence

LEARNING OUTCOMES

LO6-5 Define a data warehouse, and provide a few reasons it can make a manager more effective.

LO6-6 Explain ETL and the role of a data mart in business.

LO6-7 Define data mining, and explain the three common forms for mining structured and unstructured data.

LO6-8 Identify the advantages of using business intelligence to support managerial decision making.

THE BUSINESS BENEFITS OF DATA WAREHOUSING LO6-5

In the 1990s as organizations began to need more timely information about their business, they found that traditional management information systems were too cumbersome to provide relevant information efficiently and effectively. Most of the systems were in the form of operational databases that were

During the latter half of the 20th century, the numbers and types of operational databases increased. Many large businesses found themselves with information scattered across multiple systems with different file types (such as spreadsheets, databases, and even word processing files), making it almost impossible for anyone to use the information from multiple sources. Completing reporting requests across operational systems could take days or weeks using antiquated reporting tools that were ineffective for running a business. From this idea, the data warehouse was born as a place where relevant information could be stored and accessed for making strategic queries and reports.

A *data warehouse* is a logical collection of information, gathered from many different operational databases, that supports business analysis activities and decision-making tasks. The primary purpose of a data warehouse is to combine information, more specifically, strategic information, throughout an organization into a single repository in such a way that the people who need that information can make decisions and undertake business analysis. A key idea within data warehousing is to collect information from multiple systems in a common location that uses a universal querying tool. This allows operational databases to run where they are most efficient for the business, while providing a common location using a familiar format for the strategic or enterprisewide reporting information.

> ## " The primary purpose of a data warehouse is to combine information. "

designed for specific business functions, such as accounting, order entry, customer service, and sales, and were not appropriate for business analysis for the following reasons:

- **Inconsistent data definitions:** Every department had its own method for recording data so when trying to share information, data did not match and users did not get the data they really needed.

- **Lack of data standards:** Managers need to perform cross-functional analysis using data from all departments, which differed in granularities, formats, and levels.

- **Poor data quality:** The data, if available, were often incorrect or incomplete. Therefore, users could not rely on the data to make decisions.

- **Inadequate data usefulness:** Users could not get the data they needed; what was collected was not always useful for intended purposes.

- **Ineffective direct data access:** Most data stored in operational databases did not allow users direct access; users had to wait to have their queries or questions answered by MIS professionals who could code SQL. Users want and need answers in a timely fashion and waiting for MIS professionals to respond to queries frequently closed the window of opportunity.

Data warehouses go even a step further by standardizing information. Gender, for instance can be referred to in many ways (Male, Female, M/F, 1/0), but it should be standardized on a data warehouse with one common way of referring to each data element that stores gender (M/F). Standardizing of data elements allows for greater accuracy, completeness, and consistency as well as increases the quality of the information in making strategic business decisions. The data warehouse then is simply a tool that enables business users, typically managers, to be more effective in many ways, including:

- Developing customer profiles.
- Identifying new-product opportunities.
- Improving business operations.
- Identifying financial issues.
- Analyzing trends.
- Understanding competitors.
- Understanding product performance.

LO6-5 Define a data warehouse, and provide a few reasons why it can make a manager more effective.

PERFORMING BUSINESS ANALYSIS WITH DATA MARTS LO6-6

Businesses collect a tremendous amount of transactional information as part of their routine operations. Marketing, sales, and other departments would like to analyze these data to understand their operations better. While databases store the details of all transactions (for instance, the sale of a product) and events (hiring a new employee), data warehouses store that same information but in an aggregated form more suited to supporting decision-making tasks. Aggregation, in this instance, can include totals, counts, averages, and the like.

The data warehouse modeled in Figure 6.9 compiles information from internal databases (or transactional and operational databases) and external databases through extraction, transformation, and loading. ***Extraction, transformation, and loading (ETL)*** is a process that extracts information from internal and external databases, transforms it using a common set of enterprise definitions, and loads it into a data warehouse. The data warehouse then sends portions (or subsets) of the information to data marts. A ***data mart*** contains a subset of data warehouse information. To distinguish between data warehouses and data

marts, think of data warehouses as having a more organizational focus and data marts as having a functional focus. Figure 6.9 provides an illustration of a data warehouse and its relationship to internal and external databases, ETL, and data marts.

LO6-6   Explain ETL and the role of a data mart in business.

Multidimensional Analysis

A relational database contains information in a series of two-dimensional tables. In a data warehouse and data mart, information contains layers of columns and rows. For this reason, most data warehouses and data marts are multidimensional databases. A dimension is a particular attribute of information. Each layer in a data warehouse or data mart represents information according to an additional dimension. A ***cube*** is the common term for the representation of multidimensional information. Figure 6.10 displays a cube (cube a) that represents store information (the layers), product information (the rows), and promotion information (the columns).

After creating a cube of information, users can begin to slice-and-dice the cube to drill down into the information. The second cube (cube b) in Figure 6.10 displays a slice representing promotion II information for all products at all stores. The third cube (cube c) in Figure 6.10 displays only information for promotion III, product B, at store 2. By using multidimensional analysis, users can analyze information in a number of ways and with any number of dimensions. Users might want to add dimensions of information to a current analysis including product category, region, and even forecasted versus actual weather. The true value of a data warehouse is its ability to provide multidimensional analysis that allows users to gain insights into their information.

Data warehouses and data marts are ideal for off-loading some of the querying against a database. For example, querying a database to obtain an average of sales for Product B at Store 2 while Promotion III is under way might create a considerable processing burden for a database, increasing the time it takes another person to enter a new sale into the same database. If an organization performs numerous queries against a database (or multiple databases), aggregating that information into a data warehouse will be beneficial.

▼FIGURE 6.9 Data Warehouse Model

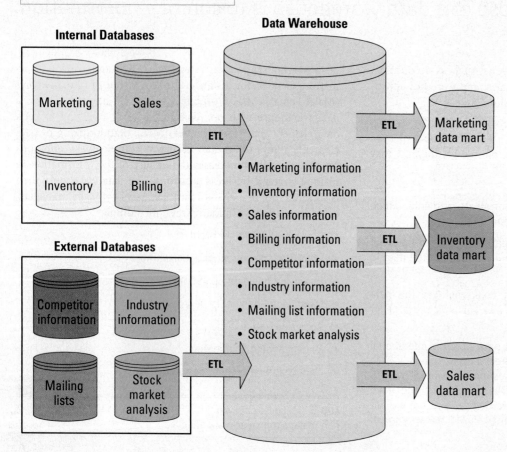

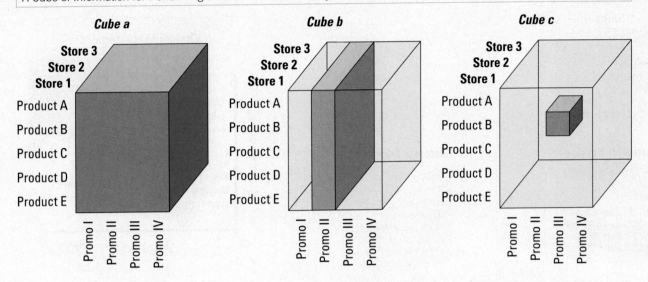

FIGURE 6.10
A Cube of Information for Performing a Multidimensional Analysis on Three Stores for Five Products and Four Promotions

Information Cleansing or Scrubbing

Maintaining quality information in a data warehouse or data mart is extremely important. To increase the quality of organizational information and thus the effectiveness of decision making, businesses must formulate a strategy to keep information clean. *Information cleansing* or *scrubbing* is a process that weeds out and fixes or discards inconsistent, incorrect, or incomplete information.

Specialized software tools exist that use sophisticated procedures to analyze, standardize, correct, match, and consolidate

data warehouse information. This step is vitally important because data warehouses often contain information from several different databases, some of which can be external to the organization. In a data warehouse, information cleansing occurs first during the ETL process and again once the information is in the data warehouse. Companies can choose information cleansing software from several different vendors including Oracle, SAS, Ascential Software, and Group 1 Software. Ideally, scrubbed information is accurate and consistent.

Looking at customer information highlights why information cleansing is necessary. Customer information exists in several operational systems. In each system, all the details could change—from the customer ID to contact information—depending on the business process the user is performing (see Figure 6.11).

Figure 6.12 displays a customer name entered differently in multiple operational systems. Information cleansing allows an organization to fix these types of inconsistencies in the data warehouse. Figure 6.13 displays the typical events that occur during information cleansing.

Achieving perfect information is almost impossible. The more complete and accurate a company wants its information to be, the more it costs (see Figure 6.14). Companies may also trade accuracy for completeness. Accurate information is correct, while complete information has no blanks. A birth date of 2/31/10 is an example of complete but inaccurate information (February 31 does not exist). An address containing Denver, Colorado, without a zip code is an example of accurate information that is incomplete. Many firms complete

FIGURE 6.11 Contact Information in Operational Systems

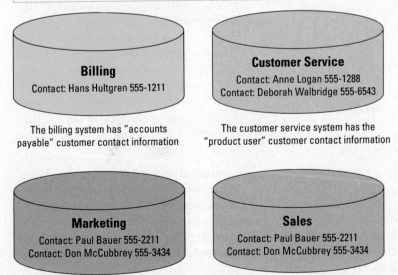

Billing
Contact: Hans Hultgren 555-1211

The billing system has "accounts payable" customer contact information

Customer Service
Contact: Anne Logan 555-1288
Contact: Deborah Walbridge 555-6543

The customer service system has the "product user" customer contact information

Marketing
Contact: Paul Bauer 555-2211
Contact: Don McCubbrey 555-3434

Sales
Contact: Paul Bauer 555-2211
Contact: Don McCubbrey 555-3434

The marketing and sales system has "decision maker" customer contact information.

FIGURE 6.12
Standardizing a Customer Name in Operational Systems

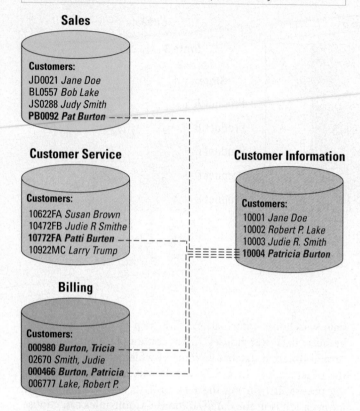

Sales

Customers:
JD0021 *Jane Doe*
BL0557 *Bob Lake*
JS0288 *Judy Smith*
PB0092 *Pat Burton*

Customer Service

Customers:
10622FA *Susan Brown*
10472FB *Judie R Smithe*
10772FA *Patti Burten*
10922MC *Larry Trump*

Billing

Customers:
000980 *Burton, Tricia*
02670 *Smith, Judie*
000466 *Burton, Patricia*
006777 *Lake, Robert P.*

Customer Information

Customers:
10001 *Jane Doe*
10002 *Robert P. Lake*
10003 *Judie R. Smith*
10004 *Patricia Burton*

FIGURE 6.13 Information Cleansing Activities

Cleansing

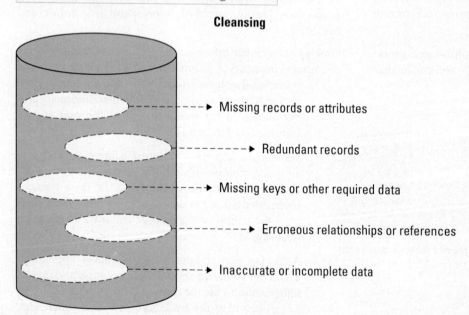

→ Missing records or attributes

→ Redundant records

→ Missing keys or other required data

→ Erroneous relationships or references

→ Inaccurate or incomplete data

data quality audits to determine the accuracy and completeness of their data. Most organizations determine a percentage of accuracy and completeness high enough to make good decisions at a reasonable cost, such as 85 percent accurate and 65 percent complete.

FIGURE 6.14
The Cost of Accurate and Complete Information

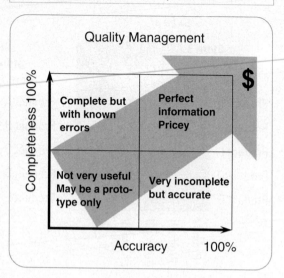

Quality Management

Completeness 100%

Complete but with known errors | Perfect information Pricey

Not very useful May be a prototype only | Very incomplete but accurate

Accuracy   100%

UNCOVERING TRENDS AND PATTERNS WITH DATA MINING LO6-7

Companies are collecting more data than ever. Historically, data were housed functionally in systems that were unable to talk to each other, such as customer service, finance, and human resources. ***Data mining*** is the process of analyzing data to extract information not offered by the raw data alone. Data mining can also begin at a summary information level (coarse granularity) and progress through increasing levels of detail (drilling down), or the reverse (drilling up). Companies use data-mining techniques to compile a complete picture of their operations, all within a single view, allowing them to identify trends and improve forecasts. Consider Best Buy, which used data-mining tools to identify that 7 percent of its customers accounted for 43 percent of its sales, so the company reorganized its stores to accommodate those customers.[10]

To perform data mining, users need data-mining tools. ***Data-mining tools*** use a variety of techniques to find patterns and relationships in large volumes of information that predict future behavior and guide decision making. Data mining uncovers trends and patterns, which analysts use to build models that, when exposed to new information sets, perform a variety of information analysis functions. Data-mining tools for data warehouses help users

BUSTED Follow the Data[11]

There is a classic line in the movie *All the President's Men,* which covers the Watergate investigation, where Deep Throat meets with Bob Woodward and coolly advises him to "follow the money." Woodward follows the money, and the Watergate investigation ends with President Nixon's resignation.

If you want to find out what is happening in today's data-filled world, you could probably change those words to "follow the data." IDC reports that the amount of information stored in the digital universe is projected to hit nearly 1.8 zettabytes by 2011, representing a tenfold increase in five years. One of the newest forms of legal requirements

emerging from the data explosion is ediscovery, the legal requirements mandating that an organization must archive all forms of software communications, including email,

text messages, and multimedia. Yes, the text message you sent four years ago could come back to haunt you.

Organizations today have more data than they know what to do with and are frequently overwhelmed with data management. Getting at such data and presenting them in a useful manner for cogent analysis is a tremendous task that haunts managers. What do you think is involved in data management? What is contained in the zettabytes of data stored by organizations? Why would an organization store data? How long should an organization store its data? What are the risks associated with failing to store organizational data?

---

uncover business intelligence in their data. Some of the key areas where businesses are using data mining include:

- Analyzing customer buying patterns to predict future marketing and promotion campaigns.

- Building budgets and other financial information.

- Detecting fraud by identifying deceptive spending patterns.

- Finding the best customers who spend the most money.

- Keeping customers from leaving or migrating to competitors.

- Promoting and hiring employees to ensure success for both the company and the individual.

Data mining enables these companies to determine relationships among such internal factors as price, product positioning, or staff skills, and external factors such as economic indicators, competition, and customer demographics. In addition, it enables companies to determine the impact on sales, customer satisfaction, and corporate profits and to drill down into summary information to view detail transactional data. With data mining, a retailer could use point-of-sale records of customer purchases to send targeted promotions based on an individual's purchase history. By mining demographic data from comment or warranty cards, the retailer could develop products and promotions to appeal to specific customer segments.

Netflix uses data mining to analyze each customer's film-viewing habits to provide recommendations for other customers with Cinematch, its movie recommendation system. Using

Cinematch, Netflix can present customers with a number of additional movies they might want to watch based on the customer's current preferences. Netflix's innovative use of data mining provides its competitive advantage in the movie rental industry.[12]

Data mining uses specialized technologies and functionalities such as query tools, reporting tools, multidimensional analysis tools, statistical tools, and intelligent agents. Data mining approaches decision making with a few different activities in mind including:

- Classification—assigns records to one of a predefined set of classes.

- Estimation—determines values for an unknown continuous variable behavior or estimated future value.

- Affinity grouping—determines which things go together.

- Clustering—segments a heterogeneous population of records into a number of more homogeneous subgroups.

Data mining occurs on **structured data** that are already in a database or a spreadsheet. **Unstructured data** do not exist in a fixed location and can include text documents, PDFs, voice messages, emails, and so on. **Text mining** analyzes unstructured data to find trends and patterns in words and sentences. Text mining a firm's customer support email might identify which customer service representative is best able to handle the question, allowing the system to forward it to the right person. **Web mining** analyzes unstructured data associated with websites to identify consumer behavior and website navigation.

Three common forms for mining structured and unstructured data are:

- Cluster analysis.
- Association detection.
- Statistical analysis.

LO6-7 Define data mining, and explain the three common forms for mining structured and unstructured data.

Cluster Analysis

Cluster analysis is a technique used to divide information sets into mutually exclusive groups such that the members of each group are as close together as possible to one another and the different groups are as far apart as possible. Cluster analysis segments customer information to help organizations identify customers with similar behavioral traits, such as clusters of best customers or onetime customers. Cluster analysis also has the ability to uncover naturally occurring patterns in information (see Figure 6.15).

A great example of using cluster analysis in business is to create target-marketing strategies based on zip codes. Evaluating customer segments by zip code allows a business to assign a level of importance to each segment. Zip codes offer valuable insight into such things as income levels, demographics, lifestyles, and spending habits. With target marketing, a business can decrease its costs while increasing the success rate of the marketing campaign.

▼**FIGURE 6.15** Example of Cluster Analysis

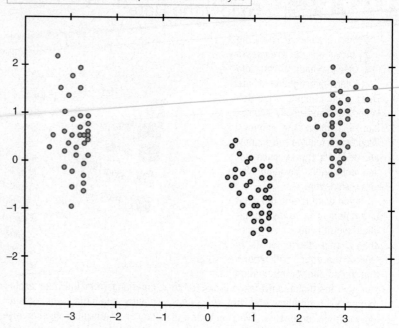

Association Detection

Association detection reveals the relationship between variables along with the nature and frequency of the relationships. Many people refer to association detection algorithms as association rule generators because they create rules to determine the likelihood of events occurring together at a particular time or following each other in a logical progression. Percentages usually reflect the patterns of these events; for example,

Want Free Books? Just Ask Google[13]

Google is scanning all or parts of the book collections of the University of Michigan, Harvard University, Stanford University, the New York Public Library, and Oxford University as part of its Google Print Library Project. It intends to make those texts searchable on Google.

The Authors Guild filed a lawsuit against Google, alleging that its scanning and digitizing of library books constitutes a "massive" copyright infringement. "This is a plain and brazen violation of copyright law," Nick Taylor, president of the New York–based Authors Guild, said in a statement about the lawsuit, which is seeking class action status.

"It's not up to Google or anyone other than the authors, the rightful owners of these copyrights, to decide whether and how their works will be copied."

A new settlement in the lawsuit is allowing Google to move forward with its Print Library Project (books.google.com). According to Google, the new agreement will allow:

- **Access to books:** Provide access to out-of-print books that were recently only available in a few libraries.
- **Online access:** Customers will be able to purchase full online access to millions of books. Customers will be able to read an entire book from any Internet-connected device.
- **Library and university access:** Libraries, universities, and other organizations will be able to purchase institutional

subscriptions, providing their users with access to the complete text of millions of titles while compensating authors and publishers for the service. The institutions can also offer terminals where users can access the full text of millions of out-of-print books for free.

- **Buying or borrowing actual books:** Customers can find print book resources directly from the site.

Do you view Google's Print Library Project as a violation of copyright laws? If you were a publisher, how would you feel about Google's project? If you were an author, how would you feel about having your book posted for free on Google Books? What do you think the future of the book publishing industry will look like based on Google's radical new Google Book's website?

"55 percent of the time, events A and B occurred together," or "80 percent of the time that items A and B occurred together, they were followed by item C within three days."

One of the most common forms of association detection analysis is market basket analysis. *Market basket analysis* analyzes such items as websites and checkout scanner information to detect customers' buying behavior and predict future behavior by identifying affinities among customers' choices of products and services (see Figure 6.16). Market basket analysis is frequently used to develop marketing campaigns for cross-selling products and services (especially in banking, insurance, and finance) and for inventory control, shelf-product placement, and other retail and marketing applications.

Statistical Analysis

Statistical analysis performs such functions as information correlations, distributions, calculations, and variance analysis. Data-mining tools offer knowledge workers a wide range of powerful statistical capabilities so they can quickly build a variety of statistical models, examine the models' assumptions and validity, and compare and contrast the various models to determine the best one for a particular business issue.

Forecasting is a common form of statistical analysis. *Time-series information* is time-stamped information collected at a particular frequency. Formally defined, *forecasts* are predictions based on time-series information. Examples of time-series information include web visits per hour, sales per month, and calls per day. Forecasting data-mining tools allow users to manipulate the time series for forecasting activities.

When discovering trends and seasonal variations in transactional information, use a time-series forecast to change the transactional information by units of time, such as transforming weekly information into monthly or seasonal information or hourly information into daily information. Companies base production, investment, and staffing decisions on a host of economic and market indicators in this manner. Forecasting models allow organizations to consider all sorts of variables when making decisions.

SUPPORTING DECISIONS WITH BUSINESS INTELLIGENCE LO6-8

Many organizations today find it next to impossible to understand their own strengths and weaknesses, let alone their biggest competitors, because the enormous volume of organizational data is inaccessible to all but the MIS department. Organization data include far more than simple structured data elements in a database; the set of data also includes unstructured data such as voice mail, customer phone calls, text messages, video clips, along with numerous new forms of data, such as tweets from Twitter.

LO6-8 Identify the advantages of using business intelligence to support managerial decision making.

The Problem: Data Rich, Information Poor

An ideal business scenario would be as follows: As a business manager on his way to meet with a client reviews historical customer data, he realizes that the client's ordering volume has substantially decreased. As he drills down into the data, he notices the client had a support issue with a particular product. He quickly calls the support team to find out all of the information and learns that a replacement for the defective part can be shipped in 24 hours. In addition, he learns that the client has visited the website and requested information on a new product line. Armed with all this information, the business manager is prepared for a productive meeting with his client. He now understands the client's needs and issues, and he can address new sales opportunities with confidence.

For many companies the above example is simply a pipe dream. Attempting to gather all of the client information would actually take hours or even days to compile. With so much data available, it is surprisingly hard for managers to get information, such as inventory levels, past order history, or shipping details. Managers send their information requests to the MIS department where a dedicated person compiles the various reports. In some situations, responses can take days, by which time the information may be outdated and opportunities lost. Many organizations find themselves in the position of being data rich and information poor. Even in today's electronic world, managers struggle with the challenge of turning their business data into business intelligence.

▼**FIGURE 6.16** Market Basket Analysis

Living the
DREAM

Ice Cream Social Takes on a Whole New Meaning[14]

When we all scream for ice cream, Ben & Jerry's screams for business intelligence and the ability to track the ingredients and life of every single pint. When a consumer calls in with a complaint, Ben & Jerry's staff matches the specific pint with its suppliers for milk, eggs, cherries, or whatever to determine where the quality issue occurred. The business intelligence (BI) tools let Ben & Jerry's officials access, analyze, and act on customer information collected by the sales, finance, purchasing, and quality assurance departments. The technology allowed Ben & Jerry's to track more than 12,500 consumer contacts, and information ranged from comments about the ingredients used in ice cream to queries about social causes supported by the company.

One of Ben & Jerry's most interesting social causes is its PartnerShop Program, a form of social enterprise in which nonprofit organizations leverage the power of business for community benefit. According to Ben & Jerry's website, PartnerShops are Ben & Jerry's scoop shops that are independently owned and operated by community-based nonprofit organizations. Ben & Jerry's waives the standard franchise fees and provides additional support to help nonprofits operate strong businesses. PartnerShops offer job and entrepreneurial training to youth and young adults that may face barriers to employment. As PartnerShop operators, nonprofits retain their business proceeds to support their programs.

Why is it important for an organization to participate in social enterprise programs?

How can Ben & Jerry's use its BI systems to help its new PartnerShops owners succeed? What types of BI would a Ben & Jerry's want to track to help run the PartnerShops? What are the ethical issues surrounding barriers to employment, and how is Ben & Jerry's helping overcome this problem?

The Solution: Business Intelligence

Employee decisions are numerous and they include providing service information, offering new products, and supporting frustrated customers. Employees can base their decisions on data, experience, or knowledge and preferably a combination of all three. Business intelligence can provide managers with the ability to make better decisions. A few examples of how different industries use business intelligence include:

- **Airlines:** Analyze popular vacation locations with current flight listings.

- **Banking:** Understand customer credit card usage and nonpayment rates.

- **Health care:** Compare the demographics of patients with critical illnesses.

- **Insurance:** Predict claim amounts and medical coverage costs.

- **Law enforcement:** Track crime patterns, locations, and criminal behavior.

- **Marketing:** Analyze customer demographics.

- **Retail:** Predict sales, inventory levels, and distribution.

- **Technology:** Predict hardware failures.

Figure 6.17 displays how organizations using BI can find the cause to many issues and problems simply by asking "Why?" The process starts by analyzing a report such as sales amounts by quarter. Managers will drill down into the report looking for why sales are up or why sales are down. Once they understand why a certain location or product is experiencing an increase in sales, they can share the information in an effort to raise enterprisewide sales. Once they understand the cause for a decrease in sales, they can take effective action to resolve the issue. Here are a few examples of how managers can use BI to answer tough business questions:

- **Where has the business been?** Historical perspective offers important variables for determining trends and patterns.

- **Where is the business now?** Looking at the current business situation allows managers to take effective action to solve issues before they grow out of control.

- **Where is the business going?** Setting strategic direction is critical for planning and creating solid business strategies.

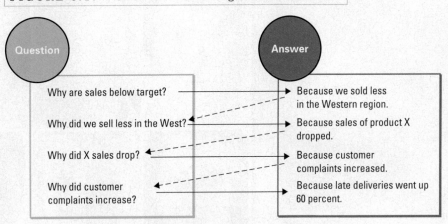

▼**FIGURE 6.17** How BI Can Answer Tough Customer Questions

Ask a simple question—such as Who is my best customer or What is my worst-selling product—and you might get as many answers as you have employees. Databases, data warehouses, and data marts can provide a single source of "trusted" data that can answer questions about customers, products, suppliers, production, finances, fraud, and even employees. They can also alert managers to inconsistencies or help determine the cause and effects of enterprisewide business decisions. All business aspects can benefit from the added insights provided by business intelligence and you, as a business student, will benefit from understanding how MIS can help you make intelligent decisions.

networks:
mobile business

What's in IT for me?

The pace of technological change never ceases to amaze as kindergarten classes are now learning PowerPoint and many elementary school children have their own cell phones. What used to take hours to download over a dial-up modem connection can now transfer in a matter of seconds through an invisible, wireless network connection from a computer thousands of miles away. We are living in an increasingly wireless present and hurtling ever faster toward a wireless future. The tipping point of ubiquitous, wireless, handheld, mobile computing is approaching quickly.

As a business student, understanding network infrastructures and wireless

continued on p. 152

CHAPTER OUTLINE

SECTION 7-1 >>
Connectivity: The Business Value of a Networked World
- Overview of a Connected World
- Benefits of a Connected World
- Challenges of a Connected World

SECTION 7-2 >>
Mobility: The Business Value of a Wireless World
- Wireless Network Categories
- Business Applications of Wireless Networks
- Benefits of Business Mobility
- Challenges of Business Mobility

continued from p. 151

technologies allows you to take advantage of mobile workforces. Understanding the benefits and challenges of mobility is a critical skill for business executives, regardless if you are a novice or a seasoned *Fortune* 500 employee. By learning about the various concepts discussed in this chapter, you will develop a better understanding of how business can leverage networking technologies to analyze network types, improve wireless and mobile business processes, and evaluate alternative networking options. ■

{SECTION 7-1}
Connectivity: The Business Value of a Networked World

LEARNING OUTCOMES

L07-1 Explain the five different networking elements creating a connected world.

L07-2 Identify the benefits of a connected world.

L07-3 Identify the challenges of a connected world.

OVERVIEW OF A CONNECTED WORLD L07-1

Computer networks are continuously operating all over the globe supporting our 24/7/365 always on and always connected lifestyles. You are probably using several different networks right now without even realizing it. You might be using a school's network to communicate with teachers, a

▼FIGURE 7.1
Networking Elements Creating a Connected World

FIGURE 7.1
Networking Elements Creating a Connected World

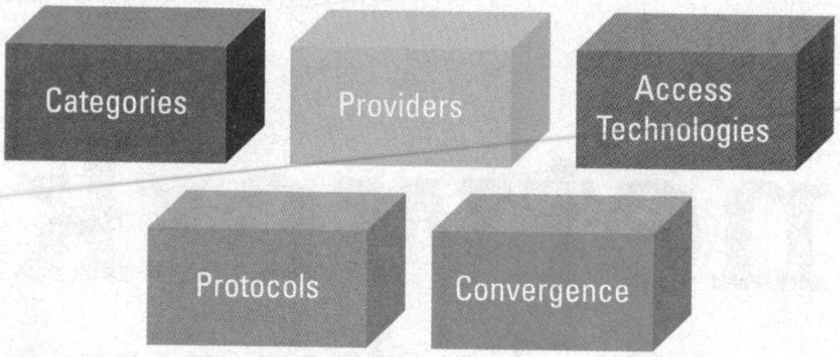

Categories · Providers · Access Technologies · Protocols · Convergence

global telephony services, satellite service, mobile radio, cable television, cellular phone services, and Internet access (all of which are detailed in this chapter). Businesses everywhere are increasingly using networks to communicate and collaborate with customers, partners, suppliers, and employees. As a manager, you will face many different communication alternatives, and the focus of this chapter is to provide you with an initial understanding of the different networking elements you will someday need to select (see Figure 7.1). A detailed technical overview of networking and telecommunications can be found in Appendix B.

L07-1 Explain the five different networking elements creating a connected world.

Network Categories

The general idea of a network is to allow multiple devices to communicate at the highest achievable speeds and, very importantly, to reduce the cost of connecting. How a particular network achieves these goals depends in part on how it is physically constructed and connected. Networks are categorized based on geographic span: local area networks, wide area networks, and metropolitan area networks. Today's business networks include a combination of all three.

["Computer networks are continuously operating all over the globe supporting our 24/7/365 always on and always connected lifestyles."]

phone network to communicate with friends, and a cable network to watch TV or listen to the radio. Networks enable telecommunications or the exchange of information (voice, text, data, audio, video). The telecommunication industry has morphed from a government-regulated monopoly to a deregulated market where many suppliers ferociously compete. Competing telecommunication companies offer local and

A *local area network (LAN)* connects a group of computers in close proximity, such as in an office building, school, or home. LANs allow sharing of files, printers, games, and other resources. A LAN also often connects to other LANs, and to wide area networks. A *wide area network (WAN)* spans a large geographic area such as a state, province, or country. Perhaps the best example is the Internet. WANs are essential for carrying out the day-to-day activities of many companies and government organizations, allowing them to transmit and receive information among their employees, customers, suppliers, business partners, and other organizations across cities, regions, and countries and around the world.

WANs often connect multiple smaller networks, such as local area networks or metropolitan area networks. A *metropolitan area network (MAN)* is a large computer network usually spanning a city. Most colleges, universities, and large companies that span a campus use an infrastructure supported by a MAN. Figure 7.2 shows the relationships and a few differences between a LAN, WAN, and MAN. A cloud image often represents the Internet or some large network environment.

While LANs, WANs, and MANs all provide users with an accessible and reliable network infrastructure, they differ in many dimensions; two of the most important are cost and performance. It is easy to establish a network between two computers in the same room or building, but much more difficult if

they are in different states or even countries. This means someone looking to build or support a WAN either pays more or gets less performance, or both.

Network Providers

The largest and most important network, the Internet has evolved into a global information superhighway. Think of it as a network made up of millions of smaller networks, each with the ability to operate independently of, or in harmony with, the others. Keeping the Internet operational is no simple task. No one owns or runs it, but it does have an organized network topology. The Internet is a hierarchical structure linking different levels of service providers, whose millions of devices, LANs, WANs, and MANs supply all the interconnections. At the top of the hierarchy are *national service providers (NSPs)*, private companies that own and maintain the worldwide backbone that supports the Internet. These include Sprint, Verizon, MCI (previously UUNet/WorldCom), AT&T, NTT, Level3, Qwest, and Cable & Wireless Worldwide. *Network access points (NAPs)*

FIGURE 7.2 Network Categories: LAN, WAN, and MAN

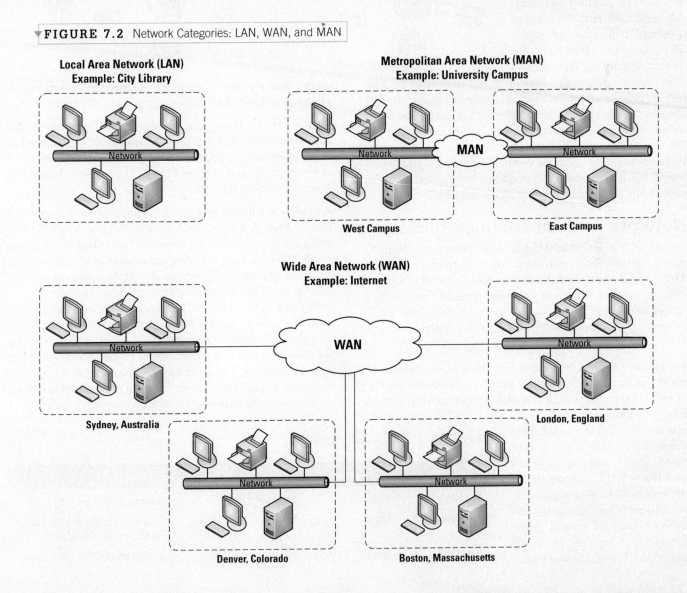

are traffic exchange points in the routing hierarchy of the Internet that connects NSPs. They typically have regional or national coverage and connect to only a few NSPs. Thus, to reach a large portion of the global Internet, a NAP needs to route traffic through one of the NSPs to which it is connected.[1]

One step down in the hierarchy is the regional service provider. *Regional service providers (RSPs)* offer Internet service by connecting to NSPs, but they also can connect directly to each other. Another level down is the Internet service providers (ISPs); recall from Chapter 3 that an ISP provides access to the Internet for a monthly fee. ISPs vary services provided and available bandwidth rates. ISPs link to RSPs and, if they are geographically close, to other ISPs. Some also connect directly to NSPs, thereby sidestepping the hierarchy. Individuals and companies use local ISPs to connect to the Internet, and large companies tend to connect directly using an RSP. Major ISPs in the United States include AOL, AT&T, Comcast, Earthlink, and NetZero. The further up the hierarchy, the faster the connections and the greater the bandwidth. The backbone shown in Figure 7.3 is greatly simplified, but it illustrates the concept that basic global interconnections are provided by the NSPs, RSPs and ISPs.[2]

Network Access Technologies

Performance is the ultimate goal of any computer, computer system, or network. Performance is directly related to the network's speed of data transfer and capacity to handle transmission. A network that does not offer adequate performance simply will not get the job done for those who rely on it. Luckily, networks can be upgraded and expanded if performance is inadequate.

We measure network performance in terms of *bandwidth,* the maximum amount of data that can pass from one point to another in a unit of time. Bandwidth is similar to water traveling through a hose. If the hose is large, water can flow through it quickly. Data differs from a hose in that it must travel great distances, especially on a WAN, and not all areas of the network have the same bandwidth. A network essentially has many different hoses of unequal capacity connected together, which will restrict the flow of data when one is

FIGURE 7.3 Internet Topology

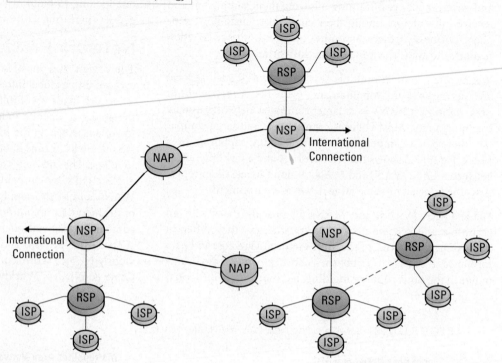

smaller than the others. Therefore, the speed of transmission of a network is determined by the speed of its smallest bandwidth.

A *bit* (short for binary digit) is the smallest element of data and has a value of either 0 or 1. Bandwidth is measured in terms of *bit rate* (or *data rate*), the number of bits transferred or received per unit of time. Figure 7.4 represents bandwidth speeds in terms of bit rates.

A *modem* is a device that enables a computer to transmit and receive data. A connection with a traditional telephone line and a modem, which most residential users had in the 1990s, is called dial-up access. Today, many users in underdeveloped countries and in rural areas in developed countries still use dial-up. It has two drawbacks. First, it is slow, providing a maximum rate of 56 Kbps. (At 56 Kbps, it takes eight minutes to download a three-minute song and more than a day to download a two-hour movie.) Second, dial-up modem access ties up the telephone line so the user cannot receive and make phone calls while online. The good news is this is not as big an issue as it once was as many people have cell phones and no longer require using the telephone line for making phone calls.[3]

FIGURE 7.4 Bandwidth Speeds

Bandwidth	Abbreviation	Bits per Second (bps)	Example
Kilobits	Kbps	1 Kbps = 1,000 bps	Traditional modem = 56 Kbps
Megabits	Mbps	1 Mbps = 1,000 Kbps	Traditional Ethernet = 10 Mbps Fast Ethernet = 100 Mbps
Gigabits	Gbps	1 Gbps = 1,000 Mbps	Gigabit Ethernet = 1,000 Mbps

Once the most common connection method worldwide, dial-up is quickly being replaced by broadband. **Broadband** is a high-speed Internet connection that is always connected. High-speed in this case refers to any bandwidth greater than 2 Mbps. Not long ago, broadband speeds were available only at a premium price to support large companies' high-traffic networks. Today, inexpensive access is available for home use and small companies.

The two most prevalent types of broadband access are digital subscriber line and cable connection. **Digital subscriber line (DSL)** allows high-speed digital data transmission over standard telephone lines. Consumers typically obtain DSL Internet access from the same company that provides their wired local telephone access, such as AT&T or Qwest. Thus, a customer's telephone provider is also its ISP, and the telephone line carries both data and telephone signals using a DSL modem.

DSL has two major advantages over dial-up. First, it can transmit and receive data much faster—in the 1 to 2 Mbps range for downloading and 128 Kbps to 1 Mbps for uploading. (Most high-speed connections are designed to download faster than they upload, because most users download more—including viewing web pages—than they upload.) The second major advantage is that because they have an "always on" connection to their ISP, users can simultaneously talk on the phone and access the Internet.[4]

While dial-up and DSL make use of local telephone infrastructure, **Internet cable connections** provide Internet access using a cable television company's infrastructure and a special cable modem. Unlike DSL, cable is a shared service, which means everyone in a certain radius, such as a neighborhood, shares the available bandwidth. Therefore, if several users are simultaneously downloading a video file, the actual transfer rate for each will be significantly lower than if only one person were doing

so. On average, the available bandwidth using cable can range from 512 Kbps to 50 Mbps for downloading, and 786 Kbps for uploading.[5]

In rural areas where neither DSL nor cable is available, a satellite link can connect to the Internet at speeds of more than 1 Mbps. Satellite technologies are discussed in Section 7.2.

Another alternative to DSL or cable is dedicated communications lines leased from AT&T or another provider. The most common are **T1 lines,** a type of data connection able to transmit a digital signal at 1.544 Mpbs. Although this speed might not seem impressive, and T1 lines are more expensive than DSL or cable, they are more reliable than either. Each is composed of 24 channels, creating 24 separate connections through one line. If a company has three separate plants that experience a high volume of data traffic, it might make sense to lease lines to connect them all with a reliable high bandwidth.[6]

A company must match its needs with Internet access methods. If it always needs high bandwidth access to communicate with customers, partners, or suppliers, a T1 line may be the most cost-effective method. Figure 7.5 provides an overview of the main methods for Internet access. The bandwidths there represent average speeds; actual speeds vary depending upon the service provider and other factors such as the type of cabling and speed of the computer.[7]

Network Protocols

A **protocol** is a standard that specifies the format of data as well as the rules to be followed during transmission. Computers using the same protocol can communicate easily, providing accessibility, scalability, and connectability between networks. Network access technologies use a standard Internet protocol

▼**FIGURE 7.5** Types of Internet Access

Access Technology	Description	Bandwidth	Comments
Dial-up	On-demand access using a modem and regular telephone line.	Up to 56 Kbps	Cheap but slow compared with other technologies.
DSL	Always-on connection. Special modem needed.	Download: 1 Mbps to 2 Mbps Upload: 128 Kbps to 1 Mbps	Makes use of the existing local telephone infrastructure.
Cable	Always-on connection. Special cable modem and cable line required.	Download: 512 Kbps to 50 Mbps Upload: 786 Kbps	It is a shared resource with other users in the area.
T1	Leased lines for high bandwidth.	1.544 Mbps	More expensive than dial-up, DSL, or cable.

FIGURE 7.6 Example of TCP/IP

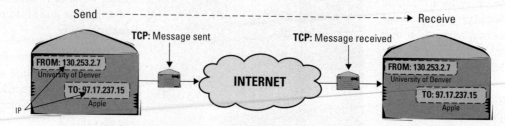

called *transmission control protocol/Internet protocol (TCP/IP)*, which provides the technical foundation for the public Internet as well as for large numbers of private networks. One of the primary reasons for developing TCP/IP was to allow diverse or differing networks to connect and communicate with each other, essentially allowing LANs, WANs, and MANs to grow with each new connection.

TCP (the TCP part of TCP/IP) verifies the correct delivery of data because data can become corrupt when traveling over a network. TCP ensures the size of the data packet is the same throughout its transmission and can even retransmit data until delivered correctly. IP (the IP part of TCP/IP) verifies the data are sent to the correct IP address, numbers represented by four strings of numbers ranging from 0 to 255 separated by periods. For example, the IP address of www.apple.com is 97.17.237.15.

Here is another way to understand TCP/IP. Consider a letter that needs to go from the University of Denver to Apple's headquarters in Cupertino, California. TCP makes sure the envelope is delivered and does not get lost along the way. IP acts as the sending and receiving labels, telling the letter carrier where to deliver the envelope and who it was from. The Postal Service mainly uses street addresses and zip codes to get letters to their destinations, which is really what IP does with its addressing method. Figure 7.6 illustrates this example. However, unlike the Postal Service, which allows multiple people to share the same physical address, each device using an IP address to connect to the Internet must have a unique address or else it could not detect which individual device a request should be sent to.

One of the most valuable characteristics of TCP/IP is how scalable its protocols have proven to be as the Internet has grown

BUSTED Never Run with Your iPod[8]

Jennifer Goebel, a 27-year-old female, was disqualified from her first place spot in the Lakefront Marathon in Milwaukee after race officials spotted her using an iPod. Officials nullified Goebel's first place time of 3:02:50 because of a controversial 2007 rule put into place banning headphones or portable music devices by U.S. Track and Field (USTAF), the governing body for running events. Race officials only decided to take action after viewing online photos of Goebel using her iPod during the last part of the race. The interesting part of this story—Goeble posted the photos herself on her website. USTAF claims the ban is required because music could give some runners a competitive advantage, as well as safety concerns when runners can't hear race announcements.

Do you agree with the USTAF's decision to disqualify Jennifer Goebel? How could an iPod give a runner a competitive advantage? With so many wireless devices entering the market, it is almost impossible to keep up with the surrounding laws. Do you think Goebel was aware of the headphone ban? In your state, what are the rules for using wireless devices while driving? Do you agree with these rules? How does a business keep up with the numerous, ever-changing rules surrounding wireless devices? What could happen to a company that fails to understand the laws surrounding wireless devices?

from a small network with just a few machines to a huge internetwork with millions of devices. While some changes have been required periodically to support this growth, the core of TCP/IP is the same as it was more than 25 years ago.[9]

If there is one flaw in TCP/IP, it is the complexity of IP addresses. This is why we use a **domain name system (DNS)** to convert IP addresses into *domains,* or identifying labels that use a variety of recognizable naming conventions. Therefore, instead of trying to remember 97.17.237.15, users can simply specify a domain name to access a computer or website, such as www.apple.com. Figure 7.7 lists the most common Internet domains.[10]

The list of domain names is expected to expand in the coming years to include entities such as .pro (for accountants, lawyers, and physicians), .aero (for the air-transport industry), and .museum (for museums). The creation of an .xxx domain was recently approved for pornographic content. Countries also have domain names such as .au (Australia), .fr (France), and .sp (Spain).

▶ FIGURE 7.7 Internet Domains

Domain Name	Use
.biz	Reserved for businesses
.com	Reserved for commercial organizations and businesses
.edu	Reserved for accredited postsecondary institutions
.gov	Reserved for U.S. government agencies
.info	Open to any person or entity, but intended for information providers
.mil	Reserved for U.S. military
.net	Open to any person or entity
.org	Reserved for nonprofit organizations

Network Convergence

In part due to the explosive use of the Internet and connectivity of TCP/IP, there is a convergence of network devices, applications, and services. Consumers, companies, educational institutions, and government agencies extensively engage in texting, web surfing, videoconference applications, online gaming, and ebusiness. *Network convergence* is the efficient coexistence of telephone, video, and data communication within a single network, offering convenience and flexibility not possible with separate infrastructures. Almost any type of information can be converted into digital form and exchanged over a

> # Network convergence is the efficient coexistence of telephone, video, and data communication within a single network, offering convenience and flexibility not possible with separate infrastructures.

Websites with heavy traffic often have several computers working together to share the load of requests. This offers load balancing and fault tolerance, so when requests are made to a popular site such as www.facebook.com, they will not overload a single computer and the site does not go down if one computer fails. A single computer can also have several host names—for instance, if a company is hosting several websites on a single server, much as an ISP works with hosting.

Domain names are essentially rented, with renewable rights, from a domain name registrar, such as godaddy.com. Some registrars only register domain names, while others provide hosting services for a fee. ICANN (Internet Corporation for Assigning Names and Numbers) is a nonprofit governance and standards organization that certifies all domain name registrars throughout the world. With the certification, each registrar is authorized to register domain names, such as .com, .edu, or .org.[11]

network. Network convergence then allows the weaving together of voice, data, and video. The benefits of network convergence allow for multiple services, multiple devices, but one network, one vendor, and one bill, as suggested by Figure 7.8.

▼ FIGURE 7.8 The Benefits of Network Convergence

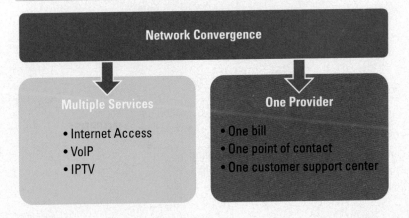

Network Convergence

Multiple Services
- Internet Access
- VoIP
- IPTV

One Provider
- One bill
- One point of contact
- One customer support center

One of the challenges associated with network convergence is using the many different tools efficiently and productively. Knowing which communication channel—PC, text message, videoconference—to use with each business participant can be a challenge. *Unified communications (UC)* is the integration of communication channels into a single service. UC integrates communication channels allowing participants to communicate using the method that is most convenient for them. UC merges instant messaging, videoconferencing, email, voice mail, and VoIP. This can decrease the communication costs for a business while enhancing the way individuals communicate and collaborate.

One area experiencing huge growth in network convergence is the use of the Internet for voice transmission. *Voice over IP (VoIP)* uses IP technology to transmit telephone calls. For the first time in more than 100 years, VoIP is providing an opportunity to bring about significant change in the way people communicate using the telephone. VoIP service providers—specialists as well as traditional telephone and cable companies and some ISPs—allow users to call anyone with a telephone number, whether local, long distance, cellular, or international.

Two ways to use VoIP for telephone calls are through a web interface that allows users to make calls from their computer and through a phone attached to a VoIP adapter that links directly to the Internet through a broadband modem. Figure 7.9 illustrates these two ways along with the use of VoIP-enabled phones, bypassing the need for an adapter.

VoIP services include fixed-price unlimited local and long-distance calling plans (at least within the United States and Canada), plus a range of interesting features, such as:

- The ability to have more than one phone number, including numbers with different area codes.
- Integrating email and voice mail so users can listen to their voice mail using their computer.
- The ability to receive personal or business calls via computer, no matter where the user is physically located.[12]

The biggest benefit of VoIP is its low cost. Because it relies on the Internet connection, however, service can be affected if the bandwidth is not appropriate or Internet access is not available.

Skype is a perfect example of IP applied to telephone use. Unlike typical VoIP systems that use a client and server infrastructure, Skype uses a peer-to-peer network. *Peer-to-peer (P2P)* is a computer network that relies on the computing power and bandwidth of the participants in the network rather than a centralized server. Skype's user directory is distributed among the users in its network, allowing scalability without a complex and expensive centralized infrastructure. Peer-to-peer networks became an overnight sensation years ago through a service called Napster that distributed digital music illegally. Skype has found a way to use this resource to provide value to its users.[13]

As the popularity of VoIP grows, governments are becoming more interested in regulating it as they do traditional telephone services. In the United States, the Federal Communications Commission requires compliance among VoIP service providers comparable to regulations for traditional telephone providers such as support for local number portability, services for the disabled, and law enforcement for surveillance, along with regulatory and other fees.

An exciting and new convergence is occurring in the area of television with *Internet Protocol TV (IPTV),* which distributes digital video content using IP across the Internet and private IP networks. Comcast provides an example of a private IP network that also acts as a cable TV provider. Traditional television sends all program signals simultaneously to the television, allowing the user to select the program by selecting a channel. With IPTV, the user selects a channel and the service provider sends only that single program to the television. Like cable TV, IPTV uses a box that acts like a modem to send and receive the content (see Figure 7.10). A few IPTV features include:

- **Support of multiple devices:** PCs and televisions can access IPTV services.
- **Interactivity with users:** Interactive applications and programs are supported by IPTV's two-way communication path.
- **Low bandwidth:** IPTV conserves bandwidth because the provider sends only a single channel.
- **Personalization:** Users can choose not only what they want to watch, but also when they want to watch it.[14]

▼FIGURE 7.9 VoIP Connectivity

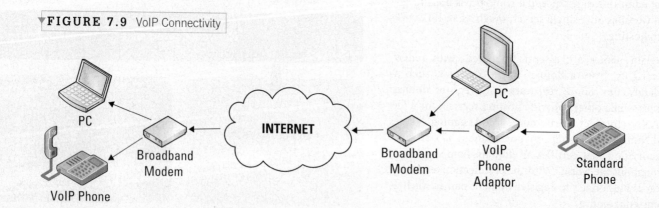

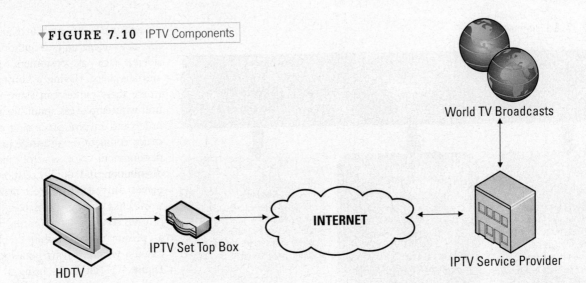

▼FIGURE 7.10 IPTV Components

World TV Broadcasts

INTERNET

IPTV Set Top Box

HDTV

IPTV Service Provider

RESOURCE SHARING MAKES ALL APPLICATIONS, EQUIPMENT, AND DATA AVAILABLE TO ANYONE ON THE NETWORK, WITHOUT REGARD TO THE PHYSICAL LOCATION OF THE RESOURCE OR THE USER.

BENEFITS OF A CONNECTED WORLD L07-2

Before networks, transferring data between computers was time-consuming and labor-intensive. People had to physically copy data from machine to machine using a disk. Networks offer many advantages for a business including:

- Sharing resources.
- Providing opportunities.
- Reducing travel.

L07-2 Identify the benefits of a connected world.

Sharing Resources

Resource sharing makes all applications, equipment (such as a high-volume printer), and data available to anyone on the network, without regard to the physical location of the resource or the user. Sharing physical resources also supports a sustainable MIS infrastructure, allowing companies to be agile, efficient, and responsible at the same time. Cloud computing (see Chapter 5) and virtualization consolidate information as well as systems that enhance the use of shared resources. By using shared resources,

cloud computing and virtualization allow for collective computing power, storage, and software, in an on-demand basis.

Perhaps even more important than sharing physical resources is sharing data. Most companies, regardless of size, depend not just on their customer records, inventories, accounts receivable, financial statements, and tax information, but also on their ability to share these, especially with operations in remote locations. Networking with a LAN, WAN, or MAN allows employees to share data quickly and easily and to use applications such as databases and collaboration tools that rely on sharing. By sharing data, networks have made business processes more efficient. For example, as soon as an order is placed, anyone in the company who needs to view it—whether in marketing, purchasing, manufacturing, shipping, or billing—can do so.

Intranets and extranets let firms share their corporate information securely. An *intranet* is a restricted network that relies on Internet technologies to provide an Internet-like environment within the company for information sharing, communications, collaboration, web publishing, and the support of business processes, as suggested in Figure 7.11. This network is protected by security measures such as passwords, encryption, and firewalls, and thus only authorized users can access it. Intranets provide a central location for all kinds of company-related information such as benefits, schedules, strategic directions, and employee directories.[15]

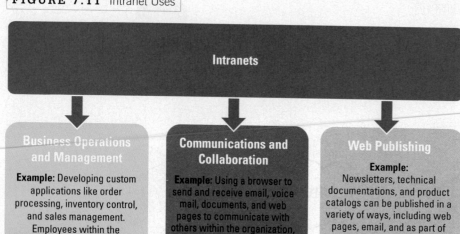

Intranets

Business Operations and Management

Example: Developing custom applications like order processing, inventory control, and sales management. Employees within the company can access and run such applications using web browsers from anywhere on the network whenever needed.

Communications and Collaboration

Example: Using a browser to send and receive email, voice mail, documents, and web pages to communicate with others within the organization, as well as externally through the Internet.

Web Publishing

Example: Newsletters, technical documentations, and product catalogs can be published in a variety of ways, including web pages, email, and as part of organizational business applications.

An ***extranet*** is an extension of an intranet that is available only to authorized outsiders, such as customers, partners, and suppliers. Having a common area where these parties can share information with employees about, for instance, order and invoice processing can be a major competitive advantage in product development, cost control, marketing, distribution, and supplier relations. Companies can establish direct private network links among themselves or create private, secure Internet access, in effect a "private tunnel" within the Internet, called a ***virtual private network (VPN).*** Figure 7.12 illustrates using a VPN to connect to a corporate server.

Extranets enable customers, suppliers, consultants, subcontractors, business prospects, and others to access selected intranet websites and other company

fyi

Music in the Clouds[16]

Years ago, if you wanted to save music to your computer you were required to have an enormous hard drive, which was rather expensive. Today, you can listen to music in the cloud. Of course we do not mean real clouds, but the term cloud is now used as a metaphor for the Internet. Most songs exist somewhere in the "cloud," and websites like YouTube, Imeem, Pandora, or HypeMachine are all services allowing you to listen to streaming music without saving a single song to your own device. Wherever those elusive songs actually live—somewhere in the cloud—you can play, collect, and share them without downloading a single thing. Five sites you can use to access music in the cloud include:

- **Fizy:** A Turkish site compiles audio from around the net into a database from which you can create your own playlists.
- **Muziic:** Developed by high school student David Nelson with help from his dad. This upstart accesses the songs on YouTube via an iTunes interface.

- **Songza:** Songza wraps the music of Imeem and YouTube in a sweet, simple web interface.
- **Spotify:** A P2P streaming architecture lets users in supported countries create collections from a massive in-house music archive.
- **Twones:** Twones allows you to download software for playback and tracks user activity on multiple online service and offline players through a single web interface.

The world of online music is a dream come true for most music lovers because you can listen to any song your heart desires with a quick Google search. What role do copyright laws play in the world of online music? If you were to start an online music business, what types of technologies would you use? Where is the future of online music headed? What are the risks associated with the online music business? If you were just starting a band, where would you post your music to gain the most exposure? What would be the risks of posting your band's music online?

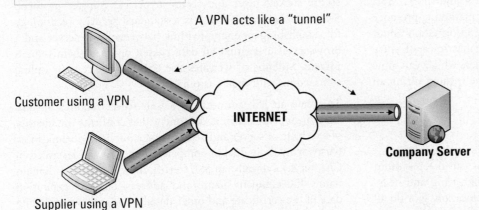

▼FIGURE 7.12 Using a VPN

A VPN acts like a "tunnel"

Customer using a VPN

INTERNET

Supplier using a VPN

Company Server

functions and check order status. The extranet links the company to the outside world in a way that improves its operations.

Extranets provide business value in several ways. First, by relying on web browsers they make customer and supplier access to company resources easy and fast. Second, they enable a company to customize interactive web-enabled services for the intended audience, to build and strengthen strategic relationships with customers and suppliers. Finally, extranets can allow and improve collaboration with customers and other business partners.

network resources that allow the sharing of information. Consultants and contractors can facilitate the design of new products or services. Suppliers can ensure that the raw materials necessary for the company to function are in stock and can be delivered in a timely fashion. Customers can access ordering and payment

Providing Opportunities

Ebusiness can enhance the opportunities of manufacturers that buy parts from a variety of suppliers. Using networks, they can order parts electronically when needed, reducing the need for large inventories and enhancing efficiency.

My **Not** To-Do List

Ding-a-Ling Took My $400![17]

Does it get any better than satellite television and radio with their endless options for entertainment choices? For some customers, these endless options just end up giving them a headache and endless frustration. One customer, Mary Cox, decided that her satellite television had terrible reception and she wanted to disconnect her service and find an alternative. This was the single decision that began her nightmare. Soon after disconnecting her service, Mary noticed a direct withdrawal on her bank account for a $430 early termination fee from her satellite provider. This unplanned expense soon cost Mary hundreds of dollars in overdraft charges from her other bills because she never anticipated this expense. To top it all off, Mary received a phone call from a satellite customer service representative asking if she was satisfied with the company and would she consider reconnecting her service, and the person said his name was Ding-a-Ling.

The number one rule you should all remember is that you never give any company your checking account number or direct access to your bank account. If you want to establish a good relationship with a company, it is best to give them your credit card number. When a relationship with a supplier turns sour, the last thing you want is for them to have direct access to your checking account.

Do you think what the satellite provider did was ethical? What could Mary do when disconnecting her service to avoid this type of issue? Can credit card companies enter your bank account and take out as much money as you owe at any time they want? Why is it important to never give a supplier direct access to your business checking account?

Networks allow companies to sell to consumers via the Internet too, offering books, clothing, airline tickets, and more. Most midsize and larger companies also have a marketing presence on the web and provide extensive online information about their products and services. The Internet has lowered entry barriers for start-ups and small companies, which can now immediately tap potential customers online without hiring an expensive marketing company.

Reducing Travel

Networks provide the means for videoconferencing. Using this technology, employees at distant locations can meet without spending time and money on travel, while seeing and hearing each other as if they were in the same location. Nor do all

Two methods for encrypting network traffic on the web are secure sockets layer and secure hypertext transfer protocol. *Secure sockets layer (SSL)* is a standard security technology for establishing an encrypted link between a web server and a browser, ensuring that all data passed between them remain private. Millions of websites use SSL to protect their online transactions with their customers.

To create an SSL connection, a web server requires an *SSL Certificate*, an electronic document that confirms the identity of a website or server and verifies that a public key belongs to a trustworthy individual or company. (Public key is described in Chapter 4.) Typically, an SSL Certificate will contain a domain name, the company name and address, and the expiration date of the certificate and other details. Verisign is the leading

> ["Even though networks provide many business advantages, they also create increased challenges in (1) security and (2) social, ethical, and political issues."]

employees have to come to the office; some can telecommute using Internet connections for both data and voice and, thanks to intranets and extranets, maintain the same access to information as they do at work. Telecommuting has been greatly enhanced by VPNs, videoconferencing, and VoIP.

CHALLENGES OF A CONNECTED WORLD L07-3

Networks have created a diverse yet globally connected world. By eliminating time and distance, networks make it possible to communicate in ways not previously imaginable. Even though networks provide many business advantages, they also create increased challenges in (1) security and (2) social, ethical, and political issues.

L07-3 Identify the challenges of a connected world.

Security

Networks are a tempting target for mischief and fraud. A company first has to ensure proper identification of users and authorization of network access. Outside suppliers might be allowed to access production plans via the company's extranet, for example, but they must not be able to see other information such as financial records. The company should also preserve the integrity of its data; only qualified users should be allowed to change and update data, and only well-specified data. Security problems intensify on the Internet where companies need to guard against fraud, invalid purchases, and misappropriation of credit card information.

Internet Certification Authority that issues SSL Certificates. When a browser connects to a secure site, it retrieves the site's SSL Certificate, makes sure it has not expired, and confirms a Certification Authority has issued it. If the certificate fails on any one of these validation measures, the browser will display a warning to the end user that the site is not secure. If a website is using SSL, a lock icon appears in the lower right-hand corner of the user's web browser.

Secure hypertext transfer protocol (SHTTP or HTTPS) is a combination of HTTP and SSL to provide encryption and secure identification of an Internet server. HTTPS protects against interception of communications, transferring credit card information safely and securely with special encryption techniques. When a user enters a web address using *https://* the browser will encrypt the message. However, the server receiving the message must be configured to receive HTTPS messages.

In summary, each company needs to create a network security policy that specifies aspects of data integrity availability and confidentiality or privacy as well as accountability and authorization. With a variety of security methods, such as SSL and SHTTP, a company can protect its most important asset, its data.

Social, Ethical, and Political Issues

Only a small fraction of the world's population has access to the Internet, and some people who have had access in the past have lost it due to changes in their circumstances such as unemployment or poverty. Providing network access to those who want or need it helps to level the playing field and removes the *digital divide,* a worldwide gap giving advantage to those with access to technology. Some organizations are trying to bridge the divide such as the Boston Digital Bridge Foundation, which concentrates on local schoolchildren and their parents, helping to make them knowledgeable about computers, programs, and the Internet. Other organizations provide inexpensive laptops and Internet access in low-income areas in developing countries.[18]

Another social issue with networking occurs with newsgroups or blogs where like-minded people can exchange messages. If the topics are technical in nature or sports related such as cycling, few issues arise. Problems can begin when social media feature topics people can be sensitive about, such as politics, religion, or sex, or when someone posts an offensive message to someone else. Different countries have different and even conflicting laws about Internet use, but because the Internet knows no physical boundaries, communication is hard to regulate, even if anyone could. Some people believe network operators should be responsible for the content they carry, just as newspapers and magazines are. Operators, however, feel that like the post office or phone companies, they cannot be expected to police what users say. If they censored messages, how would they avoid violating users' rights to free speech?

Many employers read and censor employee emails and limit employee access to distracting entertainment such as YouTube and social networks such as Facebook. Spending company time "playing" is not a good use of resources, they believe.

Social issues can even affect the government and its use of networks to snoop on citizens. The FBI has installed a system at many ISPs to scan all incoming and outgoing email for nuggets of interest. The system was originally called Carnivore but bad publicity caused it to be renamed DCS1000. While the name is much more generic, its goal is the same—locate information on illegal activities by spying on millions of people. A common conception associated with networking technologies is "Big Brother is watching!" People are wary of how much information is available on the Internet and how easily it can fall into the wrong hands.[19]

> **People are wary of how much information is available on the Internet and how easily it can fall into the wrong hands.**

{SECTION 7-2}
Mobility: The Business Value of a Wireless World

LEARNING OUTCOMES

L07-4 Explain the different wireless network categories.

L07-5 Explain the different wireless network business applications.

L07-6 Identify the benefits of business mobility.

L07-7 Identify the challenges of business mobility.

WIRELESS NETWORK CATEGORIES L07-4

As far back as 1896, Italian inventor Guglielmo Marconi demonstrated a wireless telegraph, and in 1927, the first radio-telephone system began operating between the United States and Great Britain. Automobile-based mobile telephones were offered in 1947. In 1964, the first communications satellite, Telstar, was launched, and soon after, satellite-relayed telephone service and television broadcasts became available. Wireless networks have exploded since then, and newer technologies are now maturing that allow companies and home users alike to take advantage of both wired and wireless networks.[20]

Before delving into a discussion of wireless networks, we should distinguish between mobile and wireless, terms that are often used synonymously but actually have different meanings. *Mobile* means the technology can travel with the user, for instance, users can download software, email messages, and web pages onto a laptop or other mobile device for portable reading or reference. Information collected while on the road can be synchronized with a PC or company server. *Wireless,* on the other hand, refers to any type of operation accomplished without the use of a hard-wired connection. There are many environments in which the network devices are wireless but not mobile, such as wireless home or office networks with stationary PCs and printers. Some forms of mobility do not require a wireless connection; for instance, a worker can use a wired laptop at home, shut down the laptop, drive to work, and attach the laptop to the company's wired network.

In many networked environments today, users are both wireless and mobile; for example, a mobile user commuting to work on a train can maintain a VoIP call and multiple TCP/IP connections at the same time. Figure 7.13 categorizes wireless networks by type.

L07-4 Explain the different wireless network categories.

Personal Area Networks

In addition to the three network types described in the previous section (LANs, WANs, and MANs), wireless networking includes *personal area networks (PANs)* that provide communication over a short distance that is intended for use with devices that are owned and operated by a single user. For example, a PAN can provide communication between a wireless headset and a cell phone or between a computer and a wireless mouse or keyboard. *Bluetooth* is a wireless PAN technology that transmits signals over short distances among cell phones, computers, and other devices. It eliminates the need for wires,

FIGURE 7.13 Wireless Communication Network Categories

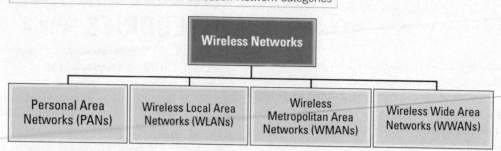

Wireless Networks

| Personal Area Networks (PANs) | Wireless Local Area Networks (WLANs) | Wireless Metropolitan Area Networks (WMANs) | Wireless Wide Area Networks (WWANs) |

docking stations or cradles, and all the special attachments that typically accompany personal computing devices. Bluetooth operates at speeds up to 1 Mbps within a range of 33 feet or less. Devices that are Bluetooth-enabled communicate directly with each other in pairs, like a handshake. Up to eight can be paired simultaneously. And Bluetooth is not just for technology devices. An array of Bluetooth-equipped appliances, such as a television set, a stove, and a thermostat, can be controlled from a cell phone—all from a remote location.[21]

Wireless LANs

Wireless LANs are everywhere in the workplace, home, educational institutions, cafés, and airports and are one of the most important access network technologies in the Internet today. A *wireless LAN (WLAN)* is a local area network that uses radio signals to transmit and receive data over distances of a few hundred feet. Most WLANs use an infrastructure in which a wireless device, often a laptop, communicates through an access point or base station by means of, for instance, wireless fidelity. *Wireless fidelity (wi-fi)* is a means by which portable devices can connect wirelessly to a local area network, using access points that send and receive data via radio waves. Wi-fi has a maximum range of about 1,000 feet in open areas such as a city park and 250 to 400 feet in closed areas such as an office building. Areas around access points where users can connect to the Internet are often called *hotspots*. By positioning hotspots at strategic locations

throughout a building, campus, or city, network administrators can keep wi-fi users continuously connected to a network or the Internet, no matter where they roam on the premises.[22]

In a wi-fi network, the user's laptop or other wi-fi-enabled device has a wireless adapter that translates data into a radio signal and transmits it to the wireless access point. The wireless access point, which consists of a transmitter with an antenna that is often built into the hardware, receives the signal and decodes it. The access point then sends the information to the Internet over a wired broadband connection, as illustrated in Figure 7.14. When receiving data, the wireless access point takes the information from the Internet, translates it into a radio signal, and sends it to the computer's wireless adapter. If too many people try to use the wi-fi network at one time, they can experience interference or dropped connections. Most laptop computers come with built-in wireless transmitters and software to enable computers to automatically discover the existence of a wi-fi network.[23]

Wi-fi operates at considerably higher frequencies than cell phones use, which allows greater bandwidth. The bandwidths associated with wi-fi are separated according to several wireless networking standards, known as *802.11,* for carrying out wireless local area network communication. Figure 7.15 outlines the bandwidths associated with a few of these standards.[24]

An increasing number of digital devices, including most laptops, netbooks, tablets such as the iPad, and even some printers

FIGURE 7.14 Wi-Fi Network

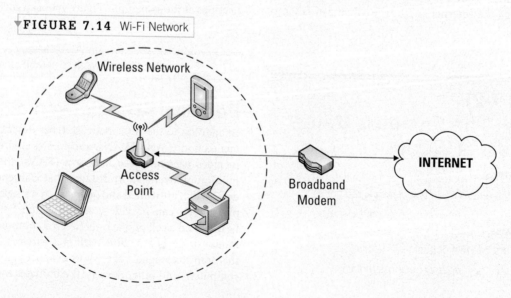

FIGURE 7.15 Wi-Fi Standards and Bandwidths

Wi-Fi Standard	Bandwidth
802.11a	54 Mbps
802.11b	11 Mbps
802.11g	54 Mbps
802.11n	140 Mbps

are incorporating wi-fi technology into their design. Cell phones are incorporating wi-fi so they can automatically switch from the cell network to a faster wi-fi network where available for data communications. BlackBerrys and iPhones can connect to an access point for data communications such as email and web browsing, but not for voice unless they use the services of Skype or another VoIP.

Wireless MANs

A *wireless MAN (WMAN)* is a metropolitan area network that uses radio signals to transmit and receive data. WMAN technologies have not been highly successful to date, mainly because they are not widely available, at least in the United States. One with the potential for success is *Worldwide Interoperability for Microwave Access (WiMAX),* a communications technology aimed at providing high-speed wireless data over metropolitan area networks. In many respects, WiMAX operates like wi-fi, only over greater distances and with higher bandwidths. A WiMAX tower serves as an access point and can connect to the Internet or another tower. A single tower can provide up to 3,000 square miles of coverage, so only a few are needed to cover an entire city. WiMAX can support data communications at a rate of 70 Mbps. In New York City, for example, one or two WiMAX access points around the city might meet the heavy demand more cheaply than hundreds of wi-fi access points. WiMAX can also cover remote or rural areas where cabling is limited or nonexistent, and where it is too expensive or physically difficult to install wires for the relatively few users.[25]

WiMAX can provide both line-of-sight and non-line-of-sight service. A non-line-of-sight service uses a small antenna on a mobile device that connects to a WiMAX tower less than six miles away where transmissions are disrupted by physical obstructions. This form of service is similar to wi-fi but has much broader coverage areas and higher bandwidths. A line-of-sight option offers a fixed antenna that points at the WiMAX tower from a rooftop or pole. This option is much faster than non-line-of-sight service, and the distance between the WiMAX tower and antenna can be as great as 30 miles. Figure 7.16 illustrates the WiMAX infrastructure.[26]

Some cellular companies are evaluating WiMAX as a means of increasing bandwidth for a variety of data-intensive applications

such as those used by smartphones. Sprint Nextel and Clearwire are building a nationwide WiMAX network in the United States. WiMAX-capable gaming devices, laptops, cameras, and even cell phones are being manufactured by companies including Intel, Motorola, Nokia, and Samsung.[27]

Wireless WAN—Cellular Communication System

A *wireless WAN (WWAN)* is a wide area network that uses radio signals to transmit and receive data. WWAN technologies can be divided into two categories: cellular communication systems and satellite communication systems.

---

show me
the MONEY

Wireless Networks and Streetlamps[28]

Researchers at Harvard University and BBN Technologies have designed CitySense, a wireless network capable of reporting real-time sensor data across the entire city of Cambridge, Massachusetts. CitySense is unique because it solves a constraint on previous wireless networks—battery life. The network mounts each node on a municipal streetlamp, where it draws power from city electricity. Researchers plan to install 100 sensors on streetlamps throughout Cambridge by 2011, using a grant from the National Science Foundation. Each node will include an embedded PC running the Linux OS, an 802.11 wi-fi interface, and weather sensors.

One of the challenges in the design was how the network would allow remote nodes to communicate with the central server at Harvard and BBN. CitySense will do that by letting each node form a mesh with its neighbors, exchanging data through multiple-hop links. This strategy allows a node to download software or upload sensor data to a distant server hub using a small radio with only a one-kilometer range.

You are responsible for deploying a CitySense network around your city. What goals would you have for the system besides monitoring urban weather and pollution? What other benefits could a CitySense network provide? How could local businesses and citizens benefit from the network? What legal and ethical concerns should you understand before deploying the network? What can you do to protect your network and your city from these issues?

FIGURE 7.16 WiMAX Infrastructure

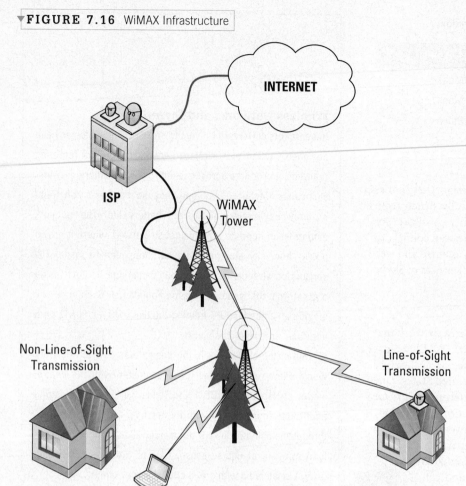

ISP

INTERNET

WiMAX
Tower

Non-Line-of-Sight
Transmission

Line-of-Sight
Transmission

Cellular systems were originally designed to provide voice services to mobile customers and thus were designed to interconnect cells to the public telephone network. Increasingly, they provide data services and Internet connectivity. There are more cell phones than landline phones in many countries today, and it is no longer uncommon for cell phones to be the only phones people have.

Cell phones have morphed into *smartphones* that offer more advanced computing ability and connectivity than basic cell phones. They allow for web browsing, emailing, listening to music, watching video, computing, keeping track of contacts, sending text messages, and taking and sending photos. The Apple iPhone and RIM BlackBerry are examples of smartphones.

Cell phones and smartphones, or mobile phones as they are collectively called, need a provider to offer services, much as computer users need an ISP to connect to the Internet. The most popular mobile phone providers in the United States are AT&T, Sprint, T-Mobile, and Verizon. They offer different cell phones, features, coverage areas, and services. One of the newer services is third-generation, or *3G,* services that bring wireless broadband to mobile phones. Figure 7.18 lists the cell phone generations. The 3G networks let users surf web pages, enjoy streaming music, watch video-on-demand programming, download and play 3D games, and participate in social media and teleconferencing. *Streaming* is a method of sending audio

Although mobile communications have been around for generations, including the walkie-talkies of the 1940s and mobile radiophones of the 1950s, it was not until 1983 that cellular telephony became available commercially. A cell phone is a device for voice and data, communicating wirelessly through a collection of stationary ground-based sites called base stations, each of which is linked to its nearest neighbor stations. Base station coverage areas are about 10 square miles and are called cells, as Figure 7.17 illustrates.[29]

The first cell phone was demonstrated in 1973 by Motorola (it weighed almost 2 pounds), but it took 10 years for the technology to become commercially available. The Motorola DynaTAC, marketed in 1983, weighed one pound and cost about $4,000. Cellular technology has come a long way since then.[30]

FIGURE 7.17 Cell Phone Communication System Overview

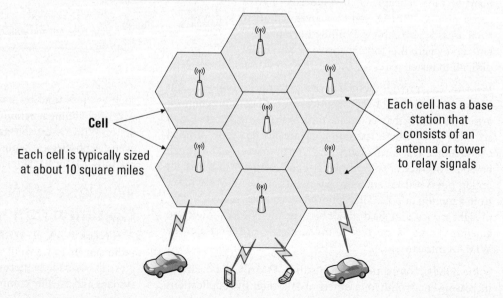

Cell

Each cell is typically sized at about 10 square miles

Each cell has a base station that consists of an antenna or tower to relay signals

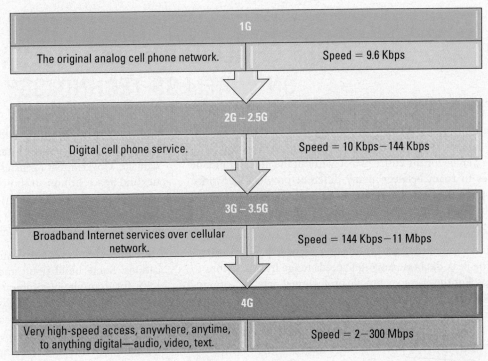

FIGURE 7.18
Cell Phone Generations

1G	
The original analog cell phone network.	Speed = 9.6 Kbps

2G – 2.5G	
Digital cell phone service.	Speed = 10 Kbps – 144 Kbps

3G – 3.5G	
Broadband Internet services over cellular network.	Speed = 144 Kbps – 11 Mbps

4G	
Very high-speed access, anywhere, anytime, to anything digital—audio, video, text.	Speed = 2 – 300 Mbps

and video files over the Internet in such a way that the user can view the file while it is being transferred. Streaming is not limited to cellular usage; all wireless and even wired networks can take advantage of this method. The most obvious advantage is speed, a direct benefit for mobile and wireless devices since they are still not as fast as their wired counterparts.[31]

Wireless WAN—Satellite Communication System

The other wireless WAN technology is a satellite communication system. A *satellite* is a space station that orbits the Earth receiving and transmitting signals from Earth-based stations

Due Diligence //:
Call 911, McNugget Outage[32]

Cellular technologies have changed the way we do business, and it is hard to imagine life without them. Just think of email. How did anyone survive without email? And let's not even talk about life before cell phones. There are so many wonderful advantages of using wireless technologies in business, but there are also some serious disadvantages, like the ability to make a bad decision faster.

A woman in Florida called 911 three times after a McDonald's employee told her they were out of Chicken McNuggets. A police report states that Latreasa Goodman, a 27-year-old female, told authorities she paid for a 10-piece McNugget meal and was later informed that the restaurant had sold out of McNuggets. Goodman says she was refused a refund and told all sales were final by the cashier. The cashier told police she offered Goodman a larger portion of different food for the same price, but Goodman became irate and called 911. "This is an emergency. If I would have known they didn't have McNuggets, I wouldn't have given my money, and now she wants to give me a McDouble, but I don't want one," Goodman told police and continued to state, "This is an emergency." Goodman was cited on a misuse of 911 charge. A McDonald's spokesman says

Goodman should have been given a refund and that she is being issued a gift card for a free meal.

It is so easy to pick up the phone, from anywhere, at anytime, and make a bad call. How many times do you see people making calls on their cell phones from inappropriate locations? If this woman had to wait in line to use a pay phone, do you think it would have given her the time to calm down and rethink her decision? With technology and the ability to communicate at our fingertips, do you agree that it is easier than ever to make a bad decision? What can you do to ensure you think before you communicate?

over a wide area. When satellite systems first came into consideration in the 1990s, the goal was to provide wireless voice and data coverage for the entire planet, without the need for mobile phones to roam between many different provider networks. But by the time satellite networks were ready for commercial use, they had already been overtaken by cellular systems.

The devices used for satellite communication range from handheld units to mobile base stations to fixed satellite dish receivers. The peak data transmission speeds range from 2.4 Kbps to 2 Mbps. For the everyday mobile professional, satellite communication may not provide a compelling benefit, but for people requiring voice and data access from remote locations or guaranteed coverage in nonremote locations, satellite technology is a viable solution.

Conventional communication satellites move in stationary orbits approximately 22,000 miles above Earth. A newer satellite medium, the low-orbit satellite, travels much closer to Earth and is able to pick up signals from weak transmitters. Low-orbit satellites also consume less power and cost less to launch than conventional satellites. With satellite networks, businesspeople almost anywhere in the world have access to full communication capabilities, including voice, videoconferencing, and Internet access. Figure 7.19 briefly illustrates the satellite communication system.[33]

BUSINESS APPLICATIONS OF WIRELESS NETWORKS LO7-5

Companies of all types and sizes have relied on wireless technology for years. Shipping and trucking companies developed some of the earliest wireless applications to help track vehicles and valuable cargo, optimize the logistics of their global operations, perfect their delivery capabilities, and reduce theft and damage. Government agencies such as the National Aeronautics and Space Administration and the Department of Defense have relied on satellite technologies for decades to track the movement of troops, weaponry, and military assets; to receive and broadcast data; and to communicate over great distances.

Wireless technologies have also aided the creation of new applications. Some build upon and improve existing capabilities. UPS, for example, is combining several types of wireless network technologies from Bluetooth to WWANs and deploying scanners and wearable data-collection terminals to automate and standardize package management and tracking across all its delivery centers. Areas experiencing tremendous growth using wireless technologies include:

- Radio-frequency identification (RFID).
- Global positioning system.
- Geographic information system.
- Location-based services.

LO7-5 Explain the different wireless network business applications.

Radio-Frequency Identification (RFID)

Radio-frequency identification (RFID) uses electronic tags and labels to identify objects wirelessly over short distances. It holds the promise of replacing existing identification technologies such as the bar code. RFID wirelessly exchanges information between a tagged object and a reader/writer. A RFID

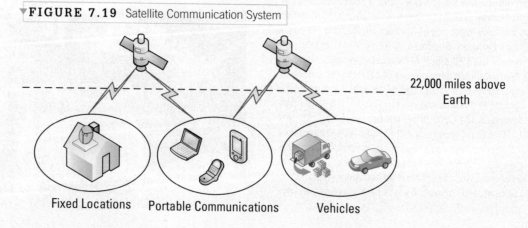

▼**FIGURE 7.19** Satellite Communication System

22,000 miles above Earth

Fixed Locations   Portable Communications   Vehicles

system is comprised of one or more tags, one or more readers, two or more antennas (one on the tag and one on each reader), RFID application software, and a computer system or server, as Figure 7.20 illustrates. Tags, often smaller than a grain of rice, can be applied to books or clothing items as part of an adhesive bar-code label, or included in items such as ID cards or packing labels. Readers can be stand-alone devices, such as for self-checkout in a grocery store, integrated with a mobile device for portable use, or built-in as in printers. The reader sends a wireless request that is received by all tags in the area that have been programmed to listen to wireless signals. Tags receive the signal via their antennas and respond by transmitting their stored data. The tag can hold many types of data, including a product number, installation instructions, and history of activity (such as the date the item was shipped). The reader receives a signal from the tag using its antenna, interprets the information sent, and transfers the data to the associated computer system or server. Examples of the innovative uses of RFID include:

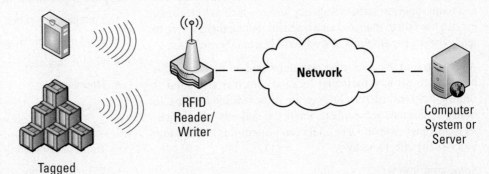

FIGURE 7.20 RFID Components

- RFID chips injected under the skin of animals using a syringe can help ranchers meet regulations, track wild animals for ecological studies, and return lost pets to their owners.

- Retail stores use RFID to track and monitor inventory. Hospitals and pharmaceutical companies meet government regulations and standards with RFID. Even local libraries are using RFID to control theft and speed up the checkout process.

- Car manufacturers install RFID antitheft systems. Toll roads use RFID to collect payments from passing cars, such as E-Pass and SunPass.

- Hospitals track patients', doctors', and nurses' locations to facilitate emergency situations and ensure safety. RFID also tracks equipment location to ensure quick response times during an emergency.

- American Express and MasterCard use RFID for automatic payments.

- Walmart and other large retailers use RFID to maintain inventory, stop shoplifting, and speed up customer checkout processes.[34]

Global Positioning System (GPS)

A *global positioning system (GPS)* is a satellite-based navigation system providing extremely accurate position, time, and speed information. The U.S. Department of Defense developed the technology in the early 1970s and later made it available to the public. GPS uses 24 global satellites that orbit Earth, sending signals to a receiver that can communicate with three or four satellites at a time. A GPS receiver can be a separate unit connected to a mobile device using cable or wireless technology such as Bluetooth, or it can be included in devices such as mobile phones or vehicle navigation systems.

The satellites broadcast signals constantly, while the receiver measures the time it takes for the signals to reach it. This measurement, which uses the speed of the signal to determine the distance, is taken from three distinct satellites to provide precise location information. The time measurements depend on high-powered clocks on each satellite and must be precise, because an error of one-thousandth of a second can result in a location variation of more than 200 miles. GPS can produce very accurate results, typically within 5 to 50 feet of the actual location (military versions have higher accuracy). GPS also provides latitude, longitude, and elevation information.[35]

GPS applications are in every kind of company vehicle these days—from police cars to bulldozers, from dump trucks to mayoral limousines. Emergency response systems use GPS to track each of their vehicles and so dispatch those closest to the scene of an accident. If a vehicle is missing, its GPS locator can help locate it.

Geographic Information System (GIS)

GPS provides the foundation for geographic information systems. A *geographic information system (GIS)* consists of hardware, software, and data that provide location information for display on a multidimensional map. This information includes building locations, street layouts, and population densities. Companies that deal in transportation combine GISs with database and GPS technology. Airlines and shipping companies can plot routes with up-to-the-second information about the location of all their transport vehicles. Hospitals can locate their medical staff with GIS and sensors that pick up transmissions from ID badges. Automobiles have GPSs linked to GIS maps that display the car's location and driving directions on a dashboard screen. GM offers the OnStar system, which sends a continuous stream of information to the OnStar center about the car's exact location.

Some mobile phone providers combine GPS and GIS capabilities so they can locate users within a geographical area about the size of a tennis court to assist emergency services such as 911. Farmers can use GIS to map and analyze fields, telling them where to apply the proper amounts of seed, fertilizer, and herbicides.

A GIS can find the closest gas station or bank or determine the best way to get to a particular location. But it is also good at finding patterns, such as finding the most feasible location to hold a conference according to where the majority of a company's customers live and work. GIS can present this information in a visually effective way.

Some common GIS uses include:

- **Finding what is nearby.** Given a specific location, the GIS finds sources within a defined radius. These might be entertainment venues, medical facilities, restaurants, or gas stations. Users can also use GIS to locate vendors that sell a specific item they want and get the results as a map of the surrounding area or an address.

- **Routing information.** Once users have an idea where they want to go, GIS can provide directions to get there using either a map or step-by-step instructions. Routing information can be especially helpful when combined with search services.

- **Sending information alerts.** Users may want to be notified when information relevant to them becomes available near their location. A commuter might want to know that a section of the highway has traffic congestion, or a shopper might want to be notified when a favorite store is having a sale on a certain item.

- **Mapping densities.** GIS can map population and event densities based on a standard area unit, such as square miles, making it easy to see distributions and concentrations. Police can map crime incidents to determine where additional patrolling is required, and stores can map customer orders to identify ideal delivery routes.

- **Mapping quantities.** Users can map quantities to find out where the most or least of a feature may be. For example, someone interested in opening a specialty coffee shop can determine how many others are already in the area, and city planners can determine where to build more parks.[36]

A GIS can provide information and insight to both mobile users and people at fixed locations. Google Earth combines satellite imagery, geographic data, and Google's search capabilities to create a virtual globe that users can download to a computer or mobile device. Not only does this provide useful business benefits, but it also allows for many educational opportunities. Instead of just talking about the Grand Canyon, an instructor can use Google Earth to view that region.

Location-Based Services (LBS)

GPS and GIS both utilize *location-based services (LBS),* applications that use location information to provide a service. LBS is designed to give mobile users instant access to personalized local content and range from 911 applications to buddy finders ("Let me know when my friend is within 1,000 feet") to games (treasure hunts) to location-based advertising ("Visit the Starbucks on the corner and get $1.00 off a latte"). Many LBS applications complement GPS and GIS, such as:

- Emergency services.
- Field service management.
- Find-it services.
- Mapping.
- Navigation.
- Tracking assets.
- Traffic information.
- Vehicle location.
- Weather information.
- Wireless advertising.[37]

Just as Facebook and Twitter helped fuel the web 2.0 revolution, applications such as Foursquare, Gowalla, and Loopt are bringing attention to LBS. Each application is a mobile phone service that helps social media users find their friends' location. Facebook and Twitter have added location-based services to complement their applications.

BENEFITS OF BUSINESS MOBILITY L07-6

Mobile and wireless development has come a long way. Consider Dr Pepper/Seven-Up Inc., of Plano, Texas, which monitors the operation of its antenna-equipped vending machines via wireless technology. The company collects inventory, sales, and "machine-health" data and polls the machines daily; managers and salespeople can access the stored information via its intranet. Dr Pepper/Seven-Up Inc. understands the business value of the data, both for daily operations and for data-mining purposes. The information collected is helpful for deciding where to place new vending machines, such as in front of a Target store or a high-traffic supermarket. Figure 7.21 lists many of the advantages of wireless networks.[38]

L07-6 Identify the benefits of business mobility.

Enhances Mobility

Enhancing mobility is one of the greatest advantages provided by wireless networks. It allows activities that were formerly tied to physical locations to be performed almost anywhere. Companies can bring employees, information, and computing resources to a job location instead of forcing the job to be located at the company's site. Consider how mobile phones alone have changed the way most companies operate. Executives and sales professionals can conduct business wherever they are, eliminating downtime during travel and speeding their response to customers. Mobility means more face-to-face contact with customers and business partners. Even people with internal jobs, such as custodians, floor salespeople, production supervisors, and emergency room doctors, keep moving throughout the day. Instead of returning periodically to their offices or other fixed location for information access or doing without, they can rely on wireless technology to bring that access to them, where and when they need it.

Mobility gives a company the power to place the right resources in the right place at the right time. It allows for the redistribution of operations to gain efficiencies or react to changing conditions. For example, a mobile checkout stand allows additional checkouts to be set up during holiday rushes and store sales events.

Provides Immediate Data Access

Mobility allows activities to be performed where needed; however, providing immediate data access offers the value. Wireless networks can support a wide variety of immediate data access options, from collecting usage data using wi-fi or RFID technologies when driving past a water meter to having full Internet access on a laptop or other mobile device. A mobile worker can submit a status report or credit card scan or be notified about a new assignment. When up-to-the-second data are required, such as for stock transactions and credit card authorizations, wireless technology is the only mobile option. Employees can "pull" data by linking to the source and requesting the desired information, or "push" it by sending an alert to a user's device or automatically refreshing data.

Whether through voice, email, or text messaging, the quality and frequency of information exchange increases with wireless access. An emergency room doctor can be notified of lab test results immediately upon completion. A service worker and appropriate information can be rerouted to a higher-priority assignment. A salesperson can submit updates right after a sales call.

Instant access to customer profiles, account history, and current order status significantly improves the quality of interactions with customers, suppliers, and business partners. A salesperson

FIGURE 7.21 Advantages of Wireless Networks

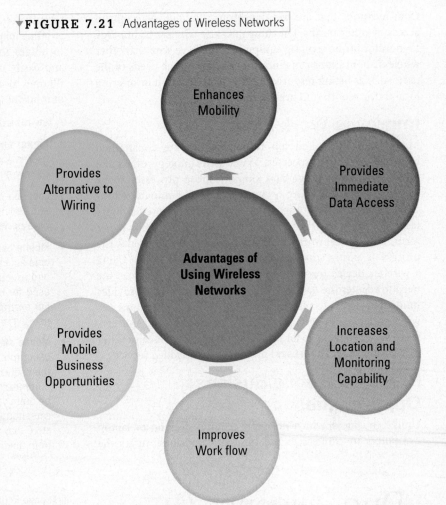

can check inventories, generate quotes, take orders, and resolve problems all at the customer's site. Field workers can identify problems with online manuals and diagnostic tools. Decision making is always improved by access to accurate and current information.

Increases Location and Monitoring Capability

The ability to locate and monitor assets reduces losses from theft and damage, gathers information from remote or difficult-to-reach locations, enhances safety, and makes possible a new wave of personalized services. RFID tags permit the tracking of assets from cattle to container shipments. LBS devices send storm data from buoys far at sea. LBS in cars provide driving directions and enable rescuers to locate the vehicle in case of an accident.

Through a combination of LBS devices and applications, companies can trace shipments from point of origin to final destination. More advanced applications can monitor their condition (e.g., ensuring that refrigeration equipment is operating) and notify users of tampering or attempted theft. Wireless applications can collect billing data, monitor operating conditions, gather scientific measurements, and relay requests for service from locations that are too dangerous, difficult, or costly to access by other means. Oil companies use wireless technology to monitor offshore oil rig equipment. We have seen that other wireless applications can tailor information to the needs of the user, such as listing resources near a given location or offering local traffic reports and driving directions.

Improves Work Flow

Many work flows and job responsibilities are constrained by paper or wired processes. Wireless technology offers the opportunity to redesign and simplify those processes to be faster, cheaper, and more responsive, and to eliminate redundant activities, integrate activities and services, and redistribute tasks. For example, when mobile workers capture data on paper forms and clerical workers enter it into computer systems, the process is costly, time-consuming, and error-prone. Using a wireless device for the original data capture eliminates the need to reenter the data, increases data accuracy, and provides immediate access to results. Rental car staff members now use wireless devices to quickly and easily check and enter mileage, fuel levels, and damage for returning cars. Drivers receive faster service and staff can focus on providing value-added services.

Provides Mobile Business Opportunities

Unlike ebusiness, which normally requires desktop or laptop computers to connect to the Internet, mbusiness offers the advantages of making a purchase via the Internet an anywhere, anytime experience. It provides consumers with the ability to obtain information and order goods and services quickly and easily using a mobile device. The growing popularity of iPhones along with iPhone apps have helped fuel the growth of mbusiness.

A few mbusiness offerings include:

- **Digital purchases.** The most suitable purchase for a mobile user is for products that can be downloaded and used immediately such as music and (electronic) books.

- **Location-based services.** The ability for merchants to capture and react to a user's current location and requirements can be a powerful tool for selling products and services.

- **Mobile banking and payments.** Using a mobile device can provide access to personal bank accounts to view account history and execute transactions. In addition, a mobile device can be used for making payments, essentially acting as digital cash. For example, someone can order and pay for a Starbucks latte using a mobile device and app.

- **Mobile shopping.** Most forms of shopping may be impractical using mobile devices; however, some forms of purchases lend themselves to mbusiness. For example, having the ability to purchase movie tickets for a show playing the same evening can be quite valuable. Mobile devices can also be used for comparison shopping. Before making a purchase, a shopper in a retail store may want to first see what the current price of a product is from another vendor to ensure he is getting a good price.[39]

Due Diligence //:
WeatherBots[40]

Warren Jackson, an engineering graduate student at the University of Pennsylvania, was not interested in the weather until he started investigating how the National Weather Service collected weather data. The weather service has collected most of its information using weather balloons that carry a device to measure items like pressure, wind, and humidity. When the balloon reaches about 100,000 feet and pressure causes it to pop, the device falls and lands a substantial distance from its launch point. The National Weather Service and researchers sometimes look for the $200 device, but of the 80,000 sent up annually, they write many off as lost.

Convinced there had to be a better way, Jackson began designing a GPS-equipped robot that launches a parachute after the balloon pops, and brings the device back down to Earth, landing it at a predetermined location set by the researchers. The idea is so inventive that the university's Weiss Tech House—an organization that encourages students to innovate and bring their ideas to market—awarded Jackson and some fellow graduate engineering students first prize in its third annual PennVention Contest. Jackson won $5,000 and access to expert advice on prototyping, legal matters, and branding.

GPS and GIS can be used in all sorts of devices, in many different industries, for multiple purposes. You want to compete and win first prize in the PennVention next year. Create a product, using a GPS or GIS, that is not currently in the market today that you will present at the fourth annual PennVention.

Provides Alternative to Wiring

Wireless networks provide an attractive alternative where physical constraints or convenience make wired solutions costly or impractical. Many office buildings already have a maze of wires in their ceilings, floors, and walls representing many generations of network technologies. Tracing existing wires or adding new lines becomes increasingly cumbersome and difficult. In other cases, building design or aesthetic considerations make wired networks unattractive. In manufacturing facilities or production lines with moving equipment or complex setups, wireless connections are simpler to implement and safer for workers. The higher per unit cost of a wireless solution may be more than offset by its advantages over physical lines.

WLANs allow MIS employees to relocate equipment at will, attractive for trade shows, temporary offices, and seasonal selling areas. In conference rooms, WLANs enable attendees to bring laptops or other wi-fi–enabled devices for Internet access.

Finally, wireless technology allows voice and data connections with ships at sea, passengers in airliners, and travelers in remote locations. In developing countries, it is a means to bypass the effort and expense of installing and maintaining telephone lines across inhospitable terrain.

CHALLENGES OF BUSINESS MOBILITY LO7-7

The mobile employee has become the norm rather than the exception, driven by lifestyle choices, productivity gains, and technology improvements. Although the advantages of using wireless networks are significant, added challenges exist such as protecting against theft, protecting wireless connections, preventing viruses on mobile devices, and addressing privacy concerns with RFID and LBS (see Figure 7.22).

LO7-7 Identify the challenges of business mobility.

Protecting Against Theft

Any mobile device is vulnerable to loss no matter how big or small it is. The company may face significant exposure from stolen IDs, passwords, encryption keys, and confidential information if the device falls into the wrong hands, especially if the theft is not discovered or reported immediately and the company does not have time to revoke access.

Power-on passwords—passwords implemented at the hardware level that must be entered before gaining access

to the computer—are the first line of defense against unauthorized use. Companies should activate these passwords before giving their workforce the devices. They should also prohibit storing passwords on devices and periodically monitor compliance with the policy. Companies need to consider encrypting and password-protecting data stored on the device, including any flash drives or other mobile storage devices. In addition, some device management tools can send messages to a device to lock it or destroy its contents, which can be an attractive security feature.

Protecting Wireless Connections

Network intrusions can occur if access codes or passwords are stored on a device that is lost or stolen. However, any time a wireless network connects to a wired one, the wireless network can serve as a conduit for a hacker to gain entry into an otherwise secure wired network. This risk is especially high if the wireless network is not sufficiently secured in its own right.

Before the emergence of the Internet, hackers generally had to be physically present within the corporate complex to gain access to a wired network. The thousands, if not millions, of access points enabled by the Internet now allow hackers to work from a distance. This threat has spawned a variety of different security techniques from firewalls to VPNs to SSL and HTTPS.

Several techniques can secure wireless networks from unauthorized access whether used separately or in combination. One method is authenticating wi-fi access points. Because wi-fi communications are broadcast, anyone within listening distance can intercept communications. Every time someone uses an unsecured website via a public wi-fi access point, his or her log-on name and password are sent over the open airwaves, with a high risk that someone might "eavesdrop" or capture log-on names, passwords, credit card numbers, and other vital information. WLANs that use wi-fi have a built-in security mechanism called **Wi-Fi Protected Access (WPA),** a wireless security protocol to protect wi-fi networks. It is an improvement on the original

▼**FIGURE 7.22** Challenges of Using Wireless Networks

Challenges of Wireless Networks			
Protecting Against Theft	**Protecting Wireless Connections**	**Preventing Viruses on Mobile Devices**	**Addressing Privacy Concerns with RFID and LBS**
Example: Mobile devices are more vulnerable to theft due to their small size.	**Example:** Wi-fi connections need to enforce data encryption.	**Example:** Mobile devices are not immune to viruses and need to be protected.	**Example:** Both RFID and LBS have the ability to share where someone is, which can cause privacy concerns.

wi-fi security standard, Wired Equivalent Privacy (WEP), and provides more sophisticated data encryption and user authentication. Anyone who wants to use an access point must know the WPA encryption key to access the wi-fi connection.

Preventing Viruses on a Mobile Device

The potential for contracting viruses on mobile devices is becoming a reality. The need for virus protection at the device level is critical. Any device that can access the Internet or receive email is at risk of catching a virus and passing it on to other devices. Because of the memory limitations of most mobile devices, antivirus software has typically been hosted on a PC or laptop, with the mobile device physically connecting to a PC or laptop to perform virus scanning. The first known mobile phone virus, named Cabir, appeared several years ago and infected only a small number of Bluetooth-enabled phones that carried out no malicious action; the virus was created by a group of malware developers to prove it could be done. The developers sent Cabir to anti-virus researchers, so they could begin to develop a solution to a problem that promises to get a lot worse. At present, mobile phone viruses do not do much damage, but if protective measures are not taken, they could be as devastating as their computer counterparts.[41]

The best way to protect against mobile phone viruses is the same way users protect themselves from computer viruses—never open anything that seems suspicious. Another method is to turn Bluetooth discoverable mode off. By setting the Bluetooth option to "hidden," other devices cannot detect it and send it the virus. In addition, install some type of security software on the mobile device. Many of the mobile phone manufacturers, such as Nokia and Samsung, have developed security software for their mobile phones that detect and remove a virus as well as protect it from getting certain viruses in the first place.

Addressing Privacy Concerns with RFID and LBS

As technology advances, the potential for privacy infringement does as well. RFID already has the capability to determine the distance of a tag from the reader location. It is not difficult to imagine that retailers could determine the location of individuals within the store and target specific advertisements to them based upon past purchases and shopping and behavior patterns. Many consumers would consider gathering such information intrusive enough, but the possibility that it could be sold to other retailers might lead consumers to refuse to give retailers any information.

Several steps are being taken to address these privacy concerns. For example, one proposal would require all RFID-tagged products to be clearly labeled. This would act as an alert mechanism to which items are being tracked. Another measure being considered is "Kill Codes," which would turn off all RFID tags when someone comes into contact with them. Another measure is "RSA Blocker Tags," which try to address privacy concerns while maintaining the integrity of the product. Only that store's authorized reader can track items with these tags; customers cannot be tracked outside the store in which they made a purchase.[42]

LBS can track and monitor objects much like RFID. Tracking vulnerable individuals and company assets is beneficial. But

---

Living the DREAM

Geoblogging for Chimpanzees[43]

As a young girl, Jane Goodall loved Tarzan and Dr. Dolittle and dreamed of living among and researching wild chimpanzees in Africa. In 1977, the Jane Goodall Institute was established to continue Dr. Goodall's pioneering research on chimpanzee behavior—research that transformed scientific perceptions of the relationship between humans and animals. Now the 100 million users of Google Earth can zoom straight into the lush awning of trees in Gombe National Park in Tanzania and read daily updates about the park's chimpanzees. This new form of innovative blog (a Google Earth "geoblog" or weblog) allows users to click on a blog entry,

causing the globe image to spin toward eastern Africa, and then slowly hones in on the 35-square-kilometer Gombe National Park. The user can then read the blog while viewing high resolution satellite images, creating an online mashup of literature and visuals. The Jane Goodall Institute was the first to create such a Google geoblog.

Now just imagine what you could do with the geoblog if you added GPS. The Jane Goodall Institute will take this next step in the evolution of its blog by adding markers and daily entries using the actual GPS coordinates provided by field staff. When a researcher posts the chimpanzees are resting on Jane's Peak, Google's pictorial Earth will spin right to Jane's Peak.

What other types of research could be accomplished using GPS? How could other nonprofits use geoblogs to help their cause? How could a business use Google Earth and GPS to create a competitive advantage? How could this type of geoblog be used unethically?

the dark side of LBS risks the invasion of privacy and security caused by indiscreet location tracking. For example, if a company is using LBS to know where each employee is on duty, it must not observe their positions when they are off duty. Advertising at random to users in a specific area may violate privacy if mobile users in the area do not want to receive these advertisements. Criminals might also take advantage of illegal location tracking. And because LBS are based on message exchange in a wireless network, there are always security risks because location information could be stolen, lost, or modified.

Security mechanisms must eliminate or minimize the potential for attacks against LBS entities and reduce exposure of the user's identity and location. One way to solve the location privacy problem is to provide strong privacy practices that counterbalance the invisible nature of location collection in the wireless world. LBS policies should specify that:

- Direct marketing purposes are permitted only with the business or service a user has a contract with.

- Electronic messages cannot hide the identity of the sender.

- Solicitation is allowed only if the user has given prior consent.

- The location service must tell the user about the type, duration, and purpose of the data they are collecting.

- The user must be given the opportunity to reject any direct marketing opportunities.

For mobile service providers, an unwelcome push can lead to increased customer care cost. When a user has issues with her PC, she tries to fix it herself. However, when a user's mobile phone is not working, she usually contacts the service provider. As a result, subscribers receiving unsolicited messages through LBS would contact their mobile service providers with complaints.

With the power of a network, business professionals can share data and resources around the globe. With the power of a wireless network, business professionals can take advantage of mobility allowing them to work from anywhere, at any time, using many different devices.

Watching people work in airports, restaurants, stores, trains, planes, and automobiles is common, and soon even remote villages in Africa, South America, and Asia will have access to the Internet along with all the power that comes with wireless networking.

GET ONLINE

mhhe.com/BaltzanM2e

for study materials including quizzes, iPod downloads, and video

coming

up

O rganizations use various types of information systems to help run their daily operations. These primarily transactional systems concentrate on the management and flow of low-level data items for basic business processes such as purchasing and order delivery. The data are often rolled up and summarized into higher-level decision support systems to help firms understand what is happening in their organizations and how best to respond. To achieve seamless and efficient handling of data and informed decision making, organizations must ensure that their enterprise systems are tightly integrated, providing an end-to-end view of operations.

This module introduces various types of enterprise information systems and their role in helping firms reach their strategic goals, including supply chain management, customer relationship management, and enterprise resource planning. Organizations that can correlate and summarize enterprisewide information are prepared to meet their strategic business goals and outperform their competitors.

This module then dives into how enterprise systems can be built to support global businesses, the challenges in that process, and how well things turn out if systems are built according to good design principles, sound management practices, and flexibility to support ever-changing business needs. Making this happen requires not only extensive planning, but also well-honed people skills. ■

ENTERPRISE MIS

module one
BUSINESS DRIVEN MIS

module two
TECHNICAL FOUNDATIONS OF MIS

module three
ENTERPRISE MIS
ch. 8 Enterprise Applications: Business Communications
ch. 9 Systems Development + Project Management:
Corporate Responsibility

eight

enterprise applications:
business communications

what's in IT for me?

This chapter introduces high-profile strategic initiatives an organization can undertake to help it gain competitive advantages and business efficiencies—supply chain management, customer relationship management, and enterprise resource planning. At the simplest level, organizations implement enterprise systems to gain efficiency in business processes, effectiveness in supply chains, and an overall understanding of customer needs and behaviors. Successful organizations recognize the competitive advantage of maintaining healthy relationships with employees, customers, suppliers, and partners. Doing so has a direct and positive effect on revenue and greatly adds to a company's profitability.

continued on p. 180

CHAPTER OUTLINE

SECTION 8-1 >>
Supply Chain Management

- Building a Connected Corporation Through Integrations
- Supply Chain Management
- The Benefits of SCM
- The Challenges of SCM
- The Future of SCM

SECTION 8-2 >>
Customer Relationship Management and Enterprise Resource Planning

- Customer Relationship Management
- The Benefits of CRM
- The Challenges of CRM
- The Future of CRM
- Enterprise Resource Planning
- The Benefits of ERP
- The Challenges of ERP
- The Future of Enterprise Systems: Integrating SCM, CRM, and ERP

continued from p. 179

You, as a business student, must understand the critical relationship your business will have with its employees, customers, suppliers, and partners. You must also understand how to analyze your organizational data to ensure you are not just meeting but exceeding expectations. Enterprises are technologically empowered as never before to reach their goals of integrating, analyzing, and making intelligent business decisions. ■

{SECTION 8-1}
Supply Chain Management

LEARNING OUTCOMES

LO8-1 Explain integrations and the role they play in connecting a corporation.

LO8-2 Describe supply chain management and its role in supporting business operations.

LO8-3 Identify the benefits and challenges of SCM along with its future.

BUILDING A CONNECTED CORPORATION THROUGH INTEGRATIONS LO8-1

Until the 1990s, each department in the United Kingdom's Ministry of Defense and Army headquarters had its own information system, and each system had its own database. Sharing information was difficult, requiring employees to manually input the same information into different systems multiple times. Often, management could not even compile the information it needed to answer questions, solve problems, and make decisions.

To combat this challenge the ministry integrated its systems, or built connections among its many databases. These connections, or *integrations* allow separate systems to communicate directly with each other, eliminating the need for manual entry into multiple systems. Building integrations allows the sharing of information across databases along with dramatically increasing the quality of that information. The army can now generate reports detailing its state of readiness and other essential intelligence, tasks that were nearly impossible before the integrations.

Two common methods are used for integrating databases. The first is to create forward and backward integrations that link processes (and their underlying databases) in the value chain. A *forward integration* takes information entered into a given system and sends it automatically to all downstream systems and processes. A *backward integration* takes information entered into a given system and sends it automatically to all upstream systems and processes. Figure 8.1 demonstrates how this method works across the systems or processes of sales, order entry, order fulfillment, and billing. In the order entry system, for example, an employee can update the customer's information. Via the integrations, that information is sent upstream to the sales system and downstream to the order fulfillment and billing systems. Ideally, an organization wants to build both forward and backward integrations, which provide the flexibility to create, update, and delete information in any of the systems. However, integrations are expensive and difficult to build and maintain, causing most organizations to invest in forward integrations only.

The second integration method builds a central repository for a particular type of information. Figure 8.2 provides an example of customer information integrated using this method across four different systems in an organization. Users can create, update, and delete customer information only in the central customer database. As users perform these tasks, integrations automatically send the new and/or updated customer

---

▼FIGURE 8.1 A Forward and Backward Customer Information Integration Example

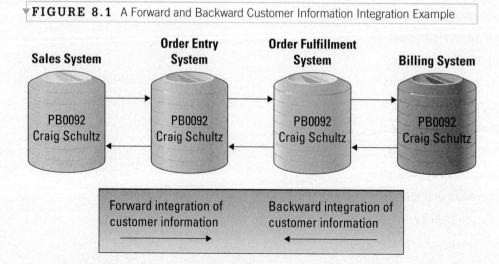

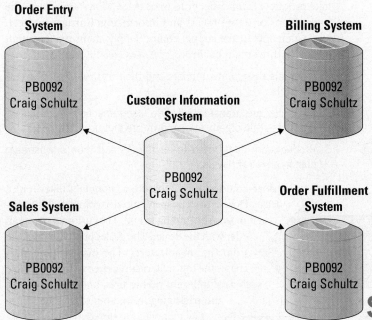

FIGURE 8.2 Integrating Customer Information among Databases

Order Entry System
PB0092 Craig Schultz

Customer Information System
PB0092 Craig Schultz

Billing System
PB0092 Craig Schultz

Sales System
PB0092 Craig Schultz

Order Fulfillment System
PB0092 Craig Schultz

information to the other systems. The other systems limit users to read-only access of the customer information stored in them. Both integration methods do not entirely eliminate information redundancy, but they do ensure information consistency among multiple systems.

LO8-1 Explain integrations and the role they play in connecting a corporation.

---

separate enterprise systems. A *legacy system* is a current or existing system that will become the base for upgrading or integrating with a new system. EAI reviews how legacy systems fit into the new shape of the firm's business processes and devises ways to efficiently reuse what already exists while adding new systems and data.

Integrations are achieved using *middleware*—several different types of software that sit between and provide connectivity for two or more software applications. Middleware translates information between disparate systems. *Enterprise application integration (EAI) middleware* takes a new approach to middleware by packaging commonly used applications together, reducing the time needed to integrate applications from multiple vendors. The remainder of this chapter covers the three enterprise systems most organizations use to integrate their disparate departments and separate operational systems: supply chain management (SCM), customer relationship management, and enterprise resource planning (see Figure 8.3).

SUPPLY CHAIN MANAGEMENT LO8-2

The average company spends nearly half of every dollar it earns on suppliers and raw materials to manufacture products. It is not uncommon to hear of critical success factors focusing on getting the right products, to the right place, at the right time, at the right cost. For this reason, tools that can help a company source raw materials, manufacture products, and deliver finished goods to retailers and customers are in high demand. A *supply chain* consists of all parties involved, directly or

---

> **"The average company spends nearly half of every dollar it earns on suppliers and raw materials to manufacture products."**

Integration Tools

Enterprise systems provide enterprisewide support and data access for a firm's operations and business processes. These systems can manage customer information across the enterprise, letting you view everything your customer has experienced from sales to support. Enterprise systems are often available as a generic, but highly customizable, group of programs for business functions such as accounting, manufacturing, and marketing. Generally, the development tools for customization are complex programming tools that require specialist capabilities.

Enterprise application integration (EAI) connects the plans, methods, and tools aimed at integrating

FIGURE 8.3 The Three Primary Enterprise Systems

Supply Chain Management

Customer Relationship Management

Enterprise Resource Planning

customer business processes infiltrating the entire value chain and helping the organization achieve greater operational efficiency (see Figure 8.20).

L08-6 Describe enterprise resource management and its role in supporting business operations.

THE BENEFITS OF ERP L08-7

The first generation of ERP systems focused on improving the manufacturing process through automation, primarily addressing back-office business processes such as inventory ordering and product distribution. The second generation of ERP systems extended its reach into the front office and

▼**FIGURE 8.20** The Organization Before and After ERP

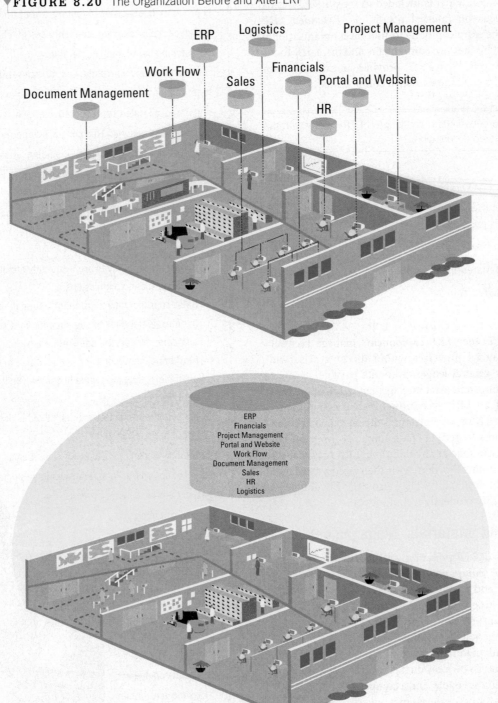

primarily addressed customer issues including marketing and sales. The third generation of ERP systems, known as ERP-II, allows a company to compete on a functional level by adopting an enterprisewide approach using the Internet to connect all participants in the value chain. Figure 8.21 shows how ERP has grown to accommodate the needs of the entire organization.

The current generation of ERP, ERP-II, is composed of two primary components—core and extended. *Core ERP components* are the traditional components included in most ERP systems and primarily focus on internal operations. *Extended ERP components* are the extra components that meet organizational needs not covered by the core components and primarily focus on external operations. Figure 8.22 provides an example of an ERP system with its core and extended components.

LO8-7 Identify the benefits and challenges of ERP along with the future of the connected corporation.

Core ERP Components

The three most common core ERP components focusing on internal operations are:

1. Accounting and finance.

2. Production and materials management.

3. Human resources.

Accounting and Finance ERP Components

Accounting and finance ERP components manage accounting data and financial processes within the enterprise with functions such as general ledger, accounts payable, accounts receivable, budgeting, and asset management. One of the most useful features of an ERP accounting/finance component is credit management. Most organizations manage their relationships with customers by setting credit limits, or limits on how much a customer can owe at any one time. ERP financial systems correlate customers' orders with their account balances to determine credit availability. They also perform all types of advanced profitability modeling techniques.

Production and Materials Management ERP Components

Production and materials management ERP components handle production planning and execution tasks such as demand forecasting, production scheduling, job cost accounting, and quality control. Demand forecasting helps determine production schedules and materials purchasing. A company that makes its own product prepares a detailed production schedule, and a company that buys products for resale develops a materials requirement plan.

▼FIGURE 8.21 The Evolution of ERP

ERP
- Materials Planning
- Order Entry
- Distribution
- General Ledger
- Accounting
- Shop Floor Control

Extended ERP
- Scheduling
- Forecasting
- Capacity Planning
- Ecommerce
- Warehousing
- Logistics

ERP-II
- Project Management
- Knowledge Management
- Work Flow Management
- Customer Relationship Management
- Human Resource Management
- Portal Capability
- Integrated Financials

| 1990 | 2000 | Present |

▼FIGURE 8.22 Core ERP Components and Extended ERP Components

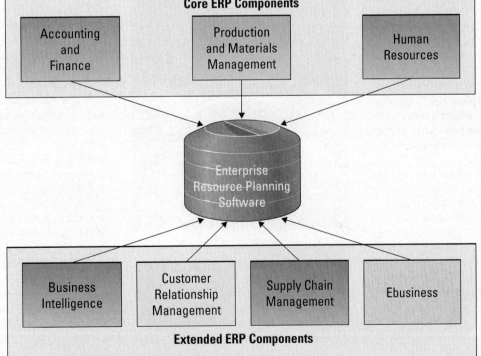

Core ERP Components

Accounting and Finance

Production and Materials Management

Human Resources

Enterprise Resource Planning Software

Business Intelligence

Customer Relationship Management

Supply Chain Management

Ebusiness

Extended ERP Components

Human Resources ERP Components *Human resources ERP components* track employee information including payroll, benefits, compensation, and performance assessment and ensure compliance with all laws. They even allow the organization to perform detailed employee analysis, such as identifying who is likely to leave the company unless additional compensation or benefits are provided, and whether the most talented people are working in areas where they can have the greatest impact. Human resource components can also identify which employees are using which resources, such as online training and long-distance telephone services.

Extended ERP Components

Extended ERP components meet the organizational needs not covered by the core components and primarily focus on external operations. Many are Internet-enabled and require interaction with customers, suppliers, and business partners outside the organization. The four most common extended ERP components are:

1. Business intelligence.
2. Customer relationship management.
3. Supply chain management.
4. Ebusiness.

Business Intelligence ERP Components Many organizations have found that ERP tools can provide even greater value with the addition of powerful business intelligence systems. The business intelligence components of ERP systems typically collect information used throughout the organization (including data used in many other ERP components), organize it, and apply analytical tools to assist managers with decisions. Data warehouses are one of the most popular extensions to ERP systems.

Customer Relationship Management ERP Components ERP vendors now include additional functionality that provides services formerly found only in CRM systems. The CRM components in ERP systems include contact centers, sales force automation, and advanced marketing functions. The goal is to provide an integrated view of customer data, enabling a firm to effectively manage customer relationships by responding to customer needs and demands while identifying the most (and least) valuable customers so the firm can better allocate its marketing resources.

fyi

Bean Integration

At Flavors, a premium coffee shop, customers receive more than just a great cup of coffee—they receive exposure to music, art, literature, and town events. Flavors' calendar for programs gives customers a quick view into this corner of the world—from live music and art displays to volunteering or a coffee tasting. Flavors offers the following:

- Music center: Information is available for all live music events occurring in the area. The store also hosts an open microphone two nights a week for local musicians.
- Art gallery: A space in the store is filled with great pieces from local artists.
- Book clubs: Customers can meet to discuss current and classic literature.
- Coffee sampler: Customers can sample coffees from around the world with the experts.
- Community events: Weekly meetings are held, where customers can find ways to become more involved in their community.
- Brewing courses: The finer details of the brewing, grinding, and blending equipment for sale in Flavors stores—from the traditional press to a digital espresso machine—are taught. There is also a trouble-shooting guide developed by brewing specialists.

Flavors' sales are great and profits are soaring; however, current operations need an overhaul. The owners of Flavors, J. P. Field

and Marla Lily, built the business piece by piece over the past 12 years. The following offers a quick look at current operations.

- Flavors does not receive any information on how many of its customers attend live music events. Musicians typically maintain a fan email listing and CD sales records for the event; however, this information is not always provided to the store.
- Book club events are booked and run through the local bookstore, Pages Up. Pages Up runs a tab during the book club and provides Flavors with a check at the end of each month for all book club events. Flavors has no access to

book club customer information or sales information.
- The artist gallery is run by several local artists who pay Flavors a small commission on each sale. Flavors has no input into the art contained in the store or information on customers who purchase art.
- Coffee sampler events are run through Flavors' primary operations.
- Community event information is open to all members of the community. Each event is run by a separate organization, which provides monthly event feedback to Flavors in a variety of formats from Word to Access files.
- Brewing and machine resource courses are run by the equipment manufacturer, and all customer and sales information is provided to Flavors in a Word document at the end of each year.

You have been hired as an integration expert by Flavors. The owners want to revamp the way the company operates so it can take advantage of marketing and sales opportunities across its many different lines of business, such as offering customers who attend book club events discounts on art and brewing and machine resource courses. They also want to gain a better understanding of how the different events affect sales. For example, should they have more open microphone nights or more book clubs? Currently, they have no way to tell which events result in higher sales. Create an integration strategy so Flavors can take advantage of CRM, SCM, and ERP across the company.

Supply Chain Management ERP Components

ERP vendors are expanding their systems to include SCM functions that manage the information flows between and among supply chain stages, maximizing total supply chain effectiveness and profitability. SCM components allow a firm to monitor and control all stages in the supply chain from the acquisition of raw materials to the receipt of finished goods by customers.

Ebusiness ERP Components

The newest extended ERP components are the ebusiness components that allow companies to establish an Internet presence and fulfill online orders. Two of the primary features of ebusiness components are elogistics and eprocurement. *Elogistics* manages the transportation and storage of goods. *Eprocurement* is the business-to-business (B2B) online purchase and sale of supplies and services. A common mistake many businesses make is jumping into online business without properly integrating the entire organization on the ERP system. One large toy manufacturer announced less than a week before Christmas that it would be unable to fulfill any of its online orders. The company had all the toys in the warehouse, but it could not organize the basic order processing function to get the toys delivered to consumers on time.

Measuring ERP Success

One of the best methods of measuring ERP success is the balanced scorecard, created by Dr. Robert Kaplan and Dr. David Norton, both from the Harvard Business School. The *balanced scorecard* is a management system, as well as a measurement system, that a firm uses to translate business strategies into executable tasks. It provides feedback for both internal and external business processes, allowing continuous improvement. Kaplan and Norton describe the balanced scorecard as follows: "The balanced scorecard retains traditional financial measures. But financial measures tell the story of past events, an adequate story for industrial age companies for which investments in long-term capabilities and customer relationships were not critical for success. These financial measures are inadequate, however, for guiding and evaluating the journey that information age companies must make to create future value through investment in customers, suppliers, employees, processes, technology, and innovation."[9] The balanced scorecard uses four perspectives to monitor an organization:

1. The learning and growth perspective.

2. The internal business process perspective.

3. The customer perspective.

4. The financial perspective (see Figure 8.23).

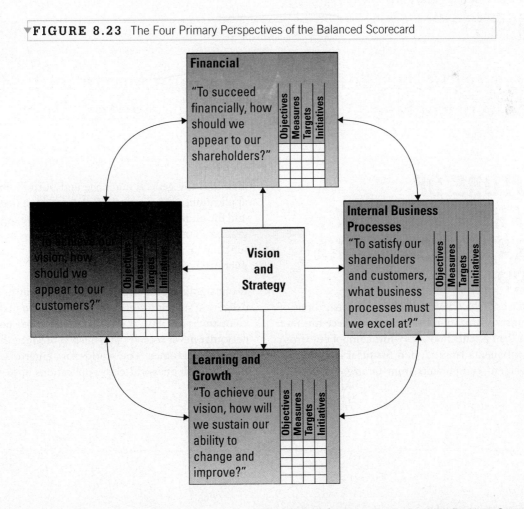

▼**FIGURE 8.23** The Four Primary Perspectives of the Balanced Scorecard

THE CHALLENGES OF ERP

One of the biggest challenges of an ERP system is cost. ERP systems contain multiple complex components that are not only expensive to purchase, but also expensive to implement. Costs can include the software itself, plus consulting charges, hardware expenses, and training fees. A large firm can easily spend millions of dollars and many years completing an ERP implementation. The biggest issue facing an ERP implementation is that it fundamentally changes the way the entire organization operates, causing employees to learn and adjust to new business processes. Many ERP failures occur because the business managers and MIS professionals underestimate the complexity of the planning, development, and training required with an ERP implementation. As a manager, you must carefully assess your company's needs and choose the right ERP system and ensure proper support for all new processes, while avoiding too much change too fast.

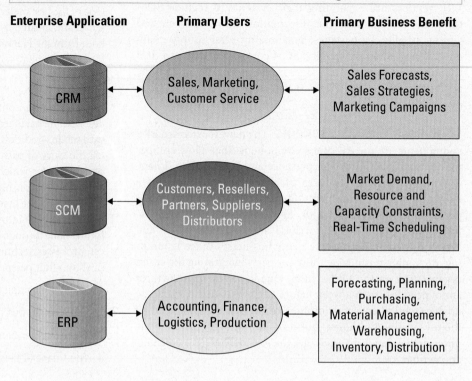

▼FIGURE 8.24 Primary Uses and Business Benefits of Strategic Initiatives

Enterprise Application	Primary Users	Primary Business Benefit
CRM	Sales, Marketing, Customer Service	Sales Forecasts, Sales Strategies, Marketing Campaigns
SCM	Customers, Resellers, Partners, Suppliers, Distributors	Market Demand, Resource and Capacity Constraints, Real-Time Scheduling
ERP	Accounting, Finance, Logistics, Production	Forecasting, Planning, Purchasing, Material Management, Warehousing, Inventory, Distribution

> "The world-class enterprises of tomorrow must be built on world-class applications implemented today."

THE FUTURE OF ENTERPRISE SYSTEMS: INTEGRATING SCM, CRM, AND ERP

Applications such as SCM, CRM, and ERP are the backbone of ebusiness, yet most organizations today have to piece together these systems. A firm might choose its CRM components from Siebel, SCM components from i2, and financial components and HR management components from Oracle. Figure 8.24 identifies the general audience and purpose for each of these applications, and Figure 8.25 shows where they are integrated and the underlying premise of an integrated organization. Integrating all of these enterprise systems allows an organization to function as a single unit meeting customer, partner, and supplier needs.

If one application performs poorly, the entire customer value delivery system is affected. For example, no matter how great a company is at CRM, if its SCM system does not work and the customer never receives the finished product, the company will lose that customer. The world-class enterprises of tomorrow must be built on world-class applications implemented today.

▼FIGURE 8.25 Integrations between SCM, CRM, and ERP

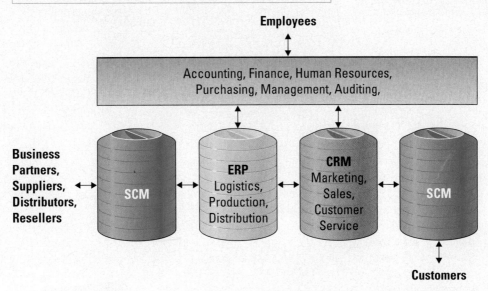

Employees

Accounting, Finance, Human Resources,
Purchasing, Management, Auditing,

Business
Partners,
Suppliers,
Distributors,
Resellers

SCM

ERP
Logistics,
Production,
Distribution

CRM
Marketing,
Sales,
Customer
Service

SCM

Customers

systems development + project management: corporate responsibility

what's in IT for me?

This chapter provides an overview of how organizations build information systems. As a business student, you need to understand this process because information systems are the underlying foundations of company operations. Your understanding of the principles of building information systems will make you a more valuable employee. You will be able to identify trouble spots early and make suggestions during the design process that will result in a better information systems project—one that satisfies both you and your business.

Building an information system is like constructing a house. You could sit back and let the developers do all the design work, construction, and testing and hope the finished product will satisfy your needs. However, participating in the process helps to guarantee that

continued on p. 206

CHAPTER OUTLINE

SECTION 9-1 >>
Developing Enterprise Applications
- Developing Software
- The Systems Development Life Cycle (SDLC)
- Traditional Software Development Methodology: The Waterfall
- Agile Software Development Methodologies
- Developing Successful Software

SECTION 9-2 >>
Project Management
- Managing Software Development Projects
- Choosing Strategic Projects
- Understanding Project Planning
- Managing Projects
- Outsourcing Projects

continued from p. 205

your needs are not only heard, but also met. It is good business practice to have direct user input steering the development of the finished product. Your knowledge of the systems development process will allow you to participate and ensure you are building flexible enterprise architectures that support not only current business needs, but also future ones. ■

{SECTION 9-1}
Developing Enterprise Applications

LEARNING OUTCOMES

L09-1 Explain the relationship between the systems development life cycle and software development along with the business benefits associated with successful software development.

L09-2 Describe the seven phases of the systems development life cycle.

L09-3 Summarize the different software development methodologies.

DEVELOPING SOFTWARE L09-1

The multimillion-dollar Nike SCM system failure is legendary as Nike CEO Philip Knight famously stated, "This is what we get for our $400 million?" Nike partnered with i2 to implement an SCM system that never came to fruition. i2 blamed the failed implementation on the fact that Nike failed to use the vendor's implementation methodology and templates. Nike blamed the failure on faulty software.[1]

It is difficult to get an organization to work if its systems do not work. In the information age, software success, or failure, can lead directly to business success, or failure. Companies rely on software to drive business operations and ensure work flows throughout the company. As more and more companies rely on software to operate, so do the business-related consequences of software successes and failures.

The potential advantages of successful software implementations provide firms with significant incentives to manage software development risks. However, an alarmingly high number of software development projects come in late or over budget, and successful projects tend to maintain fewer features and

> In the information age, software success, or failure, can lead directly to business success, or failure.

functions than originally specified. Understanding the basics of software development, or the systems development life cycle, will help organizations avoid potential software development pitfalls and ensure that software development efforts are successful.

L09-1 Explain the business benefits associated with successful software development.

THE SYSTEMS DEVELOPMENT LIFE CYCLE (SDLC) L09-2

The *systems development life cycle (SDLC)* is the overall process for developing information systems, from planning and analysis through implementation and maintenance. The SDLC is the foundation for all systems development methods, and hundreds of different activities are associated with each phase. These activities typically include determining budgets, gathering system requirements, and writing detailed user documentation.

The SDLC begins with a business need, proceeds to an assessment of the functions a system must have to satisfy the need, and ends when the benefits of the system no longer outweigh its maintenance costs. This is why it is referred to as a life cycle. The SDLC is comprised of seven distinct phases: planning, analysis, design, development, testing, implementation, and maintenance (see Figure 9.1).

1. **Planning:** The *planning phase* establishes a high-level plan of the intended project and determines project goals. Planning is the first and most critical phase of any systems development effort an organization undertakes, regardless of whether

FIGURE 9.1 The Systems Development Life Cycle

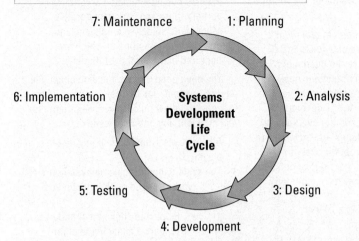

7: Maintenance

1: Planning

6: Implementation

2: Analysis

Systems Development Life Cycle

5: Testing

3: Design

4: Development

the effort is to develop a system that allows customers to order products online, determine the best logistical structure for warehouses around the world, or develop a strategic information alliance with another organization. Organizations must carefully plan the activities (and determine why they are necessary) to be successful.

2. **Analysis:** In the *analysis phase* the firm analyzes its end-user business requirements and refines project goals into defined functions and operations of the intended system. **Business requirements** are the specific business requests the system must meet to be successful, so the analysis phase is critical. The organization must spend as much time, energy, and resources as necessary to perform it accurately and in detail.

3. **Design:** The *design phase* establishes descriptions of the desired features and operations of the system including screen layouts, business rules, process diagrams, pseudo code, and other documentation.

4. **Development:** The *development phase* takes all the detailed design documents from the design phase and transforms them into the actual system. In this phase the project transitions from preliminary designs to actual physical implementation.

5. **Testing:** The *testing phase* brings all the project pieces together into a special testing environment to eliminate errors and bugs, and verify that the system meets all the business requirements defined in the analysis phase.

6. **Implementation:** In the *implementation phase* the organization places the system into production so users can begin to perform actual business operations with it.

7. **Maintenance:** Maintaining the system is the final sequential phase of any systems development effort. In the *maintenance phase* the organization performs changes, corrections, additions, and upgrades to ensure the system continues to meet its business goals. This phase continues for the life of the system because the system must change as the business evolves and its needs change, which means conducting constant monitoring, supporting the new system with frequent minor changes (for example, new reports or information capturing), and reviewing the system to be sure it is moving the organization toward its strategic goals.

LO9-2 Describe the seven phases of the systems development life cycle.

TRADITIONAL SOFTWARE DEVELOPMENT METHODOLOGY: THE WATERFALL LO9-3

Today, systems are so large and complex that teams of architects, analysts, developers, testers, and users must work together to create the millions of lines of custom-written code that drive enterprises. For this reason, developers have created a number of different systems development life cycle methodologies. A *methodology* is a set of policies, procedures, standards, processes, practices, tools, techniques, and tasks that

Have You Met Ted? If Not, You Need To![2]

You'll remember this day because it is the day you were introduced to Ted (www.ted.com). Ted, a small nonprofit started in 1984, is devoted to Ideas Worth Spreading, an annual conference focused around three worlds: Technology, Entertainment, and Design. Ted brings together the world's most fascinating thinkers and doers, who are challenged to give the talk of their lives in 18 minutes. Each talk is videotaped and posted to the Ted website including such famous speakers as:

- Chris Anderson: editor of *Wired* and author of *Technology's Long Tail.*
- Tim Berners-Lee: inventor of the World Wide Web.
- Jeff Bezos: founder of Amazon.com.
- Richard Branson: founder of Virgin.
- Bill Clinton: former President of the United States.
- Peter Diamandis: runs the X Prize Foundation.
- Sergey Brin and Larry Page: co-founders of Google.
- Malcolm Gladwell: author of *Blink* and *The Tipping Point.*
- Bill Gates: founder of Microsoft.
- Seth Godin: marketing guru.
- Steven Levitt: *Freakanomics* author.

How can you use Ted to find innovation in the business environment?

Reducing Ambiguity in Business Requirements

The number one reason projects fail is because of bad business requirements. Business requirements are considered "bad" because of ambiguity or insufficient involvement of end users during analysis and design. A requirement is unambiguous if it has the same interpretation for all parties. Different interpretations by different participants will usually result in unmet expectations. Here is an example of an ambiguous requirement and an example of an unambiguous requirement:

- **Ambiguous requirement:** The financial report must show profits in local and U.S. currencies.
- **Unambiguous requirement:** The financial report must show profits in local and U.S. currencies using the exchange rate printed in *The Wall Street Journal* for the last business day of the period being reported.

Ambiguity is impossible to prevent completely because it is

introduced into requirements in natural ways. For example:

- Requirements can contain technical implications that are obvious to the IT developers but not to the customers.
- Requirements can contain business implications that are obvious to the customer but not to the IT developers.
- Requirements may contain everyday words whose meanings are "obvious" to everyone, yet different for everyone.
- Requirements are reflections of detailed explanations that may have included

multiple events, multiple perspectives, verbal rephrasing, emotion, iterative refinement, selective emphasis, and body language—none of which are captured in the written statements.

You have been hired to build an employee payroll system for a new coffee shop. Review the following business requirements, and highlight any potential issues.

- All employees must have a unique employee ID.
- The system must track employee hours worked based on the employee's last name.
  - Employees must be scheduled to work a minimum of eight hours per day.
  - Employee payroll is calculated by multiplying the employee's hours worked by $7.25.
  - Managers must be scheduled to work morning shifts.
  - Employees cannot be scheduled to work more than eight hours per day.
  - Servers cannot be scheduled to work morning, afternoon, or evening shifts.
  - The system must allow managers to change and delete employees from the system.

people apply to technical and management challenges. Firms use a methodology to manage the deployment of technology with work plans, requirements documents, and test plans, for instance. A formal methodology can include coding standards, code libraries, development practices, and much more.

The oldest and the best known is the *waterfall methodology,* a sequence of phases in which the output of each phase becomes the input for the next (see Figure 9.2). In the SDLC, this means the steps are performed one at a time, in order, from planning through implementation and maintenance. The traditional waterfall method no longer serves most of today's development efforts, however; it is inflexible and expensive, and it requires rigid adherence to the sequence of steps. Its success rate is only about 1 in 10. Figure 9.3 explains some issues related to the waterfall methodology.[3]

▼**FIGURE 9.2** The Traditional Waterfall Methodology

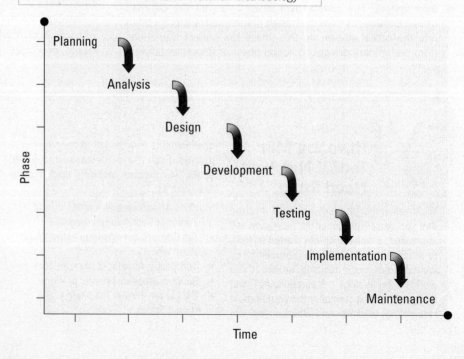

Planning → Analysis → Design → Development → Testing → Implementation → Maintenance

Phase

Time

Issues Related to the Waterfall Methodology	
The business problem	Any flaws in accurately defining and articulating the business problem in terms of what the business users actually require flow onward to the next phase.
The plan	Managing costs, resources, and time constraints is difficult in the waterfall sequence. What happens to the schedule if a programmer quits? How will a schedule delay in a specific phase impact the total cost of the project? Unexpected contingencies may sabotage the plan.
The solution	The waterfall methodology is problematic in that it assumes users can specify all business requirements in advance. Defining the appropriate IT infrastructure that is flexible, scalable, and reliable is a challenge. The final IT infrastructure solution must meet not only current but also future needs in terms of time, cost, feasibility, and flexibility. Vision is inevitably limited at the head of the waterfall.

Today's business environment is fierce. The desire and need to outsmart and outplay competitors remains intense. Given this drive for success, leaders push internal development teams and external vendors to deliver agreed-upon systems faster and cheaper so they can realize benefits as early as possible. Even so, systems remain large and complex. The traditional waterfall methodology no longer serves as an adequate systems development methodology in most cases. Because this development environment is the norm and not the exception anymore, development teams use a new breed of alternative development methods to achieve their business objectives.

LO9-3 Summarize the different software development methodologies.

AGILE SOFTWARE DEVELOPMENT METHODOLOGIES

It is common knowledge that the smaller the project, the greater the success rate. The iterative development style is the ultimate in small projects. Basically, *iterative development* consists of a series of tiny projects. It has become the foundation of multiple agile methodologies. Figure 9.4 displays an iterative approach.

An *agile methodology* aims for customer satisfaction through early and continuous delivery of useful software components developed by an iterative process using the bare minimum

▼FIGURE 9.4 The Iterative Approach

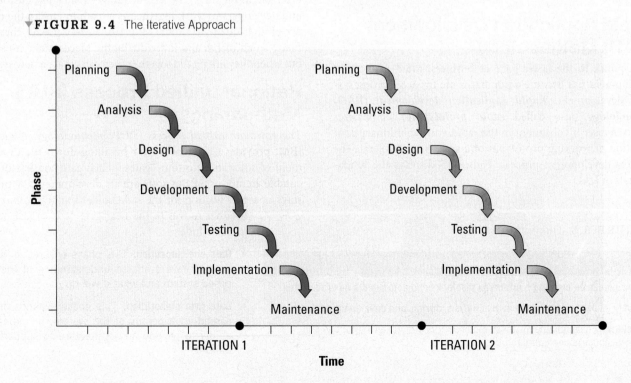

requirements. Agile methodology is what it sounds like: fast and efficient, with lower costs and fewer features. Using agile methods helps refine feasibility and supports the process for getting rapid feedback as functionality is introduced. Developers can adjust as they move along and better clarify unclear requirements.[4]

One key to delivering a successful product or system is to deliver value to users as soon as possible—give them something they want and like early to create buy-in, generate enthusiasm, and, ultimately, reduce scope. Using agile methodologies helps maintain accountability and helps to establish a barometer for the satisfaction of end users. It does no good to accomplish something on time and on budget if it does not satisfy the end user. The primary forms of agile methodologies include:

- Rapid prototyping or rapid application development methodology.
- Extreme programming methodology.
- Rational unified process (RUP) methodology.
- Scrum methodology.

It is important not to get hung up on the names of the methodologies— some are proprietary brand names, others are generally accepted names. It is more important to know how these alternative methodologies are used in today's business environment and the benefits they can deliver.

Rapid Application Development (RAD) Methodology

In response to the faster pace of business, rapid application development has become a popular route for accelerating systems development. *Rapid application development (RAD) methodology* (also called *rapid prototyping*) emphasizes extensive user involvement in the rapid and evolutionary construction of working prototypes of a system, to accelerate the systems development process. Figure 9.5 displays the fundamentals of RAD.

▼**FIGURE 9.5** Fundamentals of RAD

Fundamentals of RAD
Focus initially on creating a prototype that looks and acts like the desired system.
Actively involve system users in the analysis, design, and development phases.
Accelerate collecting the business requirements through an interactive and iterative construction approach.

A *prototype* is a smaller-scale representation or working model of the users' requirements or the proposed design for an information system. The prototype is an essential part of the analysis phase when using the RAD methodology.[5]

Extreme Programming Methodology

Extreme programming (XP) methodology, like other agile methods, breaks a project into four phases, and developers cannot continue to the next phase until the previous phase is complete. The delivery strategy supporting XP is that the quicker the feedback the more improved the results. XP has four basic phases: planning, designing, coding, and testing. Planning can include user interviews, meetings, and small releases. During design, functionality is not added until it is required or needed. During coding, the developers work together soliciting continuous feedback from users, eliminating the communication gap that generally exists between developers and customers. During testing, the test requirements are generated before any code is developed. Extreme programming saves time and produces successful projects by continuously reviewing and revamping needed and unneeded requirements.[6]

Customer satisfaction is the primary reason XP finds success as developers quickly respond to changing business requirements, even late in the life cycle. XP encourages managers, customers, and developers to work together as a team to ensure the delivery of high-quality systems. XP is similar to a puzzle; there are many small pieces and individually the pieces make no sense, but when they are pieced together they can create a new system.

Rational Unified Process (RUP) Methodology

The *rational unified process (RUP) methodology,* owned by IBM, provides a framework for breaking down the development of software into four "gates." Each gate consists of executable iterations of the software in development. A project stays in a gate waiting for the stakeholder's analysis, and then it either moves to the next gate or is canceled. The gates include:[7]

- **Gate one: inception.** This phase ensures all stakeholders have a shared understanding of the proposed system and what it will do.
- **Gate two: elaboration.** This phase expands on the agreed-upon details of the system, including the ability to provide an architecture to support and build it.

- **Gate three: construction.** This phase includes building and developing the product.

- **Gate four: transition.** Primary questions answered in this phase address ownership of the system and training of key personnel.

Because RUP is an iterative methodology, the user can reject the product and force the developers to go back to gate one. RUP helps developers avoid reinventing the wheel and focuses on rapidly adding or removing reusable chunks of processes addressing common problems.

Scrum Methodology

Another agile methodology, *scrum methodology,* uses small teams to produce small pieces of software using a series of "sprints," or 30-day intervals, to achieve an appointed goal. In rugby, a scrum is a team pack and everyone in the pack works together to move the ball down the field. In scrum methodology, each day ends or begins with a stand-up meeting to monitor and control the development effort.

DEVELOPING SUCCESSFUL SOFTWARE

Developing projects within budget and on time is challenging. The primary reasons for project failure include:

- Unclear or missing business requirements.

- Skipping SDLC phases.

- Changing technology.

- The cost of finding errors.

Unclear or Missing Business Requirements

The most common reason systems fail is because the business requirements are either missing or incorrectly gathered during the analysis phase. The business requirements drive the entire system. If they are not accurate or complete, the system will not be successful.

BUSTED Faking Your Own Death[8]

Facing insurmountable troubles, some people turn to faking their own death to escape legal issues and even the Marines. Here are a few examples:

- Marcus Schrenker, a Wall Street investor whose company was under investigation for fraud, disappeared while flying his plane over Alabama. Schrenker's plane was found in a swamp, and the last anyone heard from Schrenker was a distressed radio call—until he was discovered in a campground a few weeks later.

- A Colorado man returning from a hike reported that his friend, Lance Hering, had been injured on the hike, and rescue teams were dispatched to find the hiker. All the rescuers found was blood, a water bottle, and Hering's shoes. Two years later, Hering was arrested with his father at an airport in Washington state. Hering, a Marine, claimed he faked his death to avoid returning to Iraq, where he feared other soldiers would kill him because of something incriminating he had witnessed.

- One Florida woman, Alison Matera, informed her friends, family, and church choir that she was entering hospice be-

cause she was dying of cancer. Matera's plan unraveled when she appeared at her own funeral service, claiming to be her own long-lost identical twin sister. Police were called, and Matera admitted faking both her cancer and death.

Unexpected situations happen all the time, and the more you plan for them the better prepared you'll be when developing software. Hopefully, your employees are not faking their own deaths, but they will get into accidents, have babies, contract viruses and diseases, and face other life issues. All of these scenarios lead to unplanned absenteeism, which can throw your project plan into a tailspin. What can happen to a project when a key employee suddenly quits or is forced to go on short-term disability? When reviewing all of the different SDLC methodologies, which one offers the greatest flexibility for unplanned employee downtime? If you could choose when your employee was absent, during

which phase in the SDLC would it be the safest if your project were to still continue and achieve success? What can you do to ensure you are preparing for unplanned absenteeism on your project plan?

glossary

802.11 A set of standards carrying out wireless local area network communication.

3G A service that brings wireless broadband to mobile phones.

A

acceptable use policy (AUP) A policy that a user must agree to follow to be provided access to corporate email, information systems, and the Internet.

accessibility Refers to the varying levels that define what a user can access, view, or perform when operating a system.

accounting and finance ERP component Manages accounting data and financial processes within the enterprise with functions such as general ledger, accounts payable, accounts receivable, budgeting, and asset management.

administrator access Unrestricted access to the entire system.

adware Software, while purporting to serve some useful function and often fulfilling that function, also allows Internet advertisers to display advertisements without the consent of the computer user.

agile methodology Aims for customer satisfaction through early and continuous delivery of useful software components developed by an iterative process using the bare minimum requirements.

agile MIS infrastructure Includes the hardware, software, and telecommunications equipment that, when combined, provides the underlying foundation to support the organization's goals.

analysis phase The firm analyzes its end-user business requirements and refines project goals into defined functions and operations of the intended system.

analytical CRM Supports back-office operations and strategic analysis and includes all systems that do not deal directly with the customers.

analytical information Encompasses all organizational information, and its primary purpose is to support the performing of managerial analysis or semistructured decisions.

anti-spam policy Simply states that email users will not send unsolicited emails (or spam).

antivirus software Scans and searches hard drives to prevent, detect, and remove known viruses, adware, and spyware.

application programming interface (API) A set of routines, protocols, and tools for building software applications.

application software Used for specific information processing needs, including payroll, customer relationship management, project management, training, and many others.

arithmetic-logic unit (ALU) Performs all arithmetic operations (for example, addition and subtraction) and all logic operations (such as sorting and comparing numbers).

artificial intelligence (AI) Simulates human thinking and behavior such as the ability to reason and learn.

as-is process model Represents the current state of the operation that has been mapped, without any specific improvements or changes to existing processes.

association detection Reveals the relationship between variables along with the nature and frequency of the relationships.

asynchronous communication Communication such as email in which the message and the response do not occur at the same time.

attribute The data elements associated with an entity.

authentication A method for confirming users' identities.

authorization The process of providing a user with permission including access levels and abilities such as file access, hours of access, and amount of allocated storage space.

automation Involves computerizing manual tasks making them more efficient and effective and dramatically lowering operational costs.

availability Refers to the time frames when the system is operational.

B

backup An exact copy of a system's information.

backward integration Takes information entered into a given system and sends it automatically to all upstream systems and processes.

balanced scorecard A management system, as well as a measurement system, that a firm uses to translate business strategies into executable tasks.

bandwidth The maximum amount of data that can pass from one point to another in a unit of time.

benchmark Baseline values the system seeks to attain.

benchmarking A process of continuously measuring system results, comparing those results to optimal system performance (benchmark values), and identifying steps and procedures to improve system performance.

biometrics The identification of a user based on a physical characteristic, such as a fingerprint, iris, face, voice, or handwriting.

bit The smallest element of data and has a value of either 0 or 1.

bit rate The number of bits transferred or received per unit of time.

black-hat hacker Breaks into other people's computer systems and may just look around or may steal and destroy information.

blog, or web log An online journal that allows users to post their own comments, graphics, and video.

bluetooth Wireless PAN technology that transmits signals over short distances between cell phones, computers, and other devices.

bottleneck Occurs when resources reach full capacity and cannot handle any additional demands; they limit throughput and impede operations.

broadband A high-speed Internet connection that is always connected.

bullwhip effect Occurs when distorted product-demand information ripples from one partner to the next throughout the supply chain.

business continuity planning (BCP) Details how a company recovers and restores critical business operations and systems after a disaster or extended disruption.

business-critical integrity constraint Enforces business rules vital to an organization's success and often requires more insight and knowledge than relational integrity constraints.

business facing process Invisible to the external customer but essential to the effective management of the business; they include goal setting, day-to-day planning, giving performance feedback and rewards, and allocating resources.

business intelligence (BI) Information collected from multiple sources such as suppliers, customers, competitors, partners, and industries that analyze patterns, trends, and relationships for strategic decision making.

business model A plan that details how a company creates, delivers, and generates revenues.

business process Standardized set of activities that accomplish a specific task.

business process improvement Attempts to understand and measure the current process and make performance improvements accordingly.

business process management (BPM) system Focuses on evaluating and improving processes that include both person-to-person work flow and system-to-system communications.

business process model A graphic description of a process, showing the sequence of process tasks, which is developed for a specific purpose and from a selected viewpoint.

business process modeling (or mapping) The activity of creating a detailed flowchart or process map of a work process that shows its inputs, tasks, and activities in a structured sequence.

business process reengineering (BPR) The analysis and redesign of workflow within and between enterprises.

business requirement The specific business requests the system must meet to be successful.

business rule A statement that defines an aspect of a business.

business strategy A leadership plan that achieves a specific set of goals or objectives.

business-to-business (B2B) Applies to businesses buying from and selling to each other over the Internet.

business-to-consumer (B2C) Applies to any business that sells its products or services directly to consumers online.

buyer power One of Porter's five forces; measures the ability of buyers to directly affect the price they are willing to pay for an item.

C

cache memory A small unit of ultra-fast memory that is used to store recently accessed or frequently accessed data so that the CPU does not have to retrieve this data from slower memory circuits such as RAM.

call scripting system Gathers product details and issue resolution information that can be automatically generated into a script for the representative to read to the customer.

campaign management system Guides users through marketing campaigns by performing such tasks as campaign definition, planning, scheduling, segmentation, and success analysis

capacity planning Determines future environmental infrastructure requirements to ensure high-quality system performance.

cardinality Expresses the specific number of instances in an entity.

central processing unit (CPU) The actual hardware that interprets and executes the program (software) instructions and coordinates how all the other hardware devices work together.

certificate authority A trusted third party, such as VeriSign, that validates user identities by means of digital certificates.

change control board (CCB) Responsible for approving or rejecting all change requests.

change management Offers procedures and policies managers can use to help manage change during system development.

change management system Includes a collection of procedures to document a change request and identifies the expected impact associated with the change.

chief information officer (CIO) Responsible for (1) overseeing all uses of MIS and (2) ensuring that MIS strategically aligns with business goals and objectives.

chief knowledge officer (CKO) Responsible for collecting, maintaining, and distributing company knowledge.

chief privacy officer (CPO) Responsible for ensuring the ethical and legal use of information within a company.

chief security officer (CSO) Responsible for ensuring the security of business systems and developing strategies and safeguards against attacks from hackers and viruses.

chief technology officer (CTO) Responsible for ensuring the speed, accuracy, availability, and reliability for MIS.

clickstream data Exact pattern of a consumer's navigation through a site.

click-to-talk Allows customers to click on a button and talk with a representative via the Internet.

client A computer designed to request information from a server.

client/server network A model for applications in which the bulk of the back-end processing, such as performing a physical search of a database, takes place on a server, while the front-end processing, which involves communicating with the users, is handled by the clients.

cloud computing Refers to the use of resources and applications hosted remotely on the Internet.

cluster analysis A technique used to divide information sets into mutually exclusive groups such that the members of each group are as close together as possible to one another and the different groups are as far apart as possible.

coaxial cable Cable that can carry a wide range of frequencies with low signal loss.

cold site A separate facility that does not have any computer equipment but is a place where employees can move after a disaster.

collaboration system A set of tools that supports the work of teams or groups by facilitating the sharing and flow of information.

collective intelligence Collaborating and tapping into the core knowledge of all employees, partners, and customers.

communication device Equipment used to send information and receive it from one location to another.

competitive advantage A feature of a product or service on which customers place a greater value than on similar offerings from competitors.

competitive intelligence The process of gathering information about the competitive environment, including competitors' plans, activities, and products, to improve a company's ability to succeed.

complex instruction set computer (CISC) chips Type of CPU that can recognize as many as 100 or more instructions, enough to carry out most computations directly.

composite entities Entities that exist to represent the relationship between two other entities.

computer An electronic device operating under the control of instructions stored in its own memory that can accept, manipulate, and store data.

confidentiality The assurance that messages and information remain available only to those authorized to view them.

consolidation The aggregation of data from simple roll-ups to complex groupings of interrelated information.

consumer-to-business (C2B) Applies to any consumer who sells a product or service to a business on the Internet.

consumer-to-consumer (C2C) Applies to customers offering goods and services to each other on the Internet.

contact center or call center Where customer service representatives answer customer inquiries and solve problems, usually by email, chat, or phone.

contact management CRM system   Maintains customer contact information and identifies prospective customers for future sales, using tools such as organizational charts, detailed customer notes, and supplemental sales information.

content filtering   Occurs when organizations use software that filters content, such as emails, to prevent the accidental or malicious transmission of unauthorized information.

content management system (CMS)   Helps companies manage the creation, storage, editing, and publication of their website content.

control unit   Interprets software instructions and literally tells the other hardware devices what to do, based on the software instructions.

copyright   The legal protection afforded an expression of an idea, such as a song, book, or video game.

core ERP components   The traditional components included in most ERP systems and primarily focus on internal operations.

corporate social responsibility   Companies' acknowledged responsibility to society.

counterfeit software   Software that is manufactured to look like the real thing and sold as such.

cracker   A hacker with criminal intent.

critical path   Estimates the shortest path through the project ensuring all critical tasks are completed from start to finish.

critical success factors (CSFs)   Crucial steps companies perform to achieve their goals and objectives and implement their strategies.

CRM analysis technologies   Help organizations segment their customers into categories such as best and worst customers.

CRM predicting technologies   Help organizations predict customer behavior, such as which customers are at risk of leaving.

CRM reporting technologies   Help organizations identify their customers across other applications.

cross-selling   Selling additional products or services to an existing customer.

crowdsourcing   Refers to the wisdom of the crowd.

cube   The common term for the representation of multidimensional information.

customer facing process   Results in a product or service that is received by an organization's external customer.

customer relationship management (CRM)   A means of managing all aspects of a customer's relationship with an organization to increase customer loyalty and retention and an organization's profitability.

cybermediation   Refers to the creation of new kinds of intermediaries that simply could not have existed before the advent of ebusiness.

cyberterrorists   Seek to cause harm to people or to destroy critical systems or information and use the Internet as a weapon of mass destruction.

cycle time   The time required to process an order.

D

data   Raw facts that describe the characteristics of an event or object.

data center   A facility used to house management information systems and associated components, such as telecommunications and storage systems.

data dictionary   Compiles all of the metadata about the data elements in the data model.

data-driven website   An interactive website kept constantly updated and relevant to the needs of its customers using a database.

data element (or data field)   The smallest or basic unit of information.

data governance   The overall management of the availability, usability, integrity, and security of company data.

data inconsistency   Occurs when the same data element has different values.

data integrity issue   Occurs when a system produces incorrect, inconsistent, or duplicate data.

data mart   Contains a subset of data warehouse information.

data mining   The process of analyzing data to extract information not offered by the raw data alone.

data-mining tool   Uses a variety of techniques to find patterns and relationships in large volumes of information that predict future behavior and guide decision making.

data model   Logical data structures that detail the relationships among data elements using graphics or pictures.

data quality audit   Determines the accuracy and completeness of its data.

data redundancy   The duplication of data, or the storage of the same data in multiple places.

data warehouse   A logical collection of information, gathered from many different operational databases, that supports business analysis activities and decision-making tasks.

database   Maintains information about various types of objects (inventory), events (transactions), people (employees), and places (warehouses).

database management system (DBMS)   Creates, reads, updates, and deletes data in a database while controlling access and security.

decision support system (DSS)   Model information using OLAP, which provides assistance in evaluating and choosing among different courses of action.

demand planning system   Generates demand forecasts using statistical tools and forecasting techniques, so companies can respond faster and more effectively to consumer demands through supply chain enhancements.

dependency   A logical relationship that exists between the project tasks, or between a project task and a milestone.

design phase   Establishes descriptions of the desired features and operations of the system including screen layouts, business rules, process diagrams, pseudo code, and other documentation.

development phase   Takes all the detailed design documents from the design phase and transforms them into the actual system.

digital certificate   A data file that identifies individuals or organizations online and is comparable to a digital signature.

digital Darwinism   Implies that organizations that cannot adapt to the new demands placed on them for surviving in the information age are doomed to extinction.

digital dashboard   Tracks KPIs and CSFs by compiling information from multiple sources and tailoring it to meet user needs.

digital divide   A worldwide gap giving advantage to those with access to technology.

digital subscriber line (DSL)   Allows high-speed digital data transmission over standard telephone lines.

disaster recovery cost curve   Charts (1) the cost to the company of the unavailability of information and technology and (2) the cost to the company of recovering from a disaster over time.

disaster recovery plan   A detailed process for recovering information or a system in the event of a catastrophic disaster.

disintermediation Occurs when a business sells direct to the customer online and cuts out the intermediary.

disruptive technology A new way of doing things that initially does not meet the needs of existing customers.

domain name system (DNS) Converts IP address into domains, or identifying labels that use a variety of recognizable naming conventions.

downtime Refers to a period of time when a system is unavailable.

drill-down Enables users to view details, and details of details, of information.

dumpster diving Looking through people's trash, another way hackers obtain information.

dynamic scaling Means that the MIS infrastructure can be automatically scaled up or down based on needed requirements.

E

ebusiness Includes ecommerce along with all activities related to internal and external business operations such as servicing customer accounts, collaborating with partners, and exchanging real-time information.

ebusiness model A plan that details how a company creates, delivers, and generates revenues on the Internet.

ecommerce The buying and selling of goods and services over the Internet.

ediscovery (or electronic discovery) Refers to the ability of a company to identify, search, gather, seize, or export digital information in responding to a litigation, audit, investigation, or information inquiry.

effectiveness MIS metrics Measure the impact MIS has on business processes and activities including customer satisfaction and customer conversion rates.

efficiency MIS metrics Measure the performance of MIS itself such as throughput, transaction speed, and system availability.

egovernment Involves the use of strategies and technologies to transform government(s) by improving the delivery of services and enhancing the quality of interaction between the citizen-consumer and all branches of government.

electronic data interchange (EDI) A standard format for the electronic exchange of information between supply chain participants.

elogistics Manages the transportation and storage of goods.

email privacy policy Details the extent to which email messages may be read by others.

emergency notification service An infrastructure built for notifying people in the event of an emergency.

employee monitoring policy States explicitly how, when, and where the company monitors its employees.

employee relationship management (ERM) Provides web-based self-service tools that streamline and automate the human resource department.

encryption Scrambles information into an alternative form that requires a key or password to decrypt.

enterprise application integration (EAI) Connects the plans, methods, and tools aimed at integrating separate enterprise systems.

enterprise application integration (EAI) middleware Takes a new approach to middleware by packaging commonly used applications together, reducing the time needed to integrate applications from multiple vendors.

enterprise architect A person grounded in technology, fluent in business, and able to provide the important bridge between MIS and the business.

enterprise resource planning (ERP) Integrates all departments and functions throughout an organization into a single IT system (or integrated set of IT systems) so employees can make decisions by viewing enterprisewide information about all business operations.

enterprise system Provides enterprisewide support and data access for a firm's operations and business processes.

entity Stores information about a person, place, thing, transaction, or event.

entity-relationship diagram (ERD) A technique for documenting the entities and relationships in a database environment.

entry barrier A feature of a product or service that customers have come to expect and entering competitors must offer the same for survival.

epolicies Policies and procedures that address information management along with the ethical use of computers and the Internet in the business environment.

eprocurement The business-to-business (B2B) online purchase and sale of supplies and services.

eshop (estore or etailer) An online version of a retail store where customers can shop at any hour.

ethernet A physical and data layer technology for LAN networking.

ethical computer use policy Contains general principles to guide computer user behavior.

ethics The principles and standards that guide our behavior toward other people.

ewaste Refers to discarded, obsolete, or broken electronic devices.

executive information system (EIS) A specialized DSS that supports senior-level executives and unstructured, long-term, nonroutine decisions requiring judgment, evaluation, and insight.

executive sponsor The person or group who provides the financial resources for the project.

expert system Computerized advisory programs that imitate the reasoning processes of experts in solving difficult problems.

explicit knowledge Consists of anything that can be documented, archived, and codified, often with the help of IT.

extended ERP component The extra components that meet organizational needs not covered by the core components and primarily focus on external operations.

extraction, transformation, and loading (ETL) A process that extracts information from internal and external databases, transforms it using a common set of enterprise definitions, and loads it into a data warehouse.

extranet An extension of an intranet that is only available to authorized outsiders, such as customers, partners, and suppliers.

extreme programming (XP) methodology Breaks a project into four phases, and developers cannot continue to the next phase until the previous phase is complete.

F

fact The confirmation or validation of an event or object.

failback Occurs when the primary machine recovers and resumes operations, taking over from the secondary server.

failover A specific type of fault tolerance, occurs when a redundant storage server offers an exact replica of the real-time data, and if the primary server crashes the users are automatically directed to the secondary server or backup server.

fault tolerance A general concept that a system has the ability to respond to unexpected failures or system crashes as the backup system immediately and automatically takes over with no loss of service.

feedback Information that returns to its original transmitter (input, transform, or output) and modifies the transmitter's actions.

fiber optic (or optical fiber) Refers to the technology associated with the transmission of information as light impulses along a glass wire or fiber.

field A characteristic of a table.

firewall Hardware and/or software that guards a private network by analyzing incoming and outgoing information for the correct markings.

first-mover advantage An advantage that occurs when a company can significantly increase its market share by being first to market with a competitive advantage.

flash memory A special type of rewritable read-only memory (ROM) that is compact and portable.

folksonomy Similar to taxonomy except that crowdsourcing determines the tags or keyword-based classification system.

forecasts Predictions based on time-series information.

foreign key A primary key of one table that appears as an attribute in another table and acts to provide a logical relationship between the two tables.

forward integration Takes information entered into a given system and sends it automatically to all downstream systems and processes.

fuzzy logic A mathematical method of handling imprecise or subjective information.

G

Gantt chart A simple bar chart that lists project tasks vertically against the project's time frame, listed horizontally.

genetic algorithm An artificial intelligence system that mimics the evolutionary, survival-of-the-fittest process to generate increasingly better solutions to a problem.

geographic information system (GIS) Consists of hardware, software, and data that provide location information for display on a multidimensional map.

gigabyte (GB) Roughly 1 billion bytes.

gigahertz (GHz) The number of billions of CPU cycles per second.

global positioning system (GPS) A satellite-based navigation system providing extremely accurate position, time, and speed information.

goal-seeking analysis Finds the inputs necessary to achieve a goal such as a desired level of output.

granularity Refers to the level of detail in the model or the decision-making process.

grid computing A collection of computers, often geographically dispersed, that are coordinated to solve a common problem.

H

hackers Experts in technology who use their knowledge to break into computers and computer networks, either for profit or motivated by the challenge.

hactivists Have philosophical and political reasons for breaking into systems and will often deface the website as a protest.

hard drive A secondary storage medium that uses several rigid disks coated with a magnetically sensitive material and housed together with the recording heads in a hermetically sealed mechanism.

hardware Consists of the physical devices associated with a computer system.

high availability Occurs when a system is continuously operational at all times.

hot site A separate and fully equipped facility where the company can move immediately after a disaster and resume business.

human resources ERP component Tracks employee information including payroll, benefits, compensation, and performance assessment and ensures compliance with all laws.

hypertext markup language (HTML) Links documents allowing users to move from one to another simply by clicking on a hot spot or link.

hypertext transport protocol (HTTP) The Internet protocol web browsers use to request and display web pages using universal resource locators.

I

identity theft The forging of someone's identity for the purpose of fraud.

implementation phase The organization places the system into production so users can begin to perform actual business operations with it.

information Data converted into a meaningful and useful context.

information age The present time, during which infinite quantities of facts are widely available to anyone who can use a computer.

information architecture The set of ideas about how all information in a given context should be organized.

information cleansing or scrubbing A process that weeds out and fixes or discards inconsistent, incorrect, or incomplete information.

information compliance The act of conforming, acquiescing, or yielding information.

information ethics Govern the ethical and moral issues arising from the development and use of information technologies, as well as the creation, collection, duplication, distribution, and processing of information itself (with or without the aid of computer technologies).

information governance A method or system of government for information management or control.

information granularity The extent of detail within the information (fine and detailed or coarse and abstract).

information integrity A measure of the quality of information.

information management Examines the organizational resource of information and regulates its definitions, uses, value, and distribution ensuring it has the types of data/information required to function and grow effectively.

information MIS infrastructure Identifies where and how important information, such as customer records, is maintained and secured.

information privacy policy Contains general principles regarding information privacy.

information reach Measures the number of people a firm can communicate with all over the world.

information richness Refers to the depth and breadth of details contained in a piece of textual, graphic, audio, or video information.

information security A broad term encompassing the protection of information from accidental or intentional misuse by persons inside or outside an organization.

information security plan Details how an organization will implement the information security policies.

information security policies Identify the rules required to maintain information security, such as requiring users to log off before leaving for lunch or meetings, never sharing passwords with anyone, and changing passwords every 30 days.

information technology monitoring Tracks people's activities by such measures as number of keystrokes, error rate, and number of transactions processed.

infrastructure as a service (IaaS) The delivery of computer hardware capability, including the use of servers, networking, and storage, as a service. A service that delivers hardware networking capabilities, including the use of servers, networking, and storage over the cloud using a pay-per-use revenue model.

input device Equipment used to capture information and commands.

insiders Legitimate users who purposely or accidentally misuse their access to the environment and cause some kind of business-affecting incident.

in-sourcing (in-house development) Uses the professional expertise within an organization to develop and maintain its information technology systems.

instant messaging (sometimes called IM or IMing) A service that enables "instant" or real-time communication between people.

integration Allows separate systems to communicate directly with each other, eliminating the need for manual entry into multiple systems.

integrity constraint Rules that help ensure the quality of information.

intellectual property Intangible creative work that is embodied in physical form and includes copyrights, trademarks, and patents.

intelligent agent A special-purpose knowledge-based information system that accomplishes specific tasks on behalf of its users.

intelligent system Various commercial applications of artificial intelligence.

interactivity Measures advertising effectiveness by counting visitor interactions with the target ad, including time spent viewing the ad, number of pages viewed, and number of repeat visits to the advertisement.

intermediaries Agents, software, or businesses that provide a trading infrastructure to bring buyers and sellers together.

Internet A massive network that connects computers all over the world and allows them to communicate with one another.

Internet cable connection Provides Internet access using a cable television company's infrastructure and a special cable modem.

Internet protocol TV (IPTV) Distributes digital video content using IP across the Internet and private IP networks.

Internet protocol version 6 (IPv6) The "next generation" protocol designed to replace the current version Internet protocol, IP version 4 (IPv4)

Internet service provider (ISP) A company that provides access to the Internet for a monthly fee.

Internet use policy Contains general principles to guide the proper use of the Internet.

interoperability The capability of two or more computer systems to share data and resources, even though they are made by different manufacturers.

intranet A restricted network that relies on Internet technologies to provide an Internet-like environment within the company for information sharing, communications, collaboration, web publishing, and the support of business process.

intrusion detection software (IDS) Features full-time monitoring tools that search for patterns in network traffic to identify intruders.

iterative development Consists of a series of tiny projects.

K

key performance indicators (KPIs) Quantifiable metrics a company uses to evaluate progress toward critical success factors.

kill switch A trigger that enables a project manager to close the project before completion.

knowledge Skills, experience, and expertise coupled with information and intelligence that creates a person's intellectual resources.

knowledge management (KM) Involves capturing, classifying, evaluating, retrieving, and sharing information assets in a way that provides context for effective decisions and actions.

knowledge management system (KMS) Supports the capturing, organization, and dissemination of knowledge (i.e., know-how) throughout an organization.

knowledge workers Individuals valued for their ability to interpret and analyze information.

L

legacy system A current or existing system that will become the base for upgrading or integrating with a new system.

list generator Compiles customer information from a variety of sources and segments it for different marketing campaigns.

local area network (LAN) Connects a group of computers in proximity, such as in an office building, school, or home.

location-based services (LBS) Applications that use location information to provide a service.

logical view Shows how individual users logically access information to meet their own particular business needs.

long tail Referring to the tail of a typical sales curve.

loyalty program A program to reward customers based on spending.

M

magnetic medium A secondary storage medium that uses magnetic techniques to store and retrieve data on disks or tapes coated with magnetically sensitive materials.

magnetic tape An older secondary storage medium that uses a strip of thin plastic coated with a magnetically sensitive recording medium.

mail bomb Sends a massive amount of email to a specific person or system that can cause that user's server to stop functioning.

maintainability (or flexibility) Refers to how quickly a system can transform to support environmental changes.

maintenance phase The organization performs changes, corrections, additions, and upgrades to ensure the system continues to meet its business goals.

management information systems A business function, like accounting and human resources, which moves information about people, products, and processes across the company to facilitate decision making and problem solving.

many-to-many relationship (M:N) Between two entities in which an instance of one entity is related to many instances of another and one instance of the other can be related to many instances of the first entity.

market basket analysis Analyzes such items as websites and checkout scanner information to detect customers' buying behavior and predict future behavior by identifying affinities among customers' choices of products and services.

market share The proportion of the market that a firm captures.

mashup A website or web application that uses content from more than one source to create a completely new product or service.

mashup editor WYSIWYGs or What You See Is What You Get tools.

mass customization The ability of an organization to tailor its products or services to the customers' specifications.

megabyte (MB or M or Meg)   Roughly 1 million bytes.

megahertz (MHz)   The number of millions of CPU cycles per second.

memory cards   Contain high-capacity storage that holds data such as captured images, music, or text files.

memory sticks   Provide nonvolatile memory for a range of portable devices including computers, digital cameras, MP3 players, and PDAs.

metadata   Details about data.

Metcalfe's Law   The value of a network increases as its number of users grows.

methodology   A set of policies, procedures, standards, processes, practices, tools, techniques, and tasks that people apply to technical and management challenges.

metrics   Measurements that evaluate results to determine whether a project is meeting its goals.

metropolitan area network (MAN)   A large computer network usually spanning a city.

microblogging   The practice of sending brief posts (140 to 200 characters) to a personal blog, either publicly or to a private group of subscribers who can read the posts as IMs or as text messages.

middleware   Several different types of software that sit between and provide connectivity for two or more software applications.

MIS infrastructure   Includes the plans for how a firm will build, deploy, use, and share its data, processes, and MIS assets.

mobile business (or mbusiness, mcommerce)   The ability to purchase goods and services through a wireless Internet-enabled device.

model   A simplified representation or abstraction of reality.

modem   A device that enables a computer to transmit and receive data.

Moore's Law   Refers to the computer chip performance per dollar doubling every 18 months.

multitasking   Allows more than one piece of software to be used at a time.

multi-valued attribute   Having the potential to contain more than one value for an attribute.

N

national service providers (NSPs)   Private companies that own and maintain the worldwide backbone that supports the Internet.

nearshore outsourcing   Contracting an outsourcing arrangement with a company in a nearby country.

network   A communications system created by linking two or more devices and establishing a standard methodology in which they can communicate.

network access points (NAPs)   Traffic exchange points in the routing hierarchy of the Internet that connects NSPs.

network convergence   The efficient coexistence of telephone, video, and data communication within a single network, offering convenience and flexibility not possible with separate infrastructures.

network effect   Describes how products in a network increase in value to users as the number of users increases.

network operating system (NOS)   Operating system that runs a network, steering information between computers and managing security and users.

network topology   Refers to the geometric arrangement of the actual physical organization of the computers (and other network devices) in a network.

network transmission media   Refers to the various types of media used to carry the signal between computers.

neural network   A category of AI that attempts to emulate the way the human brain works.

nonrepudiation   A contractual stipulation to ensure that ebusiness participants do not deny (repudiate) their online actions.

null-valued attribute   Assigned to an attribute when no other value applies or when a value is unknown.

O

offshore outsourcing   Using organizations from developing countries to write code and develop systems.

one-to-many relationship (1:M)   A relationship between two entities in which an instance of one entity can be related to many instances of a related entity.

one-to-one relationship (1:1)   A relationship between two entities in which an instance of one entity can be related to only one instance of a related entity.

online analytical processing (OLAP)   The manipulation of information to create business intelligence in support of strategic decision making.

online transaction processing (OLTP)   The capturing of transaction and event information using technology to (1) process the information according to defined business rules, (2) store the information, and (3) update existing information to reflect the new information.

onshore outsourcing   Engaging another company within the same country for services.

open source   Refers to any software whose source code is made available free for any third party to review and modify.

open system   Consists of non-proprietary hardware and software based on publicly known standards that allows third parties to create add-on products to plug into or interoperate with the system.

operating system software   Controls the application software and manages how the hardware devices work together.

operational CRM   Supports traditional transactional processing for day-to-day front-office operations or systems that deal directly with the customers.

opportunity management CRM system   Targets sales opportunities by finding new customers or companies for future sales.

optimization analysis   An extension of goal-seeking analysis, finds the optimum value for a target variable by repeatedly changing other variables, subject to specified constraints.

output device   Equipment used to see, hear, or otherwise accept the results of information processing requests.

outsourcing   An arrangement by which one organization provides a service or services for another organization that chooses not to perform them in-house.

P

packet-switching   Occurs when the sending computer divides a message into a number of efficiently sized units of data called packets, each of which contains the address of the destination computer.

paradigm shift   Occurs when a new radical form of business enters the market that reshapes the way companies and organizations behave.

partner relationship management (PRM)   Discovers optimal sales channels by selecting the right partners and identifying mutual customers.

peer-to-peer (P2P) A computer network that relies on the computing power and bandwidth of the participants in the network rather than a centralized server.

performance Measures how quickly a system performs a process or transaction.

personal area networks (PANs) Provide communication over a short distance that is intended for use with devices that are owned and operated by a single user.

personalization Occurs when a company knows enough about a customer's likes and dislikes that it can fashion offers more likely to appeal to that person, say by tailoring its website to individuals or groups based on profile information, demographics, or prior transactions.

PERT (Program Evaluation and Review Technique) chart A graphical network model that depicts a project's tasks and the relationships between them.

pharming Reroutes requests for legitimate websites to false websites.

phishing A technique to gain personal information for the purpose of identity theft, usually by means of fraudulent emails that look as though they came from legitimate sources.

physical view The physical storage of information on a storage device.

pirated software The unauthorized use, duplication, distribution, or sale of copyrighted software.

planning phase Establishes a high-level plan of the intended project and determines project goals.

platform as a service (PaaS) Supports the deployment of entire systems including hardware, networking, and applications using a pay-per-use revenue model.

podcasting Converts an audio broadcast to a digital music player.

portability Refers to the ability of an application to operate on different devices or software platforms, such as different operating systems.

Porter's Five Forces Model A model for analyzing the competitive forces within the environment in which a company operates, to assess the potential for profitability in an industry.

primary key A field (or group of fields) that uniquely identifies a given record in a table.

primary storage Computer's main memory, which consists of the random access memory (RAM), cache memory, and read-only memory (ROM) that is directly accessible to the CPU.

primary value activities Found at the bottom of the value chain, these include business processes that acquire raw materials and manufacture, deliver, market, sell, and provide after-sales services.

privacy The right to be left alone when you want to be, to have control over your personal possessions, and not to be observed without your consent.

product differentiation An advantage that occurs when a company develops unique differences in its products with the intent to influence demand.

production and materials management ERP component Handles production planning and execution tasks such as demand forecasting, production scheduling, job cost accounting, and quality control.

project Temporary activity a company undertakes to create a unique product, service, or result.

project assumptions Factors considered to be true, real, or certain without proof or demonstration.

project charter A document issued by the project initiator or sponsor that formally authorizes the start of a project and provides the project manager with the authority to apply organizational resources to project activities.

project constraint Specific factors that can limit options.

project deliverable Any measurable, tangible, verifiable outcome, result, or item that is produced to complete a project or part of a project.

project management The application of knowledge, skills, tools, and techniques to project activities to meet project requirements.

Project Management Institute (PMI) Develops procedures and concepts necessary to support the profession of project management.

project management office (PMO) An internal department that oversees all organizational projects.

project manager An individual who is an expert in project planning and management, defines and develops the project plan, and tracks the plan to ensure the project is completed on time and on budget.

project milestones Represent key dates when a certain group of activities must be performed.

project objective Quantifiable criteria that must be met for the project to be considered a success.

project plan A formal, approved document that manages and controls project execution.

project scope statement Links the project to the organization's overall business goals.

project stakeholders Individuals and organizations actively involved in the project or whose interests might be affected as a result of project execution or project completion.

protocol A standard that specifies the format of data as well as the rules to be followed during transmission.

prototype A smaller-scale representation or working model of the users' requirements or the proposed design for an information system.

public key encryption (PKE) Uses two keys: a public key that everyone can have and a private key for only the recipient.

Q

query-by-example (QBE) tool Helps users graphically design the answer to a question against a database.

R

radio-frequency identification (RFID) Uses electronic tags and labels to identify objects wirelessly over short distances.

random access memory (RAM) The computer's primary working memory, in which program instructions and data are stored so that they can be accessed directly by the CPU via the processor's high-speed external data bus.

rapid application development (RAD) methodology (also called rapid prototyping) Emphasizes extensive user involvement in the rapid and evolutionary construction of working prototypes of a system, to accelerate the systems development process.

rational unified process (RUP) methodology Provides a framework for breaking down the development of software into four "gates."

read-only memory (ROM) The portion of a computer's primary storage that does not lose its contents when one switches off the power.

real simple syndication (RSS) A web format used to publish frequently updated works, such as blogs, news headlines, audio, and video in a standardized format.

real-time communication Occurs when a system updates information at the same rate it receives it.

real-time information Immediate, up-to-date information.

real-time system Provides real-time information in response to requests.

record A collection of related data elements.

recovery The ability to get a system up and running in the event of a system crash or failure that includes restoring the information backup.

reduced instruction set computer (RISC) chips Limit the number of instructions the CPU can execute to increase processing speed.

redundancy Occurs when a task or activity is unnecessarily repeated.

regional service providers (RSPs) Offer Internet service by connecting to NSPs, but they also can connect directly to each other.

reintermediation Steps are added to the value chain as new players find ways to add value to the business process.

relational database management system Allows users to create, read, update, and delete data in a relational database.

relational database model Stores information in the form of logically related two-dimensional tables.

relational integrity constraints Rules that enforce basic and fundamental information-based constraints.

reliability (or accuracy) Ensures a system is functioning correctly and providing accurate information.

reputation system Where buyers post feedback on sellers.

return on investment (ROI) Indicates the earning power of a project.

rivalry among existing competitors One of Porter's five forces; high when competition is fierce in a market and low when competitors are more complacent.

router An intelligent connecting device that examines each packet of data it receives and then decides which way to send it toward its destination.

S

sales force automation (SFA) Automatically tracks all the steps in the sales process.

sales management CRM system Automates each phase of the sales process, helping individual sales representatives coordinate and organize all their accounts.

satellite A space station that orbits the Earth receiving and transmitting signals from Earth-based stations over a wide area.

scalability Describes how well a system can scale up or adapt to the increased demands of growth.

script kiddies or script bunnies Find hacking code on the Internet and click-and-point their way into systems to cause damage or spread viruses.

scrum methodology Uses small teams to produce small pieces of software using a series of "sprints," or 30-day intervals, to achieve an appointed goal.

secondary storage Consists of equipment designed to store large volumes of data for long-term storage.

secure hypertext transfer protocol (SHTTP or HTTPS) A combination of HTTP and SSL to provide encryption and secure identification of an Internet server.

secure sockets layer (SSL) A standard security technology for establishing an encrypted link between a web server and a browser, ensuring that all data passed between them remain private.

semantic web A component of Web 3.0 that describes things in a way that computers can understand.

semistructured decision Occurs in situations in which a few established processes help to evaluate potential solutions, but not enough to lead to a definite recommended decision.

sensitivity analysis A special case of what-if analysis, is the study of the impact on other variables when one variable is changed repeatedly.

server A computer dedicated to providing information in response to requests.

shopping bot Software that will search several retailer websites and provide a comparison of each retailer's offerings including price and availability.

single-valued attribute Having only a single value of each attribute of an entity.

slice-and-dice The ability to look at information from different perspectives.

smart card A device about the size of a credit card, containing embedded technologies that can store information and small amounts of software to perform some limited processing.

smart grid Delivers electricity using two-way digital technology.

smart phones Offer more advanced computing ability and connectivity than basic cell phones.

social bookmarking Allows users to share, organize, search, and manage bookmarks.

social engineering Hackers use their social skills to trick people into revealing access credentials or other valuable information.

social media Refers to websites that rely on user participation and user-contributed content.

social media policy Outlines the corporate guidelines or principles governing employee online communications.

social network An application that connects people by matching profile information.

social networking The practice of expanding your business and/or social contacts by constructing a personal network.

social networking analysis (SNA) Maps group contacts identifying who knows each other and who works together.

social tagging Describes the collaborative activity of marking shared online content with keywords or tags as a way to organize it for future navigation, filtering, or search.

software The set of instructions the hardware executes to carry out specific tasks.

software as a service (SaaS) Delivers applications over the cloud using a pay-per-use revenue model.

source code Contains instructions written by a programmer specifying the actions to be performed by computer software.

source document The original transaction record.

spam Unsolicited email.

spyware A special class of adware that collects data about the user and transmits it over the Internet without the user's knowledge or permission.

SSL Certificate An electronic document that confirms the identity of a website or server and verifies that a public key belongs to a trustworthy individual or company.

statistical analysis Performs such functions as information correlations, distributions, calculations, and variance analysis.

streaming A method of sending audio and video files over the Internet in such a way that the user can view the file while it is being transferred.

streamlining Improves business process efficiencies simplifying or eliminating unnecessary steps.

structured data   Data already in a database or a spreadsheet.

structured decision   Involves situations where established processes offer potential solutions.

structured query language (SQL)   Users write lines of code to answer questions against a database.

supplier power   One of Porter's five forces; measures the suppliers' ability to influence the prices they charge for supplies (including materials, labor, and services).

supplier relationship management (SRM)   Focuses on keeping suppliers satisfied by evaluating and categorizing suppliers for different projects.

supply chain   All parties involved, directly or indirectly, in obtaining raw materials or a product.

supply chain execution system   Ensures supply chain cohesion by automating the different activities of the supply chain.

supply chain management (SCM)   The management of information flows between and among activities in a supply chain to maximize total supply chain effectiveness and corporate profitability.

supply chain planning system   Uses advanced mathematical algorithms to improve the flow and efficiency of the supply chain while reducing inventory.

supply chain visibility   The ability to view all areas up and down the supply chain in real time.

support value activities   Found along the top of the value chain and includes business processes, such as firm infrastructure, human resource management, technology development, and procurement, that support the primary value activities.

sustainable (or "green") MIS   Describes the production, management, use, and disposal of technology in a way that minimizes damage to the environment.

sustainable MIS disposal   Refers to the safe disposal of MIS assets at the end of their life cycle.

sustainable MIS infrastructure   Identifies ways that a company can grow in terms of computing resources while simultaneously becoming less dependent on hardware and energy consumption.

sustaining technology   Produces an improved product customers are eager to buy, such as a faster car or larger hard drive.

swim lane   Layout arranges the steps of a business process into a set of rows depicting the various elements.

switching costs   Costs that make customers reluctant to switch to another product or service.

synchronous communication   Communication that occurs at the same time such as IM or chat.

system   A collection of parts that link to achieve a common purpose.

system software   Controls how the various technology tools work together along with the application software.

systems development life cycle (SDLC)   The overall process for developing information systems, from planning and analysis through implementation and maintenance.

systems thinking   A way of monitoring the entire system by viewing multiple inputs being processed or transformed to produce outputs while continuously gathering feedback on each part.

T

T1 line   A type of data connection able to transmit a digital signal at 1.544 Mpbs.

table   Composed of rows and columns that represent an entity.

tacit knowledge   The knowledge contained in people's heads.

tags   Specific keywords or phrases incorporated into website content for means of classification or taxonomy.

taxonomy   The scientific classification of organisms into groups based on similarities of structure or origin.

telecommunication system   Enables the transmission of data over public or private networks.

terabyte (TB)   Roughly 1 trillion bytes.

testing phase   Brings all the project pieces together into a special testing environment to eliminate errors and bugs, and verify that the system meets all the business requirements defined in the analysis phase.

text mining   Analyzes unstructured data to find trends and patterns in words and sentences.

threat of new entrants   One of Porter's five forces, high when it is easy for new competitors to enter a market and low when there are significant entry barriers to joining a market.

threat of substitute products or services   One of Porter's five forces, high when there are many alternatives to a product or service and low when there are few alternatives from which to choose.

time-series information   Time-stamped information collected at a particular frequency.

to-be process model   Shows the results of applying change improvement opportunities to the current (As-Is) process model.

tokens   Small electronic devices that change user passwords automatically.

transaction processing system (TPS)   The basic business system that serves the operational level (analysts) and assists in making structured decisions.

transactional information   Encompasses all of the information contained within a single business process or unit of work, and its primary purpose is to support the performing of daily operational or structured decisions.

transmission control protocol/Internet protocol (TCP/IP)   Provides the technical foundation for the public Internet as well as for large numbers of private networks.

twisted-pair cable   Refers to a type of cable composed of four (or more) copper wires twisted around each other within a plastic sheath.

U

unavailable   When a system is not operating or cannot be used.

unified communications (UC)   The integration of communication channels into a single service.

universal resource locator (URL)   The address of a file or resource on the web such as www.apple.com.

unstructured data   Data that do not exist in a fixed location and can include text documents, PDFs, voice messages, emails, etc.

unstructured decision   Occurs in situations in which no procedures or rules exist to guide decision makers toward the correct choice.

up-selling   Increasing the value of the sale.

usability   The degree to which a system is easy to learn and efficient and satisfying to use.

user contributed content (also referred to as user generated content)   Content created and updated by many users for many users.

utility computing   Offers a pay-per-use revenue model similar to a metered service such as gas or electricity.

utility software   Provides additional functionality to the operating system.

V

value chain analysis   Views a firm as a series of business processes that each add value to the product or service.

variable   A data characteristic that stands for a value that changes or varies over time.

virtual private network (VPN)   Companies can establish direct private network links among themselves or create private, secure Internet access, in effect a "private tunnel" within the Internet.

virtual reality   A computer-simulated environment that can be a simulation of the real world or an imaginary world.

virtualization   Creates multiple "virtual" machines on a single computing device.

virus   Software written with malicious intent to cause annoyance or damage.

visualization   Produces graphical displays of patterns and complex relationships in large amounts of data.

voice over IP (VoIP)   Uses IP technology to transmit telephone calls.

volatility   Refers to RAM's complete loss of stored information if power is interrupted.

W

warm site   A separate facility with computer equipment that requires installation and configuration.

waterfall methodology   A sequence of phases in which the output of each phase becomes the input for the next.

Web 1.0   Refers to the World Wide Web during its first few years of operation between 1991 and 2003.

Web 2.0   The next generation of Internet use—a more mature, distinctive communications platform characterized by new qualities such as collaboration, sharing, and free.

web-based self-service system   Allows customers to use the web to find answers to their questions or solutions to their problems.

web browser   Allow users to access the WWW.

web conferencing   Blends videoconferencing with document-sharing and allows the user to deliver a presentation over the web to a group of geographically dispersed participants.

web mining   Analyzes unstructured data associated with websites to identify consumer behavior and website navigation.

website bookmark   A locally stored URL or the address of a file or Internet page saved as a shortcut.

website personalization   Occurs when a website has stored enough data about a person's likes and dislikes to fashion offers more likely to appeal to that person.

what-if analysis   Checks the impact of a change in a variable or assumption on the model.

white-hat hackers   Work at the request of the system owners to find system vulnerabilities and plug the holes.

wide area network (WAN)   Spans a large geographic area such as a state, province, or country.

wi-fi protected access (WPA)   A wireless security protocol to protect wi-fi networks.

wiki   A type of collaborative web page that allows users to add, remove, and change content, which can be easily organized and reorganized as required.

wire media   Transmission material manufactured so that signals will be confined to a narrow path and will behave predictably.

wireless fidelity (wi-fi)   A means by which portable devices can connect wirelessly to a local area network, using access points that send and receive data via radio waves.

wireless LAN (WLAN)   A local area network that uses radio signals to transmit and receive data over distances of a few hundred feet.

wireless MAN (WMAN)   A metropolitan area network that uses radio signals to transmit and receive data.

wireless media   Natural parts of the Earth's environment that can be used as physical paths to carry electrical signals.

wireless WAN (WWAN)   A wide area network that uses radio signals to transmit and receive data.

workflow   Includes the tasks, activities, and responsibilities required to execute each step in a business process.

World Wide Web (WWW)   Provides access to Internet information through documents including text, graphics, audio, and video files that use a special formatting language called HTML.

Worldwide Interoperability for Microwave Access (WiMAX)   A communications technology aimed at providing high-speed wireless data over metropolitan area networks.

notes

CHAPTER 1

1. Interesting Facts, www.interestingfacts.org, accessed June 15, 2011.

2. Thomas L. Friedman, *The World Is Flat* (New York: Farrar, Straus & Giroux, 2005); Thomas Friedman, "The World Is Flat," www.thomaslfriedman.com, accessed June 2010; Thomas L. Friedman, "The Opinion Pages," *The New York Times,* topics.nytimes.com/top/opinion/editorialsandoped/oped/columnists/thomaslfriedman, accessed June 2011.

3. J. R. Raphel, "The 15 Biggest Wiki Blunders," *PC World,* August 26, 2009, www.pcworld.com/article/170874/the_15_biggest_wikipedia_blunders.html.

4. Peter S. Green, "Merrill's Thain Said to Pay $1.2 Million to Decorator," *Bloomberg Businessweek,* www.bloomberg.com/apps/news?sid=aFcrG8er4FRw&pid=newsarchive, January 23, 2009, accessed April 17, 2010.

5. Frederic Paul, "Smart Social Networking for Your Small Business," www.forbes.com/2009/06/05/social-networking-interop-entrepreneurs-technology-bmighty.html, accessed July 2011.

6. Ina Fried, "Apple Earnings Top Estimates," *CNET News,* October 11, 2005, http://news.cnet.com/Apple-earnings-topestimates/2100-1041_3-5893289.html?tag=lia;rcol, accessed 2010.

7. Jon Surmacz, "By the Numbers," *CIO Magazine,* October 2009.

8. Michael E. Porter, "The Five Competitive Forces That Shape Strategy," The Harvard Business Review Book Series, *Harvard Business Review,* January 2008; Michael E. Porter, "Competitive Strategy: Techniques for Analyzing Industries and Competitors," *Harvard Business Review,* January 2002; Michael E. Porter, *On Competition,* The Harvard Business Review Book Series (Harvard Business Press, 1985); Harvard Institute for Strategy and Competitiveness, http://www.isc.hbs.edu.

9. through 17. Ibid.

18. "One Laptop per Child," http://laptop.org/en/, accessed June 2011.

19. Porter, "The Five Competitive Forces That Shape Strategy"; Porter, "Competitive Strategy"; Porter, *On Competition;* Harvard Institute for Strategy and Competitiveness, http://www.isc.

20. Robert Lenzer, "Bernie Madoff's $50 Billion Ponzi Scheme," *Forbes,* December, 12, 2008, www.forbes.com/2008/12/12/madoff-ponzi-hedge-pf-ii-in_rl_1212croesus_inl.html.

21. Porter, "The Five Competitive Forces That Shape Strategy"; Porter, "Competitive Strategy"; Porter, *On Competition;* Harvard Institute for Strategy and Competitiveness, http://www.isc.

CHAPTER 2

1. Tom Davenport, "Tom Davenport: Back to Decision-Making Basics," *Bloomberg Businessweek,* March 11, 2008.

2. Jeff Voth, "Texting and Other Bad Driving Decisions," http://ca.autos.yahoo.com/p/1960/texting-and-other-bad-driving-decisions; "Breastfeeding While Driving," *The New York Times,* March 2, 2009, http://parenting.blogs.nytimes.com/2009/03/02/breastfeeding-while-driving/.

3. Ken Blanchard, "Effectiveness vs. Efficiency," *Wachovia Small Business,* www.wachovia.com, accessed October 14, 2009.

4. Secondlife.com, accessed May 28, 2007; "Linden Lab to Open Source Second Life Software," Linden Lab, January 8, 2007, secondlife.com/community/land-islands.php, accessed May 22, 2010; Irene Sege, "Leading a Double Life," *The Boston Globe,* October 25, 2006, accessed June 22, 2010; James Harkin, "Get a (Second) Life," *Financial Times,* November, 17 2006, accessed June 15, 2010.

5. "What Is Systems Thinking," *SearchCIO.com,* http://searchcio.tech.

6. "French Trader in Scandal Ordered Behind Bars," *MSNBC,* February 8, 2008, www.msnbc.msn.com/id/23065812/.

7. www.collegehunkshaulingjunk.com/, accessed July 2011.

8. Sharon Begley, "Software au Natural"; Neil McManus, "Robots at Your Service"; Santa Fe Institute, www.dis.anl.gov/abms/, accessed June 24, 2007; Michael A. Arbib (Ed.), *The Handbook of Brain Theory and Neural Networks* (MIT Press, mitpress.mit.edu, 1995); L. Biacino and G. Gerla, "Fuzzy Logic, Continuity and Effectiveness," *Archive for Mathematical Logic.*

9. Rachel King, "Soon That Nearby Worker Might Be a Robot," *Bloomberg Businessweek,* June 1, 2010, www.businessweek.com/technology/content/jun2010/tc2010061_798891.htm.

10. through 12. Ibid.

13. Business Process Reengineering Six Sigma, www.six-sigma.com; Michael Hammer, *Beyond Reengineering: How the Process Centered Organization Is Changing Our Work and Our Lives* (New York: HarperCollins Publishers, 1996); Richard Chang, "Process Reengineering in Action: A Practical Guide to Achieving Breakthrough Results (Quality Improvement Series)," (New Jersey: Pfeiffer, John Wiley & Sons, Inc., 1996); H. James Harrington, *Business Process Improvement Workbook: Documentation, Analysis, Design, and Management of Business Process Improvement* (New York: McGraw-Hill, 1997).

16. through 18. Ibid.

19. "Reply All? World's Worst Email Blunders," http://news.sky.com/home/article/1272091, accessed July 2010.

20. Business Process Reengineering Six Sigma, www.sixsigma.com; Hammer, *Beyond Reengineering;* Chang, "Process Reengineering in Action"; Harrington, *Business Process Improvement Workbook.*

21. through 22. Ibid.

23. Phil Mansfield, "Bronx Graduate Trina Thompson Sues Monroe College for $70,000 over Unemployment," *NY Daily News,* August 3, 2009, www.nydailynews.com/ny_local/2009/08/03/2009-08-03_student_.html#ixzz1174LU5KS.

CHAPTER 3

1. "Polaroid Files for Bankruptcy Protection," www.dpreview.com/news/0110/01101201polaroidch11.asp, accessed July 2010.

2. Clayton Christensen, *The Innovator's Dilemma* (Boston: Harvard Business School, 1997).

3. Ibid.

4. Ibid.

5. Internet World Statistics, www.internetworldstats.com, January 2010.

6. info.cern.ch, accessed March 1, 2005.

7. Brier Dudley, "Changes in Technology Almost Too Fast to Follow," *The Seattle Times,* October 13, 2005.

8. Max Chafkin, "Good Domain Names Grow Scarce," *Inc.,* July 1, 2009, http://www.inc.com/magazine/20090701/good-domain-names-grow-scarce.html.

9. Chris Anderson, "The Long Tail: Why the Future of Business Is Selling Less of More," www.longtail.com/2006.

10. "Disintermediation," *TechTarget,* http://whatis.techtarget.com/ definition/0,,sid9_gci211962,00.html, accessed April 4, 2010.

11. "Reintermediation," www.pcmag.com; www.pcmag.com/encyclopedia_term/0,2542,t=reintermediation&i=50364,00.asp, accessed April 4, 2010.

12. Scott McCartney, "You Paid What for That Flight?" *The Wall Street Journal,* August 26, 2010, http://online.wsj.com/article.

13. "The Complete Web 2.0 Directory," www.go2web20.net/, accessed June 24, 2007; "Web 2.0 for CIOs," www.cio.com/article/16807; www.emarketer.com, accessed January 2006.

14. through 17. Ibid.

18. www.craigslist.org/about/, accessed July 2010.

19. "The Complete Web 2.0 Directory"; "Web 2.0 for CIOs"; www.emarketer.com.

20. Joel Holland, "Risk It When You Are Young," *Entrepreneur Magazine,* July 2010, http://www.entrepreneur.com/magazine/entrepreneur/2010/july/207174.htm.

21. Tony Bradley, "Firefox 3.6 Becomes Number Two Browser as IE6 Declines," www.pcworld.com, September 1, 2010, http://www.pcworld.com/businesscenter/article/204698.

22. Kit Eaton, "Is Facebook Becoming the Whole World's Social Network?" *Fast Company,* April 7, 2010, www.fastcompany.com/1609312/facebook-global-expansion-social-networking-privacy-world-phone-book-users.

23. About Us, "LinkedIn," http://press.linkedin.com/, accessed April 3, 2010.

24. Daniel Pink, "Folksonomy," *The New York Times,* December 11, 2005, www.nytimes.com/2005/12/11/magazine/11ideas1-21.html.

25. Daniel Nations, "What Is Social Bookmarking," *About.com:* Web Trends, http://webtrends.about.com/od/socialbookmarking101/p/aboutsocialtags.htm, accessed April 5, 2010.

26. through 31. Ibid.

32. www.eurpac.com/, *Artist2Market,* accessed July 2010.

33. John Seigenthaler, "A False Wikipedia Biography," *USA Today,* November 29, 2005, www.usatoday.com/news/opinion/editorials/2005-11-29-wikipedia-edit_x.htm.

34. Tim Berners-Lee, "Semantic Web Road Map," October 14, 1998, www.w3.org/DesignIssues/Semantic.html, accessed April 12, 2010.

35. Caroline McCarthy, "Bloomberg Mistakenly Publishes Steve Jobs Obituary," *CNET News,* August 28, 2008, http://news.cnet.com/8301-13579_3-10027886-37.html, accessed April 19, 2010.

CHAPTER 4

1. Michael Schrage, "Build the Business Case," *CIO Magazine,* www.cio.com/article/31780/Build_the_Business_Case_Extracting_Value_from_the_Customer, March 15, 2003.

2. "Kiva—Loans That Change Lives," www.kiva.org, accessed April 10, 2010.

3. Hugo Miller, "AT&T Sparks User Backlash with End to Unlimited Plans," *Bloomberg Businessweek,* June 4, 2010, www.businessweek.com/news/2010-06-04/at-t-sparks-user-backlash-with-end-to-unlimited-plans-update2-.html.

4. Scott Berinato, "The CIO Code of Ethical Data Management," *CIO Magazine,* www.cio.com, July 1, 2002, accessed April 17, 2010; Peter S. Green, "Take the Data Pledge," *Bloomberg Businessweek*, April 23, 2009, accessed May 27, 2010.

5. Richard Mason, "Four Ethical Issues of the Information Age," *Management Information Systems Quarterly* 10, no. 1 (March 1986), www.misq.org/archivist/vol/no10/10; AMA Research, "Workplace Monitoring and Surveillance," www.amanet.org, accessed March 1, 2004.

6. Jon Perlow, "New in Labs: Stop Sending Mail You Later Regret," http://gmailblog.blogspot.com/2008/10/new-in-labs-stop-sending-mail-you-later.html, accessed June 2010.

7. Raymund Flandez, "Domino's Response Offers Lessons in Crisis Management," *The Wall Street Journal,* April 20, 2009, http://blogs.wsj.com/independentstreet/2009/04/20/dominos-response-offers-lessons-in-crisis-management/.

8. FTC Spam, http://www.ftc.gov/bcp/edu/microsites/spam/, accessed June 2010.

9. Ronald Quinlan, "Ex-banker Urges Former Colleagues to Step Down," http://www.independent.ie/national-news/exbanker-urges-former-colleagues-to-step-down-1558320.html, November 2008.

10. Daniel Schorn, "Whose Life Is It Anyways?" *CBS News,* http://www.cbsnews.com/stories/2005/10/28/60minutes/main990617.shtml, February 2009.

11. Thomas Claburn, "Web 2.0. Internet Too Dangerous for Normal People," *InformationWeek,* April 1, 2009, http://www.informationweek.com/news/internet/web2.0/showArticle.jhtml?articleID=216402352&queryText = web%202.0%20security%20concerns.

12. Ibid.

13. Paige Baltzan, email received Friday, May 21, 2010.

14. Newcastle University, "Improving Password Protection with Easy to Remember Drawings," *ScienceDaily,* November 1, 2007, www.sciencedaily.com-/releases/2007/10/071030091438.htm, accessed April 15, 2010.

15. Thomas Claburn, "Web 2.0. Internet Too Dangerous for Normal People," *InformationWeek,* April 1, 2009, www.informationweek.com/news/internet/web2.0/showArticle.jhtml?articleID=216402352&queryText = web%202.0%20security%20concerns.

CHAPTER 5

1. "The New Student Excuse?" www.insidehighered.com/news/2009/06/05/corrupted, June 5, 2009.

2. "The Great 1906 San Francisco Earthquake," USGS, http://earthquake.usgs.gov/regional/nca/1906/18april/index.php, accessed July 14, 2010.

3. Doug Johnson, "When Zombies Attack," http://magazine.ufl.edu/2011/05/when-zombies-attack/, accessed June 2010.

4. EPA.gov, "eCycle Cell Phones," http://www.epa.gov/osw/partnerships/plugin/cellphone/, accessed June 2011.

5. "Moore's Law," www.intel.com/technology/mooreslaw, accessed April 2, 2010; Electronics TakeBack Coalition, "Facts and Figures on E-Waste and Recycling," www.electronicstakeback.com, accessed April 3, 2010; "EPA Report to Congress on Server and Data Center Energy Efficiency," www.energystar.gov/ia/partners/prod_development/downloads/EPA_Report_Exec_Summary_Final.pdf, accessed January 23, 2008.

6. Ibid.

7. Ibid.

8. "Switch on the Benefits of Grid Computing," h20338.www2.hp.com/enterprise/downloads/7_Benefits%20of%20grid%20computing.pdf, accessed April 2, 2010; "Talking to the Grid," www.technologyreview.com/energy/23706/, accessed April 3, 2010; "Tech Update: What's All the Smart Grid Buzz About?" www.fieldtechnologiesonline.com/download.mvc/Whats-All-The-Smart-Grid-Buzz-About-0001, accessed April 3, 2010.

9. through 13. Ibid.

14. "VMware-History of Virtualization," www.virtualizationworks.com/Virtualization-History.asp, accessed January 23, 2008.

15. Nic Cubrilovic, "The Anatomy of the Twitter Attack," *TechCrunch,* http://techcrunch.com/2009/07/19/the-anatomy-of-the-twitter-attack/, accessed June 2010.

16. Rich Miller, "Google Data Center FAQ," www.datacenterknowledge.com/archives/2008/03/27/google-data-center-faq/, accessed April 1, 2010.

CHAPTER 6

1. Julia Kiling, "OLAP Gains Fans among Data-Hungry Firms," *ComputerWorld,* January 8, 2001, p. 54.

2. Ibid.

3. Mitch Betts, "Unexpected Insights," *ComputerWorld,* April 14, 2003, www.computerworld.com, accessed September 4, 2003.

4. Ibid.

5. *BBC News,* "Grieving Relatives Find Stranger In Mum's Casket," www.bbcnews.com, accessed June 2010.

6. Steven D. Levitt and Stephen J. Dubner, "Freakonomics, The Hidden Side of Everything," http://www.freakonomics.com/, accessed July 2010.

7. "Oklahoma Leaks 10,000 Social Security Numbers," *Slashdot.org,* http://it.slashdot.org/story/08/04/15/1414223/Oklahoma-Leaks-10000-Social-Security-Numbers, accessed June 2010.

8. www.zappos.com, accessed April 9, 2010.

9. Rachel King, "Business Intelligence Software's Time Is Now," *Bloomberg Businessweek,* March 2, 2009, http://www.businessweek.com/technology/content/mar2009/tc2009032_101762.htm.

10. "IDC, Analyze the Future," www.idc.com, accessed June 2010.

11. Timothy Mullaney, "Netflix," *Bloomberg Businessweek,* May 25, 2006, www.businessweek.com/smallbiz/content/may2006/sb20060525_268860.htm.

12. www.google.com, accessed September 2010.

13. Julie Schlosser, "Looking for Intelligence in Ice Cream," *Fortune,* March 17, 2003; Leslie Goff, "Summertime Heats Up IT at Ben & Jerry's," *Computer World,* July 2001; Customer Success Stories, www.cognos.com, accessed January 2010.

CHAPTER 7

1. "Top 23 U.S. ISPs by Subscriber: Q3 2010," *ISP Planet,* www.isp-planet.com/research/rankings/usa.html.

2. Ibid.

3. "Bandwidth Meter Online Speed Test," *CNET Reviews,* http://reviews.cnet.com/internet-speed-test/, accessed June 2010; "Broadband Technology Overview," www.corning.com/docs/opticalfiber/wp6321.pdf, accessed February 1, 2008.

4. through 7. Ibid.

8. www.savetheinternet.com, accessed May 15, 2010.

9. Chris Matyszczyk, "Marathon Winner Disqualified for Wearing iPod," *CNET News,* October 11, 2009, http://news.cnet.com/8301-17852_3-10372586-71.html; Tom Held, "Second Lakefront Marathon Winner Disqualified for iPod Use," http://www.jsonline.com/blogs/lifestyle/63668622.html, accessed June 2010.

10. www.godaddy.com, accessed May 16, 2010 .

11. "IP Telephony/Voice over IP (VoIP): An Introduction," Cisco, www.cisco.com/en/US/tech/tk652/tk701/tsd_technology_support_protocol_home.html, accessed April 24, 2010; "VoIP Business Solutions," www.vocalocity.com, accessed January 21, 2008.

12. Ibid.

13. Ibid.

14. Chris Silva and Benjamin Gray, "Key Wireless Trends That Will Shape Enterprise Mobility in 2008," www.forrester.com, accessed February 12, 2008.

15. Damian Joseph, "The GPS Revolution," *Bloomberg Businessweek,* May 27, 2009, www.businessweek.com/innovate/content/may2009/id20090526_735316.htm.

16. Bob Sullivan, "Ding a Ling Took My $400," *MSNBC.com,* October 2, 2009, http://redtape.msnbc.com/2009/10/mary-coxs-consumer-nightmare-began-with-poor-satellite-television-reception-but-ended-up-costing-her-a-430-early-terminatio/comments/page/2/.

17. Boston Digital Bridge Foundation, www.digitalbridgefoundation.org/, accessed May 18, 2010.

18. The Liberty Coalition, "Carnivore—DCS 1000," July 27, 2006, www.libertycoalition.net/node/247.

19. "A Science Odyssey," *PBS,* www.pbs.org/wgbh/aso/databank/entries/btmarc.html.

20. "Rip Curl Turns to Skype for Global Communications," www.voipinbusiness.co.uk/rip_curl_turns_to_skype_for_gl.asp, July 7, 2006, accessed January 21, 2008; "Navigating the Mobility Wave," www.busmanagement.com, accessed February 2, 2008; "Sprint Plans Launch of Commercial WiMAX Service in Q2 2008," www.intomobile.com, accessed February 10, 2008; Deepak Pareek, *WiMAX: Taking Wireless to the MAX* (Boca Raton, FL: CRC Press, 2006), pp. 150–93; wimax.com, accessed February 9, 2008.

21. Ibid.

22. Ibid.

23. www.citysense.net/, accessed June 2010.

24. "Rip Curl Turns to Skype for Global Communications"; "Navigating the Mobility Wave"; "Sprint Plans Launch of Commercial WiMAX Service in Q2 2008"; Pareek, *WiMAX;* wimax.com.

25. through 29. Ibid.

30. "Woman Has 911 Meltdown over McNuggets," *MSNBC.com,* March 4, 2009, www.msnbc.msn.com/id/29498350/.

31. "Rip Curl Turns to Skype for Global Communications"; "Navigating the Mobility Wave"; "Sprint Plans Launch of Commercial WiMAX Service in Q2 2008"; Pareek, *WiMAX;* wimax.com.

32. V. C. Gungor and F. C. Lambert, "A Survey on Communication Networks for Electric System Automation, Computer Networks," *International Journal of Computer and Telecommunications Networking,* May 15, 2006, pp. 877–97.

33. Mohsen Attaran, "RFID: an Enabler of Supply Chain Operations," *Supply Chain Management: An International Journal* 12 (2007), pp. 249–57.

34. Michael Dortch, "Winning RFID Strategies for 2008," *Benchmark Report,* December 31, 2007.

35. Damian Joseph, "The GPS Revolution," *Bloomberg Businessweek,* May 27, 2009, www.businessweek.com/innovate/content/may2009/id20090526_735316.htm.

36. Natasha Lomas, "Location Based Services to Boom in 2008," *Bloomberg Businessweek,* February 11, 2008, www.businessweek.com/globalbiz/content/feb2008/gb20080211_420894.htm.

37. Ibid.

38. C. G. Lynch, "GPS Innovation Gives Weather Bots a New Ride," *CIO Magazine,* May 9, 2007, www.cio.com/article/108500/GPS_Innovation_Gives_Weather_Bots_a_New_Ride, accessed 2010.

39. Google Earth, "Jane Goodall Institute—Gombe Chimpanzee Blog," http://earth.google.com/outreach/cs_jgi_blog.html, accessed April 3, 2010.

40. RFID Security Alliance, www.rfidsa.com/, accessed June 15, 2010.

41. Ibid.

42. Ibid.

CHAPTER 8

1. Michael E. Porter, "The Five Competitive Forces That Shape Strategy," The Harvard Business Review Book Series, *Harvard Business Review,* January 2008; Michael E. Porter, "Competitive Strategy: Techniques for Analyzing Industries and Competitors," *Harvard Business Review,* January 2002; Michael E. Porter, *On Competition,* The Harvard Business Review Book Series (Harvard Business Press, 1985); Harvard Institute for Strategy and Competitiveness, www.isc.hbs.edu/, accessed June 10, 2010.

2. "Kiva—Loans That Change Lives," www.kiva.org, accessed April 10, 2010.

3. "Post Office Losses Reach $4.7B for Year," *CBS News,* August 5, 2009, http://www.cbsnews.com/stories/2009/08/05/national/main5216012.shtml.

4. "Harley-Davidson on the Path to Success," www.peoplesoft.com/media/success, accessed October 12, 2003.

5. "Integrated Solutions—The ABCs of CRM," www.integratedsolutionsmag.com, accessed November 12, 2003.

6. Rachel King, "Saving Face Online," *BusinessWeek,* www.businessweek.com/magazine/, accessed June 2010.

7. Timothy Keiningham and Lerzan Aksoy, "When Customer Loyalty Is a Bad Thing," *Bloomberg Businessweek,* May 8, 2009.

8. *Change.org,* http://www.change.org/, accessed July 2010.

9. The Balanced Scorecard, www.balancedscorecard.org, accessed February 2008.

CHAPTER 9

1. "Four Steps to Getting Things on Track," *Bloomberg Businessweek,* July 7, 2010, www.businessweek.com/idg/2010-07-07/project-management-4-steps-to-getting-things-on-track.html.

2. www.ted.com, accessed June 15, 2010.

3. "Overcoming Software Development Problems," www.samspublishing.com, accessed October 2005.

4. Agile Alliance Manifesto, www.agile.com, accessed November 1, 2003.

5. *CIO Magazine,* June 1, 2006; "The Project Manager in the IT Industry," www.standishgroup.com; G. McGraw, "Making Essential Software Work," *EETimes,* September 2010.

6. through 7. Ibid.

8. Jose Martinez, "Lesson in Fraud: NYU Employee Submitted $409K in Fake Expenses Using Receipts from Garbage," *New York Daily News,* December 23, 2009.

9. "Building Software That Works," www.compaq.com, accessed November 14, 2003.

10. http://books.google.com/googlebooks/library.html, accessed March 15, 2010.

11. *CharityFocus.org,* www.charityfocus.org/new/, accessed June 2010.

12. The Project Management Institute, www.pmi,org, accessed June 2010.

13. Martinez, "Lesson in Fraud."

14. "Overcoming Software Development Problems."

15. Karl Ritter, "Bill Murray Faces DUI after Golf-Cart Escapade in Sweden," *The Seattle Times,* August 22, 2007, http://seattletimes.nwsource.com/html/entertainment/2003848077_webmurray22.html.

APPENDIX A (www.mhhe.com/BaltzanM2e)

1. "Electronic Breaking Points," *PC World,* August 2005.

2. Tom Davenport, "Playing Catch-Up," *CIO Magazine,* May 1, 2001.

3. Hector Ruiz, "Advanced Micro Devices," *BusinessWeek,* January 10, 2005.

4. www.powergridfitness.com, accessed October 2005.

5. Denise Brehm, "Sloan Students Pedal Exercise," www.mit.edu, accessed May 5, 2003.

6. Margaret Locher, "Hands That Speak," *CIO Magazine,* June 1, 2005.

7. www.needapresent.com, accessed October 2005.

8. Aaron Ricadela, "Seismic Shift," *Information Week,* March 14, 2005.

9. www.mit.com, accessed October 2005.

10. "The Linux Counter," counter.li.org, accessed October 2005.

APPENDIX B (www.mhhe.com/BaltzanM2e)

1. Andy Patrizio, "Peer-to-Peer Goes Beyond Napster," *Wired,* www.wired.com/science/discoveries/news/2001/02/41768, accessed January 2009.

2. Intel in Communications, "10 Gigabit Ethernet Technology Overview," www.intel.com/network/connectivity/resources/doc_library/white_papers/pro10gbe_lr_sa_wp.pdf, accessed January 2009.

3. Cisco, "TCP/IP Overview," www.cisco.com/en/US/tech/tk365/technologies_white_paper09186a008014f8a9.shtml, accessed January 2009.

4. Ibid.

5. IPv6, www.ipv6.org, accessed January 2009.

6. Cisco, "TCP/IP Overview."

7. Cisco, "Network Media Types," www.ciscopress.com/articles/article.asp?p=31276, accessed January 2009.

8. Ibid.

9. Ibid.

index

A

AbsolutePoker.com, 88
Acceptable use policy (AUP), 90, 91
Accessibility (MIS infrastructure), 113, 114
Accounting and finance ERP components, 198
Accounting department, 10–12, 45
Accuracy
    information, 34, 133
    and MIS infrastructure, 115
Administrator access, 113–114
Advertising fees (ebusiness revenue model), 69
Adware, 93, 97
Adwords, 68
Affiliate programs, 66
Agent-based modeling, 43–44
Agile methodologies, 209–211
    extreme programming, 210
    rapid application development, 210
    rational unified process, 210–211
    scrum, 211
Agile MIS infrastructures, 113–116
AI; see Artificial intelligence
Aksoy, Lerzan, 240
Albertson's, 18
Alibi Network, 218
All the President's Men, 145
Altman, Eli, 63
Amazon, 6, 18, 23, 52, 64, 67, 68, 73, 79, 122, 123, 125, 126,
        185, 190, 207
Ambiguous business requirements, 208
American Express, 169
American Family Immigration History Center, 137
American Motors, 221
Analysis phase (SDLC), 207
Analytical CRM, 189, 193
Analytical information, 36, 130–131
Anderson, Chris, 64, 207, 238
Anderson, Tom, 6
Anticybersquatting Consumer Protection Act (1999), 63
Anti-spam policy, 92
Antz, 119
AOL, 23, 70, 154
API (application programming interface), 79
Appendices, online, 224
Apple, 14, 15, 61, 63, 81, 115, 116, 125, 166
Apple.com, 155, 157
Application programming interface (API), 79
Arbib, Michael A., 237
Aristotle, 70
ARPANET, 61
Artificial intelligence (AI)
    in decision support systems, 41–44
    defined, 41
    expert systems, 41–42
    genetic algorithms, 42, 43
    intelligent agents, 42–44
    neural networks, 42–43
    virtual reality, 42, 44
Artificial neural networks, 42–43
Artist2Market, 79

As-Is process models, 47–50
Ascential Software, 142
Associate programs, 66
Association detection, 146, 147
Association rule generators, 146
Assumptions, project, 215
Asynchronous communications, 75
AT&T, 70, 86, 87, 153–155, 166
ATMs (automated teller machines), 33
Attacks, detection of and response to, 102; *see also* Hackers
Attaran, Mohsen, 239
Attributes, 135–136
Auctions, online, 68
Audits, data quality, 144
AUP (acceptable use policy), 90, 91
Authentication, 98–100
Authorization, 98–100
Authors Guild, 146
Automated teller machines (ATMs), 33
Automatic call distribution, 192
Automation, 51–52
AutoTrader.com, 62
Availability (MIS infrastructure), 114, 115
Avatar, 6
Axelbank, Gary, 56

B

Back-office processes, 46
Back orders, 185
Backdoor programs, 97
Background Draw-a-Secret (BDAS), 100
Backup, 110
Backup and recovery plans, 110, 114
Backward integration, 180
Baddealings.com, 193
Balanced scorecard, 201
Baltzan, Paige, 238
Bandwidth, 154
Bank of America, 99
Bank of Ireland, 93
Banner ads, 66
Barger, Dave, 195
Barnes & Noble, 68
BBN Technologies, 165
BCP (business continuity planning), 112
BDAS (Background Draw-a-Secret), 100
Beckham, David, 9
Begley, S., 237
Ben & Jerry's, 147
Benchmarking, 34
Benchmarks, 34–35
Berinato, Scott, 238
Berners-Lee, Tim, 81, 207, 238
Best Buy, 144, 193
Betts, Mitch, 239
Bezos, Jeff, 6, 207
BI; see Business intelligence
Biacino, L., 237
Biometrics, 100
Bit, 154
Bit rate, 154

BizRate.com, 68
Black Eyed Peas, 136
Black-hat hackers, 96
Blair, Tony, 9
Blanchard, Ken, 237
Blink (Malcolm Gladwell), 207
Blockbuster, 64
Blogs, 77, 78
Bloomberg, 68, 81
Blue Marble Biking, 193
Bluetooth, 163–164
Bookmarking, social, 77
Bookmarks, 77
Bork Bill, 89
Boston Digital Bridge Foundation, 162–163
Botnets, 125
Bottlenecks, 52
Boulder, Colorado, 120
BPM (business process management) systems, 56
BPR (business process reengineering), 53–55
Bradley, Tony, 238
Branson, Richard, 207
Brehm, Denise, 240
Brick-and-mortar businesses, 68
Brin, Sergey, 9, 207
Broad cost leadership strategy, 19–20
Broad differentiation strategy, 19–20
Broadband, 155
B2B (business-to-business), 66–67
B2C (business-to-consumer), 67, 68
Bullwhip effect, 184–185
Burton, Tim, 190
Business continuity plan, 112–113
Business continuity planning (BCP), 112
Business-critical integrity constraints, 138
Business driven MIS, 5–14
    business intelligence in, 9–10
    data in, 7
    and departmental companies, 10–12
    and the information age, 6
    information in, 8–9
    knowledge in, 10
    MIS department roles and responsibilities, 13–14
    strategies for; *see* Business strategy
Business-facing processes, 46
Business intelligence (BI), 9–10, 141–149
    data marts, 142–144
    data mining, 144–147
    data warehousing, 141
    for decision support, 147–149
    defined, 9
Business intelligence ERP components, 200
Business models
    defined, 66
    for ebusiness, 66–69
    extended, 82
Business process improvement, 51–52
Business process management (BPM) systems, 56
Business process modeling/mapping, 46–50
Business process models, 46
Business process reengineering (BPR), 53–55
Business processes, 44–56
    BPM systems, 56
    changing with MIS, 50–55
    defined, 20
    evaluating, 45–46

    leveraging, 55
    managerial, 52–53
    modeling, 46–50
    operational, 51–52
    performance measures, 46–50
    strategic, 53–55
    in value chain analysis, 20–21
Business requirements
    defined, 207
    reducing ambiguity in, 208
    unclear or missing, 211
Business strategy, 14–24
    choosing a focus, 19–20
    defined, 14
    Five Forces Model, 16–19
    generic, 19–20
    identifying competitive advantages, 14–19
    value chain analysis, 20–24
Business-to-business (B2B), 66–67
Business-to-consumer (B2C), 67, 68
Business 2.0; *see* Web 2.0
Buyer power (Porter's Five Forces Model), 16
Byrd, Robert, 9

C

Cabir, 174
Cable & Wireless Worldwide, 153
Cable Communications Act (1984), 89
Café Opera, 221
California Academy of Sciences, 119
Call centers, 192
Call scripting systems, 192
Camilla, Duchess of Cornwall, 9
Campaign management systems, 190
CAN-Spam Act (2003), 89, 93
Capacity planning, 116
Carbon emissions, 118
Carfax, 67
Carnivore, 162
CCB (change control board), 219
Cell phones
    generations of, 167
    recycling, 117
    virtualization for, 124
    wireless WANs for, 165–168
Cellular technologies, 167
Certificate authority, 101
Chafkin, Max, 237
Chang, Richard, 237
Change, MIS infrastructure supporting, 113–116
Change control board (CCB), 219
Change management, 219
Change management systems, 219
Change.org, 194
CharityFocus.org, 215
Charles Schwab, 61
Charlesschwab.com, 68
Chief information officer (CIO), 13
Chief knowledge officer (CKO), 13
Chief privacy officer (CPO), 14
Chief security officer (CSO), 14
Chief technology officer (CTO), 14
China, need for jobs in, 7
Christensen, Clayton, 61, 237
Cinematch, 145

CIO (chief information officer), 13
Cisco, 60, 62
Citibank, 42, 64
Cities, smart, 119
CitySense, 165
CKO (chief knowledge officer), 13
Claburn, Thomas, 238
Classic Cars Inc., 198
Clearwire, 165
Click-and-mortar business, 68
Click-through, 66
Clickstream, 93
Clickstream data, 65, 66
Client (defined), 108
Clinton, Bill, 207
Cloud computing, 120–124, 159, 160
Cloud Computing Center, 122
Cluster analysis, 146
CMS (content management systems), 70–71
CNN.com, 68
Colby, David, 23
Cold sites, 111, 112
Collaboration
    Business 2.0 tools for, 77–79
    inside the organization, 73–74
    outside of business, 74, 75
Collaboration system (ebusiness), 73–74
Collaboration tools (Web 2.0), 77–79
Collaborative demand planning, 187
Collaborative engineering, 187
Collective intelligence, 73–74
College Hunks Hauling Junk, 41
Comcast, 70, 154
Communication(s)
    asynchronous, 75
    disaster plans for, 110
    real-time, 70
    satellite systems, 167–168
    synchronous, 75
    unified, 158
Communications Assistance for Law Enforcement Act (1994), 89
Communications management, 218–219
Communications plan, 218
Competitive advantage(s), 14–16
    defined, 14
    identifying, 14–19
    knowledge as, 73–74
    and value chain analysis, 22
Competitive forces analysis, 16–19
Competitive intelligence, 15
Competitors, rivalry among, 16, 18
Complain Complain, 193
Complaint Department, The, 193
Complaint Station, The, 193
Complaints.com Consumer Complaints, 193
Completeness of information, 132, 133
Computer use policy, ethical, 88, 90
Confidentiality, 86, 221
Conisint.com, 82
Connectivity; see also Network(s)
    benefits of, 159–162
    challenges of, 162–163
    global, 152
Consistency of information, 132
Consolidation, 40

Constraints
    integrity, 138
    project, 215
    triple, 213
Consumer protection (ebusiness), 71
Consumer-to-business (C2B), 67
Consumer-to-consumer (C2C), 67, 68
Consumer trust (ebusiness), 71
Contact centers, 192
Contact management CRM systems, 191, 192
Content filtering, 100
Content management systems (CMS), 70–71
Content providers, 68
Controlling the Assault of Non-Solicited Pornography and Marketing Act (2003), 93
Conversations.org, 215
Conversion rates, 34
Cookies, 66, 93
Copyright
    defined, 86
    and free books online, 146
    violation of, 80
Corporate culture, 79
Corporate responsibility, 205–222
    enterprise applications development, 206–212
    project management, 212–222
Corporate social responsibility, 117
Corrupted files, 111
CorruptedFiles.com, 111, 218
Cost(s)
    broad cost leadership strategy, 19–20
    of downtime, 95
    reducing, with ebusiness, 64–65
    switching, 16
Counterfeit software, 86
Cox, Mary, 161
CPO (chief privacy officer), 14
Crackers, 96
Craigslist, 23, 70
Craigslist Foundation, 70
Crib Point cemetery (Australia), 135
Critical path, 217
Critical success factors (CSFs), 32, 33
CRM; see Customer relationship management
CRM analysis technologies, 189
CRM predicting technologies, 189
CRM reporting technologies, 189
Cross-functional companies, 12, 13
Cross-selling, 190
Crowdsourcing, 74, 75
CSFs (critical success factors), 32, 33
CSO (chief security officer), 14
CTO (chief technology officer), 14
C2B (consumer-to-business), 67
C2C (consumer-to-consumer), 67, 68
Cubrilovic, Nic, 239
Customer-facing processes, 46
Customer order cycle time, 185
Customer relationship ERP components, 200
Customer relationship management (CRM), 187–196
    analytical, 189, 193
    benefits of, 188–194
    challenges of, 194
    defined, 187
    evolution of, 189
    future of, 194–196

Customer relationship management (CRM)—*Cont.*
    integrating ERP, SCM, and, 202–203
    measuring success of, 193–194
    operational, 189–193
Customer satisfaction, 34
Customer service, 192–193
Customization, mass, 64
Customreceipts.com, 218
Cyber squatting, 63
Cybermediation, 64
Cyberterrorists, 96
Cycle time, reducing, 52, 53
Cyxymu (Georgy Jakhaia), 125

D

DailyGood, 215
DARPA (Department of Defense Advanced Research Project
    Agency), 61
Darwinism, digital, 60
Data, 7; *see also* Information
    clickstream, 65, 66
    immediate access to, 171
    and information, 147
    managing, 145
    sharing, 159
    streaming, 166, 167
Data centers, 126
Data dictionary, 135
Data-driven websites, 139–140
Data elements, 135–136
Data field, 135
Data governance, 134
Data inconsistency, 132
Data integrity issues, 132
Data marts, 142–144
Data mining, 144–147
Data-mining tools, 144–145
Data models, 135
Data quality audits, 144
Data rate, 154
Data redundancy, 138
Data warehouses, 141
    data marts, 142–144
    data-mining tools for, 144–145
    model of, 142
Data warehousing, 141
Database, 134, 135
Database management system (DBMS)
    defined, 135
    relational, 134–139
Davenport, Tom, 237, 240
DCS1000, 162
DDoS (distributed denial-of-service attacks), 97
Death, faking, 211
DEC, 61
Decision making
    business intelligence support for, 147–149
    challenges in, 28
    at managerial level, 30, 31
    at operational level, 29–30
    process of, 29
    at strategic level, 30, 31
Decision support systems (DDSs), 27–44
    artificial intelligence in, 41–44
    and challenges in decision making, 28

    and decision-making process, 29
    defined, 36
    EISs vs., 38
    interaction of TPS and, 38
    at managerial level, 30, 31
    OLAP modeling in, 36, 37
    at operational level, 29–30
    and organizational structure, 29
    at strategic level, 30, 31
    and success measures, 32–35
    systems thinking in, 38
    using MIS for, 35–40
Del.icio.us, 77
Deliverables, project, 213
Dell, 6, 60, 65
Dell, Michael, 6
Dell.com, 82
Demand planning systems, 185
Denial-of-service attacks (DoS), 97, 125
Department of Defense Advanced Research Project Agency
    (DARPA), 61
Departmental companies, 10–12
Dependencies, 216
Design phase (SDLC), 207
Detroit, Michigan, 134
Development phase (SDLC), 207
DeWolfe, Chris, 6
Diamandis, Peter, 207
Diapers.com, 185
Differentiation
    broad differentiation strategy, 19–20
    product, 18
Digg, 75
Digital certificates, 101
Digital Darwinism, 60
Digital dashboards, 38, 40
Digital divide, 162–163
Digital subscriber line (DSL), 155
Disaster recovery cost curve, 112
Disaster recovery plans, 110–111, 114
Disasterhelp.gov, 82
Discovery, electronic, 88
Disintermediation, 64
Disruptive technologies, 60–62
    defined, 60
    Internet and World Wide Web as, 61–63
Distributed denial-of-service attacks (DDoS), 97
DNS (domain name system), 157
Dole Organic, 79
Domain name system (DNS), 157
Domain names, 63, 157
Domain squatting, 63
Domains, 157
Domino's Pizza, 91
Donotbuydodge.ca, 195
Doodling passwords, 100
Dortch, Michael, 239
DoS (denial-of-service attacks), 97, 125
Downtime, 94
    cost of, 95
    unplanned, 94
Dr Pepper/Seven-Up Inc., 170
DreamWorks Animation, 119, 120
Drill-down, 40
Driving, poor decisions made while, 32
Drucker, Peter, 32, 33

DSL (digital subscriber line), 155
Dubner, Stephen J., 239
Dudley, Brier, 237
Dumpster diving, 98

E

EAI (enterprise application integration), 181
EAI (enterprise application integration) middleware, 181
Earthlink, 70, 154
Eaton, Kit, 238
eBay, 23, 49, 64, 68, 73, 79, 82
Ebusiness, 59–82
    advantages of Web 2.0, 72–75
    challenges of, 71–72
    collaboration tools, 77–79
    cost reduction with, 64–65
    defined, 62
    disruptive technologies, 60–62
    effectiveness improvement with, 65–66
    global reach with, 63–64
    and Internet/World Wide Web, 61–62
    models for, 66–69
    and networking communities, 75–77
    new markets opened by, 64
    operations improvement with, 65
    tools for, 69–71
    Web 1.0 as catalyst for, 62
    Web 3.0, 80–82
Ebusiness ERP components, 201
Ebusiness models, 66–69
    business-to-business, 66–67
    business-to-consumer, 67, 68
    consumer-to-business, 67
    consumer-to-consumer, 68
    defined, 66
    and revenue-generating strategies, 68–69
Ecommerce, 62
EC2 (Elastic Compute Cloud), 122, 123
EDI (electronic data interchange), 184
Ediscovery, 88
Edmunds.com, 68
Effectiveness
    efficiency vs., 33–35
    improving, 45, 65–66
Effectiveness MIS metrics, 33, 34
Efficiency
    effectiveness vs., 33–35
    improving, 45
Efficiency MIS metrics, 33, 34
egov.com, 82
Egovernment, 82
802.11 standard, 164
EISs (executive information systems), 37–39
Elastic Compute Cloud (EC2), 122, 123
Electric Sheep Company, 36
Electronic Communications Privacy Act (1986), 89
Electronic data interchange (EDI), 184
Electronic discovery, 88
Electronic waste, 117, 118
Elevation of privilege, 97
Ellisisland.org, 137
Elogistics, 201
Email, 70
    content filtering, 100
    Mail Goggles for, 91

personal use of company email, 53
Email privacy policy, 91–92
Emergency notification service, 113
Employee monitoring policy, 94
Employee relationship management (ERM), 194, 196
Encryption, 101
Enemies, online, 78
Enemybook, 78
Energy consumption, 118
Enterprise application integration (EAI), 181
Enterprise application integration (EAI) middleware, 181
Enterprise applications development, 206–212
    agile methodologies, 209–211
    software, 206
    success in, 211–212
    systems development life cycle, 206–207
    waterfall methodology, 207–209
Enterprise architects, 108–109
Enterprise Rent-A-Car, 193
Enterprise resource planning (ERP), 196–203
    benefits of, 197–201
    challenges of, 202
    core components of, 198, 199
    defined, 196
    extended components of, 200
    generations of, 197–198
    integrating SCM, CRM, and, 202–203
Enterprise systems, 181
    customer relationship management, 187–196
    enterprise resource planning, 196–203
    integration of, 180–181, 202–203
    supply chain management, 181–187
Entities, 135–136
Entry barriers, 18
Environmental MIS infrastructures, 117–118
Eprocurement, 201
Equifax, 86, 87
ERM (employee relationship management), 194, 196
ERP; see Enterprise resource planning
Eshops, 67
Etailers, 67
Ethical computer use policy, 88, 90
Ethics, 86–94
    acceptable use policy, 90, 91
    defined, 86
    email privacy policy, 91–92
    ethical computer use policy, 88, 90
    information, 86–88
    and information management policies, 88, 89
    information privacy policy, 90
    and Internet access, 162–163
    legality vs., 87, 88
    social media policy, 92
    workplace monitoring policy, 93–94
ETL (extraction, transformation, and loading), 142
Etrade.com, 68
Eurpac, 79
Ewaste, 118
Executive information systems (EISs), 37–39
Executive sponsor, 213–214
Executives, and alignment with company goals, 10
Expedia.com, 62
Expense reports, 218
Expert systems, 41–42
Explicit knowledge, 74
Export.gov, 82

Extraction, transformation, and loading (ETL), 142
Extranets, 159–161
Extreme programming (XP) methodology, 210

F

Facebook, 6, 75, 78, 91, 115, 121, 125, 131, 157, 162, 170, 190
Facts, 6
Failback, 110
Failover, 110
Fair and Accurate Credit Transactions Act (2003), 89
Fair Credit Reporting Act (FCRA), 87
Faking your own death, 211
Family Education Rights and Privacy Act (1974), 89
Fault tolerance, 110
FBI, 162, 190
FCRA (Fair Credit Reporting Act), 87
Federal Communications Commission, 158
FedEx (Federal Express), 15, 46, 53, 192
Feedback, 13
Fidelity.com, 68
Field, J. P., 200
FileMaker, 135
Finance department, 10–12, 45
Financial analysis, 215
Financial metrics, 34
FireFighter AI Robot, 41
Firefox, 61, 73
Firewalls, 101, 102
Firm infrastructure, as support value activity, 22
First-mover advantage, 15
FirstGov.gov, 82
Five Forces Model; see Porter's Five Forces Model
Fizy, 160
Flandez, Raymund, 238
Flavors, 200
Flexibility (MIS infrastructure), 115
Flickr, 63, 68, 73, 76, 79
Focus, choosing, 19–20
Focused strategy, 19–20
Folksonomy, 76
Ford, Henry, 185
Forecasts, 147
Foreign key, 136
Forrester Research, 62
Forward integration, 180
Foursquare, 170
FoxPro, 135
Freakonomics (Steven Levitt), 137, 207
Freedom of Information Act (1967, 1975, 1994, 1998), 89
Fried, Ina, 237
Friedman, Nick, 41
Friedman, Thomas, 7, 237
Frito-Lay, 15
Front-office processes, 46
Fuzzy logic, 43

G

Gantt charts, 217
Gap, The, 63, 67
"Garbage in, garbage out," 40
Gates, Bill, 6, 81, 207
General Motors (GM), 60, 77, 169
Generic business strategies, 19–20
    and decision support, 28

and value chain analysis, 23
Genetic algorithms, 42, 43
Geoblogging, 174
Geographic information systems (GIS), 169–170
Gerla, G., 237
Germanotta, Stefani Joanne Angelina, 6; see also Lady Gaga
GIS (geographic information systems), 169–170
Gladwell, Malcolm, 207
Global connectivity, 152
Global Kids, 36
Global positioning system (GPS), 169
Global reach, expanding, 63–64
Globalization, supply chain complexity and, 186
GM; see General Motors
Gmail, 53, 122
Goal-seeking analysis, 37
Godin, Seth, 207
Goebel, Jennifer, 156
Gombe National Park (Tanzania), 174
Goodall, Jane, 174
Goodman, Latreasa, 167
Google, 9, 53, 68, 79, 81, 91, 115, 122, 124, 126, 146, 160, 207
Google Application Engine, 123, 124
Google Calendar, 122
Google Docs & Spreadsheets, 122
Google Earth, 79, 170, 174
Google Print Library Project, 146
Gore, Al, 81
Governance
    data, 134
    information, 88, 134
Gowalla, 170
GPS (global positioning system), 169
Granularity
    defined, 38
    information, 130, 131
Gray, Benjamin, 239
Green, Peter S., 237, 238
Green MIS, 117; see also Sustainable MIS infrastructure
Grid computing, 119–120
Group 1 Software, 142
Gungor, V. C., 239

H

Hackers, 96, 97
    common types of, 96
    defined, 96
    phishing by, 101
    Twitter attack by, 125
Hactivists, 96
Hammer, Michael, 237
Hardware, 108
Hardware key logger, 93
Harkin, James, 237
Harley, 63
Harley-Davidson, 187–188
Harley's Owners Group (HOG), 187
Harrington, H. James, 237
Harvard Business School, 16, 201
Harvard University, 146, 165
Health Insurance Portability and Accountability Act (HIPAA) (1996), 89
HealthVault, 122
Hefner AI Robot Cleaner, 41
Held, Tom, 239

HelpOthers, 215
Hering, Lance, 211
Hewlett-Packard, 61, 93
High availability, 114
High-speed Internet connections, 155
HIPAA (Health Insurance Portability and Accountability Act) (1996), 89
Hit metrics (websites), 67
Hitler, Adolf, 9
Hoaxes, 97
HOG (Harley's Owners Group), 187
Holland, Joel, 238
Home Depot, 60
Homeland Security Act (2002), 89
Hot sites, 111, 112
Hotmail, 53, 93, 122
How to Train Your Dragon, 119
HTML (hypertext markup language), 61
HTTP (hypertext transport protocol), 61
HTTPS (secure hypertext transfer protocol), 162
Human resources department, 11, 12, 45
Human resources ERP components, 199
Human resources management, 22, 23
Hundred Monkeys, A, 63
HypeMachine, 160
Hypertext markup language (HTML), 61
Hypertext transport protocol (HTTP), 61

I

IaaS (Infrastructure as a Service), 123
IBM, 42, 44, 61, 65, 122, 220
ICANN (Internet Corporation for Assigning Names and Numbers), 157
IDC, 145
Ideas Worth Spreading, 207
Identity theft, 98
Identity Theft and Assumption Deterrence Act (1998), 89
IDS (intrusion detection software), 102
Ignasinski, Paul, 79
Illuminate Live, 70
Imeem, 160
IMing (instant messaging), 70
Implementation phase (SDLC), 207
Implicit knowledge, 74
In-house development, 219
In-sourcing, 219
Inbound logistics, 21, 22
Inconsistency, data, 132
Infomediaries, 68
Information, 8–9
    analytical, 36
    completeness of, 132, 133
    consistency of, 132
    and data, 147
    governance, 88, 134
    levels, formats, and granularities of, 131
    quality of, 130, 132–134
    real-time, 132
    time-series, 147
    timeliness of, 131–132
    transactional and analytical, 130–131
Information accuracy, 34, 133
Information age, 6
    business intelligence in, 9–10
    core drivers of, 6
    data in, 7

    information in, 8–9
    knowledge in, 10
Information architecture, 71
Information cleansing, 143–144
Information compliance, 88
Information ethics, 86–88
Information governance, 88, 134
Information granularity, 130, 131
Information integrity, 138
Information management, 88
Information management policies, 88, 89
Information MIS infrastructures, 109–113
Information privacy policy, 90
Information reach, 63–64
Information richness, 63
Information security, 94–102
    authentication and authorization, 98–100
    defined, 96
    detection and response to attacks, 102
    hackers, 96, 97
    people issues with, 98
    prevention and resistance technologies, 100–102
    protecting intellectual assets, 94–96
    with relational databases, 138–139
    technology for, 98–102
    viruses, 97
Information security plans, 98
Information security policies, 98
Information technology monitoring, 93, 94
Information vandalism, 80
Infosys, 220
Infrastructure
    disaster plans for, 111
    MIS; see MIS infrastructures
    as support value activity, 22
Infrastructure as a Service (IaaS), 123
Innovator's Dilemma The, (Clayton M. Christensen), 61
Inovant, 90
Insider crime, 40
Insiders, 98
Instant messaging (IMing), 70
Integration(s), 180–181
    defined, 180
    of ERP, SCM, and CRM, 202–203
    tools for, 181
Integrity
    data, 132
    information, 138
Integrity constraints, 138
Intel, 61, 117, 165
Intellectual assets, protecting, 94–96
Intellectual property, 86
Intelligence; see also Business intelligence (BI)
    collective, 73
    competitive, 15
Intelligent agents, 42–44
Intelligent systems, 41; see also Artificial intelligence (AI)
Intelligent web applications, 80; see also Web 3.0
Interactive voice response (IVR), 192
Interactivity, 65
Intermediaries, 64
Internet
    as catalyst for ebusiness, 62
    defined, 61
    as disruptive technology, 61–63

Internet cable connections, 155
Internet Certification Authorities, 162
Internet Corporation for Assigning Names and Numbers (ICANN), 157
Internet Explorer, 61, 62, 73
Internet protocol (IP), 156
Internet Protocol TV (IPTV), 158–159
Internet service providers (ISPs), 70
Internet use policy, 91
Intranets, 159, 160
Intrusion detection software (IDS), 102
Intuit, 61
Inventory cycle time, 185
Inventory turnover, 185
IP (Internet protocol), 156
iPad, 14, 15
iPod, 14, 15
IPTV (Internet Protocol TV), 158–159
IRS, 102
ISPs (Internet service providers), 70
Iterative development, 209
iTunes, 14, 62, 68, 115, 116, 160
i2, 202, 206
IVR (interactive voice response), 192

J

Jackson, Warren, 172
Jakhaia, Georgy (Cyxymu), 125
Jane Goodall Institute, 174
JetBlue, 195
Jobs, Steve, 14
Johnson, Doug, 238
Johnson, J., 240
Johnson & Johnson, 60
Joseph, Damian, 239

K

Kaplan, Robert, 201
KarmaTube, 215
Kay, Vernon, 9
Keiningham, Timothy, 240
Kelkoo, 64
Kennedy, John F., 9, 80
Kennedy, Robert F., 9, 80
Kennedy, Ted, 9
Key logger software, 93
Key performance indicators (KPIs), 32, 33
Key trapper software, 93
Keys, 136
Kiling, Julia, 239
Kill switch, 216
King, Rachel, 237, 239, 240
Kiva Mobile Fulfillment System (Kiva MFS), 185
Kiva Systems, 185
Kiva.org, 87
KM (knowledge management), 74
KMS (knowledge management system), 74
Knight, Philip, 206
Knowledge, 10
    as competitive advantage, 73–74
    explicit and implicit, 74
Knowledge management (KM), 74
Knowledge management system (KMS), 74
Knowledge workers, 10
KPIs (key performance indicators), 32, 33
Kroger, 18, 138

L

Lady Gaga, 6, 81, 136
Lambert, F. C., 239
LANs; see Local area networks
LBS (location-based services), 170–172, 174–175
Leadership, business strategy and, 14
Lee, Tommy, 79
Legacy system, 181
Lending Tree, 62
Lenzer, Robert, 237
Level3, 153
Leveraging business processes, 55
Levi Strauss, 64
Levitt, Steven D., 137, 207, 239
License fees (ebusiness revenue model), 69
Lily, Marla, 200
LinkedIn, 75, 76, 91
List generators, 190
LiveJournal, 125
Local area networks (LANs), 152, 153, 164–165
Location-based services (LBS), 170–172, 174–175
Locher, Margaret, 240
Lockheedmartin.com, 82
Logical view (of information), 137
Logistics, 21, 22
Lomas, Natasha, 239
Long tail, 64
Loopt, 170
Loyalty programs, 17
Lulu.com, 62, 64
Lutz, Bob, 77
Lynch, C. G., 240

M

Madagascar, 119
Madoff, Bernard, 23
Mail Goggles, 91
Main Grid, 36
Maintainability (MIS infrastructure), 114, 115
Maintenance phase (SDLC), 207
Malicious code, 97
Management information systems (MIS), 12–14; see also specific
        topics, e.g.: MIS infrastructures
    business driven, 5–14
    in changing business processes, 50–55
    for decision support systems, 35–40
    defined, 13
    value added by, 22–23
Managerial business processes, streamlining, 52–53
Managerial decision making, 2, 30, 31
Managing people, 217–218
Manchester Airport (England), 41
MANs (metropolitan area networks), 153, 165
Mansfield, Phil, 237
Mapping, business process, 46–50
Mapquest.com, 68
Marconi, Guglielmo, 162
Market basket analysis, 147
Market segmentation, business strategy and, 20
Market segments (ebusiness), 71
Market share, 32
Marketing
    as primary value activity, 22
    via ebusiness, 66

Marketing department, 11, 12, 45
Martinez, Jose, 240
Mashup editors, 79
Mashups, 79
Mason, Richard, 238
Mass customization, 64
Massachusetts, 119
MasterCard, 42, 169
Matera, Alison, 211
Matsushita, 41
Matyszczyk, Chris, 239
Mbusiness, 82; *see also* Mobile business (mbusiness, mcommerce)
McCarthy, Caroline, 238
McCartney, Scott, 238
McDonald's, 18, 167, 190–191
McGraw, G., 240
MCI, 153
McManus, Neil, 237
Mcommerce; *see* Mobile business (mbusiness, mcommerce)
Measurement; *see also* Metrics
    of business process performance, 46–50
    of success, 32–35
Medicare.gov, 82
Merrill Lynch, 10
Metadata, 135
Methodologies, 207, 208
Metrics
    CRM, 193–194
    defined, 32
    effectiveness, 33, 34
    efficiency, 33, 34
    of website success, 67
Metropolitan area networks (MANs), 153, 165
Microblogging, 78
Microsoft, 6, 44, 61, 62, 73, 79, 93, 121, 122, 126, 207
Microsoft Access, 135
Microsoft Project, 217
Middleware, 181
Milestones, project, 213
Miller, Hugo, 238
Miller, Rich, 239
Miller, Sienna, 9
Ministry of Defense and Army (UK), 180
MIS; *see* Management information systems
MIS department, 13–14
MIS infrastructures, 107–126
    agile, 113–116
    business benefits of, 108–109
    defined, 108
    environmental, 117–118
    information, 109–113
    sustainable, 118–126
MIT Media Lab, 21
Mizy, 122
Mobile business (mbusiness, mcommerce), 82, 163–175
    applications of wireless networks, 168–170
    benefits of, 170–173
    challenges of, 173–175
    wireless network categories, 163–168
Mobile technology, 163
Model(s)
    business process, 46
    defined, 35
    granularity of, 38
Modeling
    agent-based, 43–44
    business process, 46–50

Modems, 154
Monroe College, 56
Moore, Gordon, 117
Moore's Law, 117, 118, 212
Motorola, 165, 166
Mozilla, 61, 73
Mozy, 122
MSN.com, 68, 93
Mullaney, Timothy, 239
Multiagent systems, 43–44
Multidimensional analysis, 142–143
Multipoint videoconferences, 70
Murray, Bill, 221
Muziic, 160
MySpace, 6, 15, 75, 121
MySQL, 135

N

NAPs (network access points), 153, 154
Napster, 14, 158
National Aeronautics and Space Administration, 168
National Arbitration Forum, 63
National Science Foundation, 165
National Semiconductor, 46
National service providers (NSPs), 153
National Weather Service, 172
Nations, Daniel, 238
Nearshore outsourcing, 220
Neeleman, David, 195
Negroponte, Nicholas, 21
Neiman Marcus, 20
Nelson, David, 160
Nestlé, 133
Netflix, 6, 23, 62, 64, 68, 73, 87, 145
Netscape Navigator, 62
Network(s), 152–163
    access technologies, 154–155
    benefits of connectivity, 159–162
    categories of, 152–153
    challenges of connectivity, 162–163
    defined, 108
    global connectivity, 152
    network convergence, 157–159
    network providers, 153–154
    protocols, 155–157
    wireless, 163–170
Network access points (NAPs), 153, 154
Network access technologies, 154–155
Network convergence, 157–159
Network effect, 79
Network protocols, 155–157
Network providers, 153–154
Networking communities, 75–77; *see also* Social networking
NetZero, 70, 154
Neural networks, 42–43
New entrants, threat of, 16
New markets, opening, 64
New York City, 165
New York Public Library, 146
Newcastle University, 100
NIIT, 220
Nike, 206
Nixon, Richard, 145
Nokia, 165, 174
Nonprofits, virtual, 36
Nonrepudiation, 90

Norton, David, 201
NSPs (national service providers), 153
NTT, 153

O

Obesity policies, 95
Objectives, project, 215
O'Brien, Conan, 9
Office 2010, 122
Offshore outsourcing, 220
Oklahoma, 139
OLAP (online analytical processing), 36
OLTP (online transaction processing), 35, 36
One Laptop per Child, 21
Onion, The, 10
Online analytical processing (OLAP), 36
Online appendices, 224
Online auctions, 68
Online information, accessibility of, 15
Online marketplaces, 68
Online transaction processing (OLTP), 35, 36
Onshore outsourcing, 220
OnStar, 169–170
Oooooc, 63
Open source, 73
Open systems, 73
Operational business processes, improving, 51–52
Operational CRM, 189–193
    and customer service, 192–193
    defined, 189
    and sales, 191–192
Operational decision making, 29–30
Operations
    improving with ebusiness, 65
    information MIS infrastructure for, 109–113
    as primary value activity, 22
Operations management, 45
Operations management department, 11, 12
Opportunity management CRM systems, 191, 192
Optimization analysis, 37
Oracle, 61, 135, 142, 202
Organizational goals, 215
Organizational structure, decision support systems and, 29
Outbound logistics, 22
Outsourcing, 219–222
Oxford University, 146

P

PaaS (Platform as a Service), 123–124
Packet tampering, 97
Page, Larry, 207
Pages Up, 200
Pandora, 80, 160
PANs (personal area networks), 163–164
Paradigm shift
    created by ebusiness, 62
    defined, 62
Pareek, Deepak, 239
Partner relationship management (PRM), 194
PartnerShop Program, 148
Passwords, 100
Patrizio, Andy, 240
Patterns, uncovering, 144–147

Paul, Frederic, 237
Payless, 20
PC World, 9
Peer-to-peer (P2P) networks, 158
PennVention, 172
People, managing, 217–218
Performance, system, 116, 137–138
Performance measures, 46–50
Perlow, Jon, 238
Personal area networks (PANs), 163–164
Personalization, 64, 193
PERT (Program Evaluation and Review Technique) charts, 216–217
Pharming, 99
Phillips Petroleum, 60
Phishing, 98–99, 101
Phoenix, Arizona, 134
Physical view (of information), 137
Picasa, 122
Ping of Death, 97
Pink, Daniel, 238
Pirated software, 86
PKE (public key encryption), 101
Plagiarism, 80
Planning phase (SDLC), 206–207
Plans
    backup and recovery, 110, 114
    business continuity, 112–113
    communications, 218
    disaster recovery, 110–111, 114
    information security, 98
    project, 216
Platform as a Service (PaaS), 123–124
PMI (Project Management Institute), 213
PMO (project management office), 213
Podcasting, 70
Point-to-point videoconferences, 70
Polaroid, 17–18, 60
Political issue, Internet access as, 162–163
Polymorphic viruses and worms, 97
Pop-Tarts, 131
Pop-up ads, 66
Portability (MIS infrastructure), 114, 115
Portals, 68
Porter, Michael E., 14, 16, 18–21, 23, 28, 45, 60, 237, 240
Porter's Five Forces Model
    in airline industry analysis, 18–19
    buyer power in, 16–17
    and decision support, 28
    rivalry among existing competitors in, 18
    SCM's effect on, 183, 184
    supplier power in, 17
    threat of new entrants in, 18
    threat of substitute products or services in, 17–18
    and value chain, 22, 23
Predictive dialing, 192
Prevention and resistance technologies, 100–102
Prezi, 123
Priceline.com, 67, 68, 82
Primary key, 136
Primary value activities, 21, 22
Priorities, business, 215
Privacy, 89
    chief privacy officer, 14
    defined, 86

email privacy policy, 91–92
information privacy policy, 90
with RFID and LBS, 174–175
Privacy Act (1974), 89
PRM (partner relationship management), 194
Procter & Gamble, 60, 183, 221
Procurement, 22
Product differentiation, 18
Production and materials management ERP components, 198
Productivity, 33
Profitability
and SCM systems, 185
variables in, 9
Progressive Insurance, 55
Project assumptions, 215
Project charter, 215
Project constraints, 215
Project deliverables, 213
Project management, 212–222
activities involved in, 217
change management, 219
choosing strategic projects, 214–215
communications management, 218–219
defined, 213
managing people, 217–218
outsourcing, 219–222
project planning, 215–217
software development projects, 212–214
Project Management Institute (PMI), 213
Project management office (PMO), 213
Project manager, 213
Project milestones, 213
Project objectives, 215
Project plan, 216
Project planning, 215–217
Project scope statement, 215
Project stakeholders, 213
Projects
defined, 32
outsourcing, 219–222
strategic, 214–215
Protocols, 155–157
Prototype, 210
P2P (peer-to-peer) networks, 158
Public key encryption (PKE), 101
Pure-play (virtual) businesses, 68

Q

QBE (query-by-example) tool, 135
Quality of information, 130, 132–134, 138
Quantum, 61
Query-by-example (QBE) tool, 135
Quinlan, Ronald, 238
Qwest, 153, 155

R

RAD (rapid application development) methodology, 210
Radio-frequency identification (RFID), 168–169, 174–175
Raphel, J. R., 237
Rapid application development (RAD) methodology, 210
Rapid prototyping, 210
Rational unified process (RUP) methodology, 210–211
Real People magazine, 133

Real Simple Syndication (RSS), 78
Real-time communication, 70
Real-time information, 132
Records (data), 136
Recovery, 110
Recycling cell phones, 117
Redundancy, 52, 138
Reengineering; *see* Business process reengineering (BPR)
Regional service providers (RSPs), 154
Reidenberg, Joe, 86, 87
Reintermediation, 64
Reiser, Paul, 9
Relational database management system, 134–139
Relational database model, 135
Relational integrity constraints, 138
Reliability (MIS infrastructure), 114, 115
Reputation system, 73
Response time, 34
Responsible technology use, 23
Restaurant Maloney & Porcelli's, 218
Return on investment (ROI), 33
RFID (radio-frequency identification), 168–169, 174–175
Ricadela, Aaron, 240
RIM, 166
Ritter, Karl, 240
Rivalry among existing companies (Porter's Five Forces Model), 16
Robots, 185
Rochester, New York, 134
ROI (return on investment), 33
Rowdii, 63
RSPs (regional service providers), 154
RSS (Real Simple Syndication), 78
Ruiz, Hector, 240
RUP (rational unified process) methodology, 210–211
RustyBrick, 190

S

SaaS (Software as a Service), 123
Safeway, 18
Sales
and operational CRM, 191–192
as primary value activity, 22
Sales department, 11, 12, 45
Sales force automation (SFA), 191
Sales management CRM systems, 191
Salesforce.com, 123
Samsung, 165, 174
San Francisco, 119
San Francisco earthquake (1906), 112–113
Sandler, Adam, 80–81
Sarbanes-Oxley Act (2002), 89, 134
SAS, 142
Satellite communication systems, 167–168
Satellite radio and TV, 161
Satellites
defined, 167–168
for GPS, 169
Satyam, 220
Scalability
information, 137–138
MIS infrastructure, 114–116
Scams, 40
ScanR.com, 124
SCEM (supply chain event management), 187

Schlosser, Julie, 239
Schmidt, Eric, 81
Schorn, Daniel, 238
Schrage, Michael, 238
Schrenker, Marcus, 211
Schwartz, Barry, 190
Schwartz, Jonathan, 77
SCM; *see* Supply chain management
Scope statement, 215
Script bunnies, 96
Script kiddies, 96
Scrubbing, 143–144
Scrum methodology, 211
SDLC (systems development life cycle), 206–207, 212
Sears, 60, 61
Second Life, 36
Secure hypertext transfer protocol (SHTTP, HTTPS), 162
Secure sockets layer (SSL), 162
Security
    information; *see* Information security
    network, 162
    with wireless devices, 173–175
Sege, Irene, 237
Seigenthaler, John, 9, 238
Seigenthaler, John, Sr., 80
Selling chain management, 187
Semantic web, 81
Semistructured decisions, 30, 38
Sensitivity analysis, 37
Server, 108
Service providers, 68
Sex.com, 63
SF Recycling & Disposal, 119
SFA (sales force automation), 191
Shanghai, 119
Sharing resources, 159–161
Shell Oil, 41
Shopping bots, 43
Shrek, 119
SHTTP (secure hypertext transfer protocol), 162
Siebel, 202
Silva, Chris, 239
Sinbad, 9
Skinner, Mike, 79
Skype, 158
Slice-and-dice, 40
Smart cards, 100
Smart cities, 119
SMART criteria, 215
Smart grids, 120
Smartphones, 166
SmartPump, 41
Smoking policies, 95
SNA (social networking analysis), 75–76
Sneakware, 93
Sniffers, 97
Social activism, 194
Social bookmarking, 77
Social engineering, 98
Social issue, Internet access as, 162–163
Social media, 75
Social media policy, 92
Social network, 75
Social networking
    defined, 75

employees terminated for overuse of, 75
    fraudulent use of, 190
Social networking analysis (SNA), 75–76
Social tagging, 76
Socializr, 63
Soden, Michael, 93
Software
    defined, 108
    pirated, 86
Software as a Service (SaaS), 123
Software development, 206
    agile methodologies, 209–211
    business requirements for, 211
    changing technology in, 212
    and cost of errors in SDLC, 212
    project management for; *see* Project management
    skipping phases of, 212
    successful, 211–212
    waterfall methodology, 207–209
Soloway, Robert, 93
Songza, 160
Sony, 60–61
Source code, 73
Source documents (TPS), 36
Spam, 92, 93, 100
Spam blogs, 97
Spider-Man, 23
Splogs (spam blogs), 97
Sponsor, project, 213–214
Spoofing, 97
Spotify, 160
Sprint, 153, 166
Sprint Nextel, 165
Spyware, 93, 97
SQL (structured query language), 135
SQL Server, 135
SRM (supplier relationship management), 194
SSL (secure sockets layer), 162
SSL Certificate, 162
Stakeholders, project, 213
Stamps.com, 186
Stanford University, 146
Staples, 185
Starbucks, 78, 170, 172
Statistical analysis, 147
Stealthware, 93
Stockholm, 119
Strategic business process reengineering, 53–55
Strategic decision making, 30, 31
Strategic projects, choosing, 214–215
Strategic vision, 46
Strategy; *see* Business strategy
Streaming, 166, 167
Streamlining, 52–53
Streetlamps, 165
Strong forces (Five Forces Model), 18
Structured data, mining, 145, 146
Structured decisions, 29, 30
Structured query language (SQL), 135
StumbleUpon, 77
Subscription fees (ebusiness revenue model), 69
Substitute products or services, threat of, 16–18
Success measures, 32–35
Sullivan, Bob, 239
Sun Microsystems, 77

Super Bowl advertising, 6
Supplier power
    defined, 17
    in Porter's Five Forces Model, 16, 17
Supplier relationship management (SRM), 194
Supply chain
    basic activities of, 182
    defined, 17, 181, 182
    and Porter's Five Forces Model, 17
Supply chain event management (SCEM), 187
Supply chain execution systems, 184
Supply chain management (SCM), 181–187
    benefits of, 183–185
    challenges of, 186
    defined, 182
    future of, 186–187
    integrating ERP, CRM, and, 202–203
Supply chain management ERP components, 201
Supply chain planning systems, 184
Supply chain visibility, 183–184
Support value activities, 22, 23
Surmacz, Jon, 237
Sustainability, 36
Sustainable MIS disposal, 118
Sustainable MIS infrastructure, 118–126
    cloud computing, 120–124
    defined, 117
    grid computing, 119–120
    virtualized computing, 124–126
Sustaining technology, 60
Switching costs, 16
Synchronous communications, 75
System(s)
    defined, 12, 13
    intelligent, 41
    multiagent, 43–44
System availability, 34
System thinking (BPR), 55
Systems development life cycle (SDLC), 206–207, 212
Systems thinking, 13
    in DSS, 38
    in TPS, 37

T

T-Mobile, 166
T1 lines, 155
Tags, 76
Takelessons.com, 79
Taxes (ebusiness), 72
Taxonomies, 71
Taylor, Nick, 146
TCP (transmission control protocol), 156
TCP/IP (transmission control protocol/Internet protocol), 156, 157
TCS, 220
Technology(ies); *see also specific technologies*
    cellular, 167
    dependence on, 80
    disruptive, 60–62
    for information security, 98–102
    mobile, 163
    network access, 154–155
    responsible use of, 23
    sustaining, 60
    wireless, 163–170

Technology development, 22
Technology's Long Tail (Chris Anderson), 207
Ted (ted.com), 207
Teen Grid, 36
Telstar, 162
Testing phase (SDLC), 207
Text mining, 145
Thain, John, 10
Theft
    identity, 98
    of mobile devices, 173
Thompson, Trina, 56
Threat of new entrants, 16
Threat of substitute products/services, 16–18
Throughput, 34
Thunderbird, 73
Thurman, Howard, 215
Tiffany & Co., 20
Time-series information, 147
Timeliness of information, 131–132
Tipping Point The, (Malcolm Gladwell), 207
Titchmarsh, Alan, 9
T.J. Maxx, 68
To-Be process models, 47–49
Tokens, 100
TPSs (transaction processing systems), 36–39
Trackur.com, 91
Transaction brokers, 68
Transaction fees (ebusiness revenue model), 69
Transaction processing systems (TPSs), 36–39
Transaction speed, 34
Transactional information, 35, 130–131, 142
Transmission control protocol (TCP), 156
Transmission control protocol/Internet protocol (TCP/IP), 156, 157
Transportation, disaster plans for, 111
Travelocity.com, 19
Trends, uncovering, 144–147
Triple constraint, 213
Trojan-horse viruses, 97
Twitter, 75, 78, 91, 125, 170, 190
Twones, 160

U

UC (unified communications), 158
Unambiguous business requirements, 208
Unavailable systems, 114
Unified communications (UC), 158
Uniform Domain-Name Dispute-Resolution Policy, 63
Union Bank of California, 113
Unisys, 42
United Nations, 63
U.S. Department of Defense, 61, 168, 169
U.S. Postal Service, 155, 186
U.S. Track and Field (USTAF), 156
Universal resource locator (URL), 61
University of Cincinnati, 9
University of Denver, 155
University of Florida, 114
University of Michigan, 146
Unplanned downtime, 94
Unstructured data, mining, 145, 146
Unstructured decisions, 30
Up-selling, 190–191
URL (universal resource locator), 61

USA Patriot Act (2001 and 2003), 89
Usability
    as effectiveness metric, 34
    and MIS infrastructure, 114, 116
User-contributed content, 73
User-generated content, 73
User IDs, 99, 100
USTAF (U.S. Track and Field), 156
Utilities damage, disaster plans for, 111
Utility computing, 122
UUNet/WorldCom, 153

V

Value-added services fees (ebusiness revenue model), 69
Value chain
    and efficiency/effectiveness, 45
    and Porter's Five Forces Model, 22, 23
Value chain analysis, 20–24
    for business processes, 45–46
    and decision support, 28
    defined, 21
Value chain map, 46
Value driven business, 27–56
    business process in; see Business processes
    decision support systems for; see Decision support systems
Variables, 9
Verizon, 153, 166
Video Privacy Protection Act (1988), 89
Videoconferencing, 70, 162
Viral marketing, 66
Virgin airlines, 207
Virtual (pure-play) businesses, 68
Virtual data centers, 126
Virtual nonprofits, 36
Virtual private networks (VPNs), 160, 161
Virtual reality, 42, 44
Virtual supercomputer, 119
Virtual workforce, 44
Virtualization, 124–126, 159
Virtualized computing, 124–126
Viruses, 97
    and corrupted files, 111
    defined, 97
    on mobile devices, 174
Visa, 42, 90
Visibility, supply chain, 183–184
Visitor metrics (websites), 67
Visualization, 38
Vitale, Adam, 23
Voice over IP (VoIP), 158
Voth, Jeff, 237
VPNs (virtual private networks), 160, 161

W

Wales, Jimmy, 9
Walgreens, 186, 187
Wall Street Journal, The, 208
Walmart, 20, 34, 60, 65, 131, 169, 183
WANs (wide area networks), 152–153, 165–168
Warm sites, 111, 112
Waterfall methodology, 207–209
Watergate, 145
Weak forces (Five Forces Model), 18

Weatherbots, 172
Web 1.0, 62
Web 2.0 (Business 2.0), 72–80
    advantages of, 72–75
    and capacity planning, 116
    challenges of, 80
    characteristics of, 73
    collaboration tools, 77–79
    networking communities, 75–77
Web 3.0, 80–82
Web-based self-service systems, 192
Web conferencing, 70
Web logs (blogs), 77
Web logs (for monitoring), 93
Web mining, 145
Webinars, 70
Website bookmarks, 77
Website personalization, 193
Websites
    analyzing, 72
    data-driven, 139–140
    domain names, 63
    for ebusiness, 64
Weiss Tech House, 172
Wellpoint, 23
Weyco Inc., 95
Weyers, Howard, 95
What-if analysis, 37
White-hat hackers, 96
Wi-fi (wireless fidelity), 164–165
Wi-Fi Protected Access (WPA), 173–174
Wide area networks (WANs), 152–153, 165–168
Wikipedia, 9, 73, 78–79, 115
Wikis, 78–79
Williams, Robbie, 9
WiMAX (Worldwide Interoperability for Microwave Access), 165
Windows Live, 122
Wipro, 220
Wired magazine, 64, 207
Wireless connections, protecting, 173–174
Wireless fidelity (wi-fi), 164–165
Wireless LANs (WLANs), 164–165
Wireless MANs (WMANs), 165
Wireless networks
    applications of, 168–170
    categories of, 163–168
Wireless technologies, 163
Wireless WANs (WWANs), 165–168
Wishes, 72
WLANs (wireless LANs), 164–165
WMANs (wireless MANs), 165
Woodward, Bob, 145
Workflow, 50
    defined, 50
    and wireless technology, 172
Workforce, virtual, 44
Workplace monitoring policy, 93–94
World Intellectual Property Organization, 63
World Is Flat The, (Thomas Friedman), 7
World Wide Web (WWW)
    as catalyst for ebusiness, 62
    defined, 61
    as disruptive technology, 61–62
    reasons for growth of, 62

Worldwide Interoperability for Microwave Access (WiMAX), 165
Worms, 97
WPA (Wi-Fi Protected Access), 173–174
WWANs (wireless WANs), 165–168
WWW; *see* World Wide Web

X

X Prize Foundation, 207
Xcel Energy, 120
Xerox, 61
XP (extreme programming) methodology, 210

Y

Yahoo!, 68, 79, 126
Yelp, 73

YouSendIt, 123
YouTube, 15, 68, 73, 78, 91, 160, 162
Yuuguu, 63

Z

Zappos, 6, 139, 140, 185
Zillow.com, 68
Zoho Office, 123
Zoomr, 63
Zuckerberg, Mark, 6